PROFESSIONAL BURNOUT IN HUMAN SERVICE ORGANIZATIONS

PROFESSIONAL BURNOUT IN HUMAN SERVICE ORGANIZATIONS

CARY CHERNISS

Foreword by
Seymour Sarason

PRAEGER SPECIAL STUDIES • PRAEGER SCIENTIFIC

Library of Congress Cataloging in Publication Data

Cherniss, Cary.
    Professional burnout in human service organizations.

    Bibliography: p.
    1. Social workers--United States--Longitudinal
studies. 2. Social service--Pschological aspects--
United States. 3. Helping behavior. 4. Professional
socialization. 5. Social workers, Professional ethics
for. I. Title.
HV10.5.C47   331.7'613613'0973   80-12136
ISBN 0-03-056912-5

Published in 1980 by Praeger Publishers
CBS Educational and Professional Publishing
A Division of CBS, Inc.
521 Fifth Avenue, New York, New York 10017 U.S.A.

© 1980 by Praeger Publishers

0123456789   038   987654321

Printed in the United States of America

For Deborah and Joshua

FOREWORD

"Professional burnout" is a phrase that in a few short years has become part of our jargon. Some use it as an excuse, some as a badge of honor, and others as a negative symptom of our times and a fast changing society. Like so many other catch phrases it encapsulates a kernel of truth wrapped in attractive language. Reading the literature, scholarly and popular, one might gain the impression that we are dealing with a new phenomenon, although a little reflection would suggest that that is not likely to be the case. It is like "discovering" the problems of aging, as if they were newly minted by contemporary society. But there is another and more insidiously fateful consequence of these catch phrases, and that is that their metaphorical quality directs attention away from the structure of the social contexts in which the phenomenon occurs. What are the characteristics of these contexts in which the phenomenon occurs? What are the characteristics of these contexts in which burnout appears to be frequent? Why do contexts vary in this respect? Can one understand professional burnout only in terms of their interconnections with other contexts? Can one understand a human service agency by looking only at it or must one see it in its place in a federal-state-local complex? Is professional burnout understandable primarily by an individual psychology or by an orientation that takes account of the characteristics of clients and colleagues, the distribution of resources, and the nature and weight of the traditions of professionalism? And, finally, can one understand professional burnout without looking at where and how professionals receive their formal training? How much of the disillusionment that the young professional experiences can be attributed to a faulty preparation that simply does not reflect the realities he or she will encounter? It is easy, too easy, to blame "bureaucracy," but is it not indulging scapegoating to place all the blame there and to ignore the contribution of the weaknesses of professional education and training?

We owe a real debt to Carry Cherniss for raising and discussing these and other important questions. Far from simplifying the antecedents, nature, and consequences of burnout, he has the courage to face up to what is a very complex social-cultural problem. He is no armchair theorist or a mindless collector of questionnaires. He is *thoughtful*, and that is the word that characterizes this book. He uses group data very sensitively and he does not stand in the way of letting his interviewees talk to us.

This book has been several years in the writing. Those of us who have interest in this area have been waiting for this book. The wait has been worth it.

That this book should be read by people in human service agencies goes without saying. If only this book could be put into the hands of every student newly entering the human service scene! My students will read it.

Seymour B. Sarason
Yale University

PREFACE

This book describes and analyzes what happens to people when they become "professionals." More specifically, it is a study of new professionals who have begun their careers working in public human service agencies such as mental health clinics, schools, public health departments, and poverty law agencies. It is these professionals on whom many rely for education or aid, especially when under physical or emotional stress; it is these professionals who seem to have much influence on important life decisions and events. Yet all too often, the person-in-need encounters "helping" professionals who are distant or disdainful, "human service" workers who seem unresponsive to human need and pain.

It is generally true that these professionals have entered service fields with ideals and goals of contributing directly to the welfare of others and that their training is aimed at providing the tools with which to do this. How then does the paradox of the aloof, uncaring helper occur? This book addresses the paradox by exploring two general questions. First, what important experiences and changes occur in a person during the earliest phase of a professional career in a public institution? And second, what forces produce the observed reactions and changes? To put it another way, how do professionals get to be the way they are?

In order to begin answering these questions, we studied the lives of 28 new professionals in the process of moving from advanced training to first jobs in their chosen fields. The early years of a professional career are often seen rather romantically as a time of challenge, struggle, and change, a kind of initiation period. The shared experience creates bonds among newer members of a profession, and older ones seem to enjoy exchanging stories about the trials and tribulations of this time before they established ways of negotiating the demands of their work. However, we wanted to know what it was actually like, beyond the current bonds or remembered struggles. What was the experience of being a new professional working in a large, public, human service agency, and how did that experience affect the new professional?

Imagine the typical individual who has completed close to 20 years of formal schooling—public school, college, perhaps several years of graduate training. Finally, after being a student longer than one can remember, one emerges from the "ivory tower" and assumes a new role, a new identity, a new status. One is now a professional, responsible for the welfare of other people, probably in a way one has never been before. Ability, expertise, and effectiveness are assumed. One may have worked previously "as" a professional in student-teaching or internship experiences. But, until now, one has not *been* a professional, with all the rights, responsibilities, and obligations implied by that status. What is this experience like for those who live through it? How does it change them? What do those changes mean to their personal and professional development, to the welfare of their clients, to their co-workers, agencies, and families, and to society in general? These were the first and most basic questions we considered in our intensive study of new public professionals.

We soon found that the answers to these questions were complex. Each individual's experience clearly differs. Most of the material on which this book is based came from intensive study of 28 individuals from four professional groups: law, public health nursing, mental health, and high school teaching. Even within our restricted sample, there was much variety in experience. There was not a single experience but rather 28 experiences, each unique and each poignant in its own way. We could have simply described those 28 individuals and their initial work experience in turn, letting their firsthand, personal accounts speak for themselves. But it seemed important to at least attempt a distillation and synthesis of that human experience, to discover underlying patterns and themes that occurred in most of the cases we studied. Thus, we looked beyond the surface of each individual story and sought common issues, problems, and feelings. This book presents the results of that search.

As one might expect, the choice of topic and focus was not fortuitous. There were personal reasons for doing this study. All of those who worked on the project were either relatively new professionals themselves or were planning to become new professionals in the not too distant future. We were all concerned about what was happening to us and our friends, and we were curious about why things were happening as they were. Those of us who had been new professionals in public institutions knew that the experience was difficult and stressful. We also sensed that the way in which we dealt with the stress of our work had had a strong impact on our attitudes and behavior. We believed that the pressures to change in ways that we were not always very happy about were even stronger in the initial period of our careers than they had been during our training, a belief supported by others who have studied and written about "professional socialization." Thus, our study of new public professionals was, for many of us, a quest for self-understanding, with all of the advantages and pitfalls that such an undertaking involves.

This study's formal inception was in 1973, when I began a graduate research seminar with the purpose of initiating more systematic study of the experience of new professionals working in human service organizations. Several graduate students of psychology, social work, and education participated in that ongoing seminar and contributed to the study on which this book is based. Research proposals were prepared by members of the seminar, and funding for the study was secured from the University of Michigan's Horace Rackham School of Graduate Studies in the form of a faculty research grant to me. During the next three years, interviews were conducted with the new professionals. As the interviews progressed, members of the research team met regularly to discuss, analyze, and speculate about the emerging material. Several preliminary papers were published. Finally, in 1976, we concluded the data collection phase of our research and began the lengthy process of analysis, interpretation, and writing.

During the period of this study, there were related studies initiated by myself and others. One was a survey of job satisfaction and other attitudes toward work in staffs of community mental health centers. The results were based on the responses of 164 staff members working in 23 community mental health centers in Michigan. Another study examined job satisfaction and work alienation in more than 700 public employees at all occupational levels of a state government. All of these studies have been concerned with the work experiences of public professionals, and their findings have increasingly tended to converge. Although this book is based primarily on the intensive, longitudinal study of 28 new public professionals, findings from the other research are referred to when appropriate.

I have written this book with the belief that its contents will be of interest and use to a variety of readers. First, I have tried to write for a more general readership, since virtually everyone is affected by public professionals. As I suggest in Chapter 1, human welfare in this society is increasingly influenced by public professionals and the institutions that employ them. Further, because the institutions are publicly supported, all of us have the responsibility and the right to participate in making policy decisions affecting them. However, I am also writing for those professionals who work in these settings or who manage them as administrators. They should be particularly concerned about the contents of this book and will undoubtedly make up a large part of the readership. It is my hope that the results of our study and the contents of this book will also be useful to students in professional training programs, the new public professionals of the future whose plight will hopefully be made a little easier because of the findings of our research. Finally, this book should also be of interest to scholars, for the study represents a contribution to theory and research on professional career development and organizational socialization.

In writing any book, one must make certain decisions about scope. In other words, one must decide what the book will *not* include as well as what it will. In this book, my primary purpose is to define a problem and describe and analyze an experience in a way that touches the concerns of professional practitioners, administrators, policy makers, and the general reading public. There is a voluminous literature containing research and theory on related topics (professional socialization, adult development, job stress, job satisfaction), which I have made no attempt to review. Such a review would be interesting and useful, but it goes beyond the scope of this book.

As noted, many individuals have contributed to this work, and I would now like to acknowledge their invaluable help. First, there were the graduate students at the University of Michigan who ably transcended the student role and became my research collaborators. Edward Egnatios and Sally Wacker became involved in the original research seminar and continued with the proposal writing, data collection, and data analysis. Some of the material in Chapters 6 and 7 came from Wacker's doctoral dissertation, and I am grateful to her for allowing me to use it here.

Once the study was under way, we were joined by Bill O'Dowd and Bert Maguire, who helped with the interviewing and participated in our discussions and analyses of the data. Bill O'Dowd's second-year doctoral research project was based on the study, and his work was a valuable conceptual contribution to the thinking of the rest of us.

I would also like to acknowledge the continuing support and stimulation of my friends and colleagues. Especially helpful has been Seymour B. Sarason, whose work, friendship, and teaching prepared me for the task. Also important was Richard H. Price, who, as my colleague at Michigan, has provided both the intellectual and organizational conditions necessary for doing a study such as this. Without his administrative ability, intellectual stimulation, and sustained emotional support, I could never have completed this work. I would also like to thank Baron Perlman of the University of Wisconsin, Oshkosh, who read the manuscript and offered many useful suggestions. I am grateful as well to those who typed the thousands of pages of interview transcripts and the manuscript drafts, especially Laura Spitz and Barb Toler.

Special thanks are due to the new public professionals who participated in this study. They gave of their time without any compensation during a period of their lives when time was an all too scarce resource. Their sensitivity and self-insight contributed enormously to the final conclusions. They were truly collaborators as well as subjects.

Finally, I would like to thank my closest friend, colleague, confidante, and companion, Deborah Cherniss, who, despite the formidable demands of her own career, was able to contribute an inestimable amount of criticism, support, and love, without which this work—and I—would be far poorer. She painstakingly read and edited every page of this book, and, because of her efforts, this work is much better in every possible way.

CONTENTS

LIST OF TABLES AND FIGURE

PROFESSIONAL BURNOUT IN HUMAN SERVICE ORGANIZATIONS

1

NEW PUBLIC PROFESSIONALS AND THE PROBLEM OF BURNOUT

Imagine two professionals (teachers, social workers, lawyers) who have been engaged in practice for about five years. One is committed, idealistic, concerned about clients, and more interested in doing good work than in making large amounts of money. The other is cynical, not very interested in the work, and considers most clients to be ignorant, dishonest, or apathetic. The primary goals of this second professional are higher salary, career advancement, and security.

Most people in our society would regard the first professional as "better" than the second. This first professional fits the ideal of what a professional should be. Also, many people in our society probably believe that there are too many professionals like the second one. Further, many of us think that, as professionals become older and more experienced, they are more likely to become like the second example.

The purpose of the research reported here was to understand why many professionals, especially those working in public institutions, become more like the second example over time. What is it about that experience that "hardens" them? On the other hand, why is it that some manage to sustain their sense of commitment and concern over time? Finally, can something be done to increase the number of professionals who resemble the "good" example? As our reliance on professionals and public human service agencies grows, these questions become ever more pressing.

THE SOCIAL SIGNIFICANCE
OF PROFESSIONAL HUMAN SERVICE

We live in an increasingly professionalized society, one in which many human needs are met through the intervention of highly trained professional personnel. Whatever their number relative to the rest of the population, professionals have always been an important segment of society. As Schein (1972, p. 2) noted, "The professions have always been the agent by which society dealt with its major problems." However, during the past nine decades, their significance has grown even more. For instance, the proportion of professionals in the population has increased more than threefold according to census data. In 1890, 3.78 percent of the population between the ages of 25 and 64 were professionals. In 1920, the percentage had increased to 4.4 percent. But, by 1960, it had risen to 13 percent (Veysey, 1975).

Also, during recent decades, the number of professionals and specialities within professions has mushroomed. The original three professions of law, medicine, and the clergy have greatly expanded in size, influence, and internal differentiation. For instance, medical care now is provided by dozens of allied professional groups; at one time, only physicians, midwives, and surgeons comprised the entire health care establishment. And, as the original three professions have grown and differentiated, distinctly new professional and "semiprofessional" fields have emerged (for example, social work, public school teaching, psychotherapy, engineering, and so on).

As the number of professions and professionals has increased, so too has society's reliance on their work. During the past century, many of the caring and socializing functions formerly provided by family, church, neighborhood, and work place have been assumed by formal institutions such as schools, hospitals, day care centers, social welfare programs, and mental health agencies. As these new institutions have proliferated and assumed new functions, their social, political, and economic impact on our lives has increased. The statistics are compelling. For instance, in 1974, Americans spent 8.5 percent less of their total personal expenditures on food than they had in 1965. However, they spent 17.5 percent more for medical care, education, and welfare services during this same period. In other words, an ever increasing proportion of expenditures has gone into human service during the last decade. In economic terms alone, human service agencies and the professionals who run them have become more important and probably will continue to become so in the future. Lynn (1965) was apparently not exaggerating when he wrote that the professions are "triumphant in American life."

At the same time that the social and economic importance of the professions and of human services generally have grown, public concern and criticism also seem to have increased. As Hasenfeld and English (1974) noted, there has been growing dissatisfaction with the fairness and effectiveness of many human service organizations, often reaching the level of a "consumer revolt." The growing demand for "accountability" has not occurred simply because someone decided it is a good principle. Rather, the demand for accountability reflects a growing suspicion that something is wrong and must be brought to public light. Because of this growing dissatisfaction, both the general public and professionals themselves have become conscious of human services as a social institution that performs a critical function in our society and that can all too often be ineffective and inhumane.

In the current indictment of the professions, many criticisms have been put forth: they have not been accountable enough; they tend to neglect the poor and dispossessed; they focus too much on individual change and adjustment and not enough on change in social systems; they obstruct self-development and expression for their members; they are too concerned with status, money, and security for themselves; the monopoly of professional credentials limits our capacity to meet demands for service in the most effective ways; professional education is too long, too specialized, and too much tied to the classroom; and professional care leads to an unhealthy over-dependency and passivity in the client (Gross & Osterman, 1972).

Although the validity of these criticisms has been and undoubtedly will continue to be debated, the increasingly important role that professionals play in our lives almost guarantees that there will be growing concern with professional responsibility, commitment, and effectiveness. Professionals constitute one of the fastest growing and most important sectors of American society. To a very great extent, the welfare of society has come to depend on their work. For these reasons, the study of how professionals get to be the way they are is of great practical significance.[1]

THE "PUBLIC" PROFESSIONAL

As the role of the professions in society has grown, the proportion of professionals "on their own" has declined. Increasingly, they work in public agencies rather than in private practice. They are still professionals, but they are also salaried workers. This situation creates great potential for strain and conflict between the professional and the organization, a strain that can strongly influence the attitudes and performance of the professional.

Traditionally, professions have been distinctive in their autonomy and self-regulation. By definition, professions have been groups regulated by special occupational norms rather than external client pressure or organizational restraints. The professions have functioned as an aristocracy of knowledge. Because their work required the creative application of highly specialized knowledge, they were allowed to work with very little external control. Instead, the professional was allegedly monitored by colleagues who knew enough to evaluate the individual's work. As an added protection to society, professionals were in-doctrinated in an ethical system, often formalized into an actual "code of ethics" in which social service and client welfare were placed above narrow self-interest. Strong ethical commitment and evaluation by peers were the primary means by which professional work was controlled.

However, certain changes in the nature of professional work imposed new values and constraints. For instance, as the practice of medicine became more technologically sophisticated and complex, hospitals grew in size and scope. Working as part of a team in a hospital, the physician's time and effort became more regulated. The institution has its own needs, and professionals were in-creasingly forced to serve those needs as well as the more traditional needs of client and society. Bureaucratic control came to play an increasingly important role in the professional's work life, and at times the demands of this bureaucratic control conflicted with the needs of individual clients and the humanitarian values to which professionals had been indoctrinated.

Financial support from local, state, and federal governments has tended to further regulate and transform the nature of professional work. The institutions in which public professionals work frequently receive funds from multiple sources. (One community mental health program I recently visited received funding from 17 different sources.) Each source of funds prescribes a certain role for the professional; because these funding agencies are increasingly hetero-genous in goals, it is not uncommon for their role prescriptions to conflict. This state of affairs produces great role conflict for the public professional and further restricts the professional's control over his or her work. Sarason (1977, p. 214), in describing the plight of the professional in community mental health pro-grams, accurately portrayed the situation experienced by virtually all public pro-fessionals: "The professional in the community mental health center has become part of a 'complex bigness' in which he is a very subordinate part and which puts predictable and unpredictable constraints on how he functions as a professional."

Some professional groups have worked almost exclusively within bureau-cratically organized public institutions for some time, while others have only begun to do so in significant numbers relatively recently. Although it is still true that the proportion of public professionals in some groups (social work, teach-ing) is higher than in others (medicine, law), the phenomenon of the public professional is not unknown to any profession in this country today.

The ramifications of professionals working in public institutions are in-creasing in significance, not only because of the percentage of the professional work force involved, but also because of the inherent strains and dilemmas, such as role conflict and loss of personal autonomy. The growing urge toward unioni-zation among professionals working in public human service agencies is but one concrete reaction against the strains that occur when individual workers in our society are professional, salaried employees (Oppenheimer, 1975). An even more important reaction to these strains and dilemmas is the phenomenon of "burnout."

THE CONCEPT OF BURNOUT

As our understanding of the new public professional's world developed in our study, the concept of "burnout" became central. Burnout refers to a process in which the professional's attitudes and behavior change in negative ways in response to job strain. We found that many of the new public professionals we studied *did* change during the first year or so of their careers. They lost much of their idealism. They became less trusting and sympathetic toward clients or students or patients. They became less committed and invested in their jobs. However, not all of the professionals we studied changed to the same degree. Also, the extent to which they changed seemed to be strongly influenced by the nature of their work settings. Those who worked in extremely demanding, frustrating, or boring jobs tended to change more negatively than those whose jobs were interesting, supportive, and stimulating. In other words, negative changes in attitude seemed to be associated with high job stress.

Perhaps the best way to convey what the experience of burnout is like is through concrete examples. The following are typical.

Example 1.   Mary Smith was a social worker employed in a community mental health center. It was her first job since receiving her M.S.W., and she had been working there for about eight months. As most new social workers, she had begun with "great expectations." She was idealistic, committed, and hopeful. But, after eight months on the job, she had become discouraged and demoralized about the lack of motivation and change in so many of her clients. She wanted to do family therapy, but she could never get a whole family to come in together for treatment. She was expected to spend part of her time doing consultation and education in the community, but she was not even sure what that was and certainly did not feel competent when she tried to do it. And she did not like feeling incompent. Going to work became more and more unpleasant. She began getting colds and the flu frequently. She was less empathic and responsive in sessions with clients, except in one or two cases that were more interesting and successful than the others. She had expected that being a therapist and counselor in a mental health agency would be fascinating, just like the books she had read in college. But she found herself feeling bored during many sessions with clients. She eventually quit and went back to graduate school to work on a Ph.D. in psychology.

Example 2.   In its early days, this group home for youth had an exciting, innovative program. The staff seemed like one big happy family. No one cared about the extra hours they worked. There was tremendous dedication to the teenagers, who were seen as having great potential to change and grow. However, over time, the staff became frustrated. Staff members were irritated by what they considered to be insensitive and inept administrators who were never around, made all the important decisions, and got paid twice as much as the rest for working half as hard. The frequent delays in their paychecks and the red tape they had to go through whenever they wanted to do something for a youth seemed to be further indication of the lack of administrative support. There was also increasing jealousy and rivalry among the staff. Cliques and conflicts emerged: afternoon staff versus morning staff, professionals versus paraprofessionals, black versus white. Motivation and commitment to the organization declined. Absenteeism and turnover increased. Staff members rarely worked a minute over their regular shifts and became furious if they had to stay a few minutes longer because someone on the next shift was late. At staff meetings, they began to ask how much physical force was permitted in dealing with disruptive behavior and why tranquilizers were not used more to help control the youths' behavior. Many staff members were drinking heavily at home. Many were having marital problems.

As these examples suggest, burnout involves a change in attitude and behavior in response to a demanding, frustrating, unrewarding work experience. The dictionary defines "to burn out" as "to fail, wear out, or become exhausted by making excessive demands on energy, strength, or resources." This term all too aptly describes the experience of many human service professionals. However, the term "burnout" has come to have an additional meaning in recent research and writing on the topic; it refers to negative changes in work-related attitudes and behavior in response to job stress. What are these negative changes? A major one is loss of concern for the client and a tendency to treat clients in a detached, mechanical fashion (Maslach, 1976). Other changes include increasing discouragement, pessimism, and fatalism about one's work; decline in motivation, effort, and involvement in work; apathy; negativism; frequent irritability and anger with clients and colleagues; preoccupation with one's own comfort and welfare on the job; a tendency to rationalize failure by blaming the clients or "the system"; and resistance to change, growing rigidity, and loss of creativity.

In moderation, some of these changes associated with burnout may not be entirely negative. For instance, it is probably desirable for an extremely idealistic and naive new professional to develop a more realistic and balanced view of clients and their problems. Also, adopting more modest goals and expectations for one's self and one's clients is certainly desirable if one's goals were unrealistically high. Tempering one's involvement in work with outside commitments, rather than remaining totally absorbed in the job, is to be recommended. Even assuming a somewhat detached, objective, and "professional" stance toward clients is probably useful in many helping occupations. However, there is clearly a point at which these desirable changes in attitude and behavior become undesirable for all concerned. Burnout has come to be associated with that point at which the changes are no longer positive.

On a concrete day-to-day level, there are many signs of professional burnout. For instance, one might feel great inner resistance to going to work each day. Frequent "clock watching" is another sign, as is postponement of appointments with clients. An inability to concentrate on or listen to what a client is saying may be a sign of burnout. Increasing reliance on rules in dealing with client demands may be a sign.

In addition to these negative changes in thought and behavior related to the job, there are physical and behavioral signs. These include chronic fatigue; frequent colds; the flu, headaches, gastrointestinal disturbances, and sleeplessness; excessive use of drugs; decline in self-esteem; and marital and family conflict. Of course, not all of these symptoms need to be present to say that a person is burning out. Some may be present and some not in any particular case. However, when there are several of these signs and changes in a professional, the work situation is all too likely the source of this burnout. This will be elaborated upon in later chapters of this book.[2]

Based on our research with new professionals, burnout is different in important ways from three related phenomena. First, burnout is not the same as temporary fatigue or strain, although such feelings may be an early sign of burnout. As used here, burnout involves change in attitudes toward one's work and clients as well as the feelings of exhaustion and tension that sometimes occur. Second, burnout is different from socialization or acculturation, the process in which a staff person's attitudes and behavior change in response to social influence exerted by colleagues or clients. For instance, McPherson (1972) described how older teachers influence newer ones to emphasize order and maintain control in their classrooms. The same negative changes that occur in burnout may also occur in response to the socializing influence of supervisors or coworkers. But in burnout these changes are a direct response to overload and stress caused by the job. Both burnout and socialization involve change in attitudes and behavior over time as a function of one's role in a system, but burnout refers to an individual adaptation to stress. (We shall return to this distinction in Chapters 6 and 7.)

Finally, burnout should be distinguished from turnover. Burnout may cause staff members to quit, but they may burn out and remain on the job. (The image that comes to mind is of the attendant in a state institution who remains because the job pays well, is not too demanding, and has great security.) Also, people may leave jobs for positive or irrelevant reasons rather than as a flight from a bad work situation. So while high turnover in an agency *may* be a sign of high burnout, it need not be.

Burnout adversely affects the professional's performance in a variety of ways. First, the loss of enthusiasm, idealism, and hope often diminishes the professional's effectiveness. While excessive idealism and enthusiasm may even lead to the loss of objectivity and excessive demands on one's clients and one's self, enthusiasm, commitment, and hope seem to be valuable ingredients in many fields. For instance, in an extensive review of the research on classroom teaching,

Lortie (1973) concluded that the enthusiasm of the teacher is strongly associated with higher rates of student learning. And in a comparative study of
healing and psychotherapy, Frank (1973) concluded that the healer's faith,
conviction, and zeal concerning what he is doing is probably the most critical
ingredient in the process.

Thus, although a professional's knowledge and skill are important for
effective performance, his emotional state, especially the level of enthusiasm
and commitment brought to the helping relationship, seems to be as important
as the specific methods and techniques used. Further, a professional's emotional
responsiveness and effectiveness can be adversely affected by the negative
changes in attitude that tend to occur when he is exposed to stress for a sustained period of time.

Burnout in public professionals affects the delivery of service in other
ways as well. It contributes to staff absenteeism and turnover, which can disrupt
program continuity and adversely affect clients because of frequent change in
primary caregivers. Also, because burned out professionals are less responsive to
clients, clients wait longer and receive less attention. In some cases, burnout may
lead to physical abuse of clients. Thus, burnout in professionals does seem to
affect professional performance and is therefore a critical problem for research
and policy in the human services.

THE CRITICAL FIRST YEARS

The loss of idealism and commitment in response to stressful working
conditions can and does occur at any point in a professional's career. No one
is immune. However, the initial period of the career—that time immediately
following professional training and certification when one abandons the student
role and assumes the new role of professional—is often the time of greatest
change in attitudes and behavior. It seems to be the time when many of the core
values and attitudes that will persist throughout the career are formed. For this
reason, the first year or two of the professional career seems to be a particularly
important point for studying professional development in general and burnout
in particular.

The importance of the first years to professional development has been
recognized by many scholars. For instance, Becker, Geer, Hughes, and Strauss
(1961), in their classic study of socialization in medical students, argued that
formal training plays a relatively minor role in the formation of professional
perspectives. More important are the forces that come into play following
graduation. The student role socializes the novice for being a student as much as
for being a professional. If physicians become less idealistic and more cynical,
they do so primarily in response to situational constraints and forces they
confront when they leave school and become practicing physicians.

The importance of the first years of work to the development of work-related attitudes was also supported by Hall and Schneider (1973) in an extensive study of career development in priests. Their data suggested that the first year of the priest's career is especially critical to subsequent career development. The "career sub-identity" grows at a faster rate during this period than in subsequent years. What happens to priests during this time was found to be associated with the levels of commitment, performance, and success observed in later years.

Research on early career development and socialization also suggests that the changes in attitude that occur during the early part of a professional career are often less than desirable. For instance, Hall and Schneider found that new priests became less idealistic and more "realistic" and less enthusiastic about creating change in the church and more aware of the importance of interpersonal and political aspects of their work, including problems with other priests and the laity. They also found that self-esteem and job satisfaction tended to decline during the early years of the priest's career. An initial decline in job satisfaction and self-esteem has also been found in public school teachers, and there is a tendency for professionals to become more resistant to change and experimentation (Anderson, 1968; Sarason, 1971) and more preoccupied with technique and procedure, often losing sight of the larger purpose and meaning of their work (Anderson, 1968).

There is also evidence that the nature of attitude change differs with the professional group. For instance, in comparative research on professional students, Eron (1958) found that medical students became more cynical about life during their training, but law students did not. Medical and nursing students became less humanitarian, but law students remained the same. The attitudes formed as a result of becoming a professional can even overcome the effects of earlier socialization. For instance, in a study of administrator attitudes toward racial imbalance, student discipline, and judicial intervention in the public schools, Cohn (1978) found that the degree of *professional socialization* was even more strongly correlated with one's opinions on these issues than was one's *race*. The higher one's educational level and the longer one had been a public school administrator, the more resistant one was to judicial intervention or system change affecting integration, no matter what one's race happened to be. In other words, black administrators who initially might have been more likely to support judicial intervention on behalf of racial integration became more resistant to such intervention and more like white administrators in their attitudes as they became more "professionalized."

Thus, the first years of a professional career seem to be critical to the development of attitudes and behavior that are likely to persist. The molding of a professional identity clearly does not end with the completion of formal training. The experiences of those critical first years are fateful not only for the professional, but for all who live in the "professional service society." Therefore, the problem of burnout in *new* public professionals is especially important for all of us.

THE RESEARCH METHOD

To understand this phenomenon, we developed a research method[3] that had several distinct features. First, it was longitudinal. We studied new professionals at various points during the first two years of their professional careers. In this way, we were able to observe the *process* of coping and adjustment; changes in attitude that occurred during this period could be clearly attributed to this process, rather than to a confounding factor such as selective attrition. Second, we chose a comparative approach, studying novices from four fields (law, public health nursing, mental health, and high school teaching). Consequently, we were able to determine what was common to the professional experience, as well as important differences that might not have been noticed if only one field were studied.

A third feature of our method was the use of multiple, in-depth interviews with a small group of subjects. The interviews were unstructured, designed to let the subjects tell their own stories as much as possible. There were several rationales for this. The lack of previous research on the topic and the exploratory nature of the study led us to use a method that was suited for discovery, one that allowed us to identify important patterns and processes that could not have been anticipated. A less structured, in-depth interview procedure allowed us to study the total pattern of experience, the way in which various aspects of human existence fit together, rather than specific variables in isolation from the rest. The problem of candor was another important consideration. A study of how people feel about their work is immediately confronted by the problem of openness, for work is one of the most significant aspects of people's lives, a major source of self-esteem, meaning, and identity. And professionals, even more than most workers, are particularly invested in seeing themselves and their occupations in the most positive light possible and in presenting this view to the public world (Sarason, 1977). We believed that repeated, in-depth, relatively unstructured interviews, conducted by trained interviewers who first sought to develop trust and rapport with the subjects, would best overcome the subjects' initial reticence. Thus, several considerations led us to adopt a longitudinal, comparative method utilizing unstructured, in-depth interviews with a small group of subjects.

The final sample for the study consisted of 28 new professionals, seven from each field. (Details on how the sample was selected and on the subjects' backgrounds can be found in Appendix A.) The subjects worked in a variety of settings, but all of the settings were publicly funded agencies or institutions accountable to legislatures or citizen boards. The lawyers worked in neighborhood legal aid offices, state appellate defender offices, and reform law agencies representing the interests of indigent groups. The mental health professionals worked in community mental health agencies, small family counseling agencies, councils on alcoholism, large state institutions for the mentally retarded and mentally ill, and public school systems. The public health nurses worked in visiting nurse associations and public health departments. And the high school teachers taught math, business, science, and art history in both urban and rural schools of varying size.

The interviews were conducted between October, 1974 and May, 1976. Each subject was interviewed at least twice initially with a follow-up interview conducted several months later. The average length of time between the initial interviews and the follow-up was five months. The interviewers attempted to keep the interviews informal. The primary task in each case was to put the subjects at ease and encourage them to discuss their work experiences as freely as possible. The interviewers sought to communicate a sympathetic, accepting interest in the subject, assuming the role of learner and inviting the subject to participate as a colleague in the investigation. Interviews were tape-recorded, and most of the recordings were transcribed. The transcripts were studied, discussed, and analyzed by our research group, using a procedure of thematic analysis (described in Appendix A).

AN OVERVIEW OF THE STUDY

Surprisingly little research has been conducted on the problem of stress and burnout in new public professionals, the group in which the incidence may well be highest. While psychologists and sociologists have devoted much energy to the study of stress and anxiety in others (elementary school children, college sophomores, industrial workers, and survivors of disasters), they have neglected the study of stress in themselves and other professionals. However, stress and anxiety exist at high levels in most new public professionals. The individual's attempts to cope with this role-related stress often lead to burnout, and thus have profound implications for professional career development and public welfare.

Theoretically, our research was strongly influenced by what has come to be called the "social ecological perspective." In this approach, human behavior is seen as a dynamic interaction between the individual and the social environments of which he or she is a part. The social environment, whether it is a classroom, the family, or a work organization, imposes certain demands on individuals at the same time that individuals attempt to influence their environment to conform to their needs and wishes. The pattern of any human life at any point in time represents a response by the individual to the demands and constraints—as well as the opportunities—provided by the social environment. Thus, a study that focuses only on the structure of the environment will produce a distorted, one-sided picture of human existence and will not allow us to predict and constructively influence human behavior with much success. The similar limitation holds for research focusing exclusively on the needs, personalities, or motivations of individuals. Only the study of individuals, their social environment, and the interaction or "fit" between the two will suffice.

Using this social ecological perspective for a study of new public professionals led to a certain emphasis in our approach. We were especially sensitive to the structure of the job and work setting, including its roles, norms, traditions, patterns of authority and control, organizational climate, and so on. We also assumed that much of the change occurring in new professionals would be the result of adaptation to strain produced by exposure to a new set of environmental contingencies. We were aware from the beginning that the initial period of a professional career is usually marked by significant tension, anxiety, and frustration, and we believed that the individual's efforts to cope with this unpleasant situation would play an important role in the development of professional attitude and behavior patterns. However, while we had certain notions about the situation, we attempted to remain close to the observable, allowing our data to influence our own emerging perspective.

More specifically, our study of what happens to new public professionals focused on four basic questions. First, what are the major sources of stress in the new professional working in a public institution? Second, how do new public professionals cope with this stress? Third, how does the coping process lead to change in professional attitudes and behavior? And fourth, how do differences in work settings influence the process?

Sources of Strain

The first question addressed by the study is considered in Chapters 2-5. I examine the major sources of stress experienced by new public professionals, describing the issues that preoccupied the novices we interviewed, the issues that they discussed at greatest length and with most feeling. Phenomenologically, these are the themes that characterize the new professional experience.

The first and most critical source of stress for the novice was the problem of competence (Chapter 2). Despite many years of formal schooling, most new public professionals did not feel completely prepared for their roles. This insecurity about competence and a persistent sense of uncertainty about performance became a major source of stress. Another major source of stress, frustration, and disappointment was that clients were not always motivated, cooperative, or grateful (Chapter 3). Most of the new public professionals we studied were not prepared for the reception from their clients. They were easily hurt, disappointed, and/or resigned by this unexpected facet of their work lives.

Bureaucratic interference was a third source of stress (Chapter 4). Politics and paperwork figured prominently in the complaints made by professionals working in public institutions. The new professionals were not at all prepared for dealing with this aspect of the job. Bitter conflicts between agencies that were supposed to work in concert, the interference of administrators who often knew little about the day-to-day problems affected by their decisions, the intricate and laborious procedures that must be followed to get things done, and the general lack of autonomy and control over one's work created considerable stress and frustration for many new public professionals.

Boredom was a related source of stress and dissatisfaction. To their amazement, many new public professionals found that their work was not as stimulating or meaningful as they had thought it would be. Anxious to finish their schooling and get out into the "real world," many soon began to miss the opportunities for learning and intellectual stimulation that occurred more frequently in school. They also found that much of their work was routine, and the lack of variety and challenge became another source of discontent. Understimulation can be as stressful as overstimulation, and, for many new public professionals, lack of variety, meaning, and intellectual discovery in their jobs became yet one more strain contributing to burnout.

The relationship between the new public professionals and their peers was another crucial aspect of the job (Chapter 5). The new professionals desired collegial relations with co-workers; in the face of stress they turned to their colleagues for support. Unfortunately, many factors frustrated their efforts. The structure of their jobs and agencies, the prevailing social climate of the institution, and organizational conflict often interfered with the development of supportive and collaborative relations among professionals working in the public institutions. Rather than a source of help, professional colleagues sometimes become yet one more source of stress and strain.

Coping and Change

After examining these major sources of stress, Chapters 6 and 7 consider the ways in which the new professionals coped with this stress and the ultimate impact of this coping on professional attitudes and behavior. Previous research on what happens to new professionals has tended to focus on the process of socialization. Both burnout and socialization involve change in attitudes and behavior as a function of one's role in a system. Both processes probably contribute to change in new public professionals. However, our research has suggested that the process of adjusting to the demands and pressures of the job is more significant.

New professionals in public human service institutions tend to cope with the stress and strain in their work by modifying their attitudes toward work. Specifically, six changes in attitude were observed. First, the novices changed their work goals. In some cases, this involved lowering their personal standards. For instance, new teachers who initially believed they were not successful unless they "reached" every student came to accept reaching a few students as adequate.

A second important change in attitude involved personal responsibility for outcomes. While they initially were more likely to consider the impact of their own behavior on the outcome of their work, over time, many new public professionals blamed their clients or "the system" when they failed. A third change was a decline in idealism. Few new professionals continued to regard clients as positively as they had initially. They also gave up many of their more progressive and humanistic beliefs about people. For instance, a new high school teacher initially believed that, if she treated her students with respect, they would treat her with respect. Six months later, she told us that she had been naive. "Don't ever count on the students," she said. "They'll stab you in the back every time if you do." For her and many of the other new public professionals, idealism was one of the first casualties.

Emotional detachment also occurred. As did the other changes in attitude and behavior, emotional detachment seemed to reduce some of the stress and strain associated with work. One poverty lawyer provided an especially clear example of this change. She stated that initially she had taken a personal interest in her clients and their problems. However, she simply could not cope with the extra demands created by the warmer, more personal style of interaction, and this personal involvement was replaced by a more distant, "professional" orientation. Many of the new teachers reported changing in the same way and for the same reason.

Yet another change that occurred during the early phase of the career was a decrease in psychological involvement in work. Most new professionals began their careers with the belief that their work should be one of the primary commitments of their lives. However, one way that many novices seemed to cope with the strains and disappointments of their work was to withdraw psychologically from the job and to seek meaning, creativity, and self-actualization elsewhere. In the beginning, many novices lived to work; after working in a public agency for a year, many merely worked to live. What had begun as a vocation or calling had become only a job.

The final change in outlook concerned self-interest. Over time, many novices seemed to adopt a "me first" attitude. Their ideas about work-related rewards changed. For instance, many novices were initially unconcerned about the size of their paychecks. Most were satisfied with their salaries. However, after four months many had become more dissatisfied with the size of their paychecks. Because so many of the intrinsic rewards they had hoped to receive from work were missing, because they so often felt that their work involved much "giving" and little "getting," they increasingly placed their own welfare above their commitment to clients, colleagues, and organizations. Thus, in the process of coping with the crisis of competence, the lack of collegial support, and other work-related strains, the new public professionals began to change their attitudes.

Sources of Variation in Experience

Chapters 8-12 are concerned with sources of variation in the subjects we studied. Why were a few fortunate novices able to escape burnout early in their careers? Was there something unique about their initial outlooks, the structure of their jobs and work settings, and the quality of their lives outside of work? Chapter 8 begins the explanation of these questions by presenting four case studies of early professional career development in public human service institutions. Two of the subjects—a high school teacher and a poverty lawyer—followed the pattern of job stress and burnout previously described. However, the other two subjects, though they came from the same professional groups, were striking in the degree to which they were able to sustain commitment, compassion, and enthusiasm. In describing these four individuals at some length, I hope that the complexity of the problem of burnout will be conveyed at the same time that the specific factors contributing to its incidence will begin to emerge.

The next three chapters consider a set of factors in the individual and the work place associated with differences in early career development. First are factors in the work setting. These include the presence or absence of special orientation experiences for new professionals, the nature of the workload, the degree to which institutional goals are clearly articulated, the strength and vitality of the program's guiding philosophy, and organizational leadership. When the most successful and satisfied novices are compared with those who had the most difficult experiences, they tend to differ on these dimensions.

There are two factors that individuals bring to their first professional jobs. The first is what we came to call the career orientation. What work-related rewards are most important to the individual? What are the individual's future aspirations and goals? The answers to these questions define the career orientation of a new public professional. For example, work is primarily seen by some as a vehicle for bringing about institutional change. They are guided by a strong, conscious, ideological commitment. Others are more interested in the intrinsic rewards obtained from the process of performing their work than in the ultimate outcomes. For them, professional work is a craft to be studied, pursued, and enjoyed with unwavering loyalty. Our research suggested that a new professional's career orientation influenced the degree of stress and the likelihood of burnout during the initial phase of the career.

The second important factor that individuals brought to the job was the quality of their lives outside of work. The work lives and personal lives of our subjects were intimately connected. What happened in one sphere influenced the other. Generally, those new professionals who were not involved in a stable, satisfying relationship outside of work were more vulnerable to stress on the job and more likely to burn out. Those who had just moved from another community or who were involved in a stormy, unsatisfying relationship were especially at risk. Of course, heavy demands and pressures in their jobs could spill over and adversely affect life outside of work. For the new public professionals we interviewed, work life and personal life were mutually dependent.

Implications and Conclusions

Although the findings of this study are tentative, many who make social policy and direct human service programs will want to use what is known about professional burnout to make changes in training and the work place that might alleviate the problem. Chapters 13 and 14 present a number of practical ideas for preventing burnout and promoting positive career development.

Unfortunately, many of the forces that contribute to burnout in new public professionals are beyond the control of individual professionals in their work organizations. The concluding chapter identifies cultural and historical factors that must be addressed by the larger society if professional burnout is to be overcome. These factors include the "professional mystique," a set of beliefs concerning professionals and the nature of their work that contributes to unrealistic expectations. The decline of community and the weakening of professional credibility are two other important factors. Resistance to change within the professions has also played a role. The book ends with the message that these larger social forces can and should be addressed.

NOTES

1. There is a large body of literature on professionals and professionalization. The interested reader would do well to consult Vollmer and Mills (1966), Sarason (1977), Becker et al. (1961), Corwin (1961), Abrahamson (1967), Kramer (1974), Moore (1970), Freidson (1970), and Bucher and Stelling (1977).

2. Those familiar with research and theory on psychological stress will recognize burnout as a particular kind of stress response. Caplan, Cobb, French, Harrison, and Pinneau (1975) proposed that an imbalance between job demands and the individual's resources for meeting those demands (stress) will lead to various kinds of strain, defined as any deviation from normal responses in the person. Strain can be psychological (for instance, job dissatisfaction, anxiety, frustration, low self-esteem), physiological (such as high blood pressure), or behavioral (for example, smoking). Lazarus (1966) has concentrated on the coping process, showing that when an individual experiences stress and strain, efforts to reduce the threatening imbalance between demand and resources are activated. These efforts can take the form of active problem solving (such as increased information seeking, direct action), withdrawal, or psychological defense (for instance, denial, repression). Burnout would thus appear to be a process in which job stress leads to strain, which takes the form of emotional exhaustion and other physical and psychological symptoms. This strain may initially lead to active problem-solving efforts in the worker; however, the worker eventually gives up and instead withdraws emotionally from the stressful work situation. There is a large literature on stress (for example, McGrath, 1970; Kahn, Wolfe, Quinn, Snoel, & Rosenthal, 1964; Dohrenwend

& Dohrenwend, 1974; Coelho, Hamburg, & Adams, 1974; Pearlin & Schooler, 1978) that would contribute much to current attempts to define and conceptualize burnout.

3. An extensive description and rationale for our procedures can be found in Appendix A.

PART I

SOURCES OF STRAIN

2

THE CRISIS OF COMPETENCE

The one theme that most strongly shaped and colored the experiences of new professionals was a deep concern with personal competence. So profound and pervasive was the self-doubt and insecurity concerning personal efficacy that we began referring to the new professional experience as the "crisis of competence." The concern was felt more strongly by some subjects in our study than by others, and it was manifested in different ways. However, every new professional interviewed expressed concern about the adequacy of his or her performance. This concern was a major source of stress for new public professionals and thus a potential cause of burnout. If the new professional's sense of inadequacy and self-doubt became too great or was sustained too long, he or she might eventually burn out, withdrawing from the field of conflict, blaming others for mishaps and failures, and giving up the idealism and commitment that are often necessary for effective performance.

The dictionary defines "competence" as "having all the natural powers, physical or mental, to meet the demands of a situation or work." White (1979, p. 11) defined competence simply as "effective in work." The new professionals frequently questioned whether their abilities were sufficient for the demands of their work during this initial period of their careers. This concern about competence was not a neurotic quest for perfection. They knew that there would be failures. They knew that they would not be able to reach every client. However, they often felt that they lacked some of the abilities required to perform in the way that their profession and organization expected. Their concern with their own performance, the self-doubt and insecurity they felt, and the way it affected their work and personal lives proved to be one of the most poignant and important themes to emerge.

THE QUEST FOR COMPETENCE

Achieving a sense of competence in one's work is a goal for most workers. As a special government commission on the quality of work life in America pointed out in its report, *Work in America* (O'Toole, 1973), a person's work strongly influences her self-esteem. Individuals in our society tend to measure themselves by what they do. If their work is challenging and they are able to meet the challenge successfully, self-esteem is enhanced. Conversely, if they are unemployed or underemployed or if they believe they are not performing competently, self-esteem is likely to suffer.

Professionals employed in human service agencies are no exception. In fact, competence is a distinguishing characteristic of "professionalism" in our culture. To be considered a true professional is to be regarded as particularly able and competent in one's work. Once they complete their training and receive certification, new professionals are *expected* to be competent. Not only do others expect it of them; they expect it of themselves.

When the new professionals interviewed for our study discussed what being a professional meant to them, competence was often mentioned as a major aspect. For instance, in an interview with Sherman Reynolds,* a new clinical social worker employed in a family counseling agency, the interviewer asked, "Do you see yourself now as a professional?" Sherman answered, "A *real* professional, not just somebody with the title, would be someone who feels right on top of things. Right when I started, I didn't really see myself as a new professional. I saw myself as a new social worker." For Sherman and the other new professionals, to be a "real" professional was to be "right on top of things," to know what to do in all situations, to be in control, to be knowledgeable and wise—in a word, to be competent.

When the new professionals in our study described other professionals whom they most admired and most wanted to be like, competence emerged as a major distinguishing attribute. For instance, Gloria Bennet, a new public health nurse, described another nurse with whom she had been working:

> I met this consultant who I found out graduated two years before I did. She's come back as a mental health consultant for the Visiting Nurses Association. She got out of school, worked for a year, and then went to get her master's in family counseling within nursing. She's really the only person in our agency who does this kind of work. So you go to her when you have problem patients, psychologically, that you would like help with, and this girl, I have so much

---

*All names used in this book are pseudonyms, and details about work situations are disguised.

admiration for her. She's unreal, what she does. To watch her work! You have a family with trouble, and you go in and she sits them all down and she says, "Now, look your father in the eye and tell him you love him. You love him? Tell him you love him." She solves a tremendous amount of problems. She has gone so far. I guess I look at her, and I think that's the way it should be. I think when I saw her, it kind of made me fit in a lot of little pieces of things I know I would like to do, but I didn't know where to go with them. And I've really never met another nurse that I felt I could use as a role model so much.

In describing the mental health consultant, Gloria suggested that it was her almost magical *competence* in dealing with difficult problems that she most admired and most wanted to emulate. A good professional, one worthy of admiration and respect, was above all an effective professional. For Gloria Bennet and virtually all of the other new professionals we interviewed, to be an effective professional was a primary goal in work—and in life.

THE BURDEN OF BEING RESPONSIBLE FOR OTHERS

For the new public professionals, competence in work was a major goal. They wanted a sense of accomplishment in their work. Self-esteem seemed constantly to be on the line. But for professionals in human service agencies, more than their own self-esteem is at stake. The personal well-being of numerous individuals may be affected by one's actions. When the new professional makes a mistake, others may suffer greatly. Even if no one else were aware that a mistake had been made, the professional would know.

When they were students, these individuals were responsible only for themselves. If they did poorly on an exam or a paper, their grade in the course might suffer. Perhaps their future could be jeopardized. However, only they would be affected. As professionals, they affected others through their actions as well. Much more seemed to be at stake. Thus, morale was strongly affected by how much they were able to help their clients. In a study of job satisfaction in the mental retardation field, Sarata (1972) found that lack of client progress was a major source of dissatisfaction. Cherniss and Egnatios (1978a), in a study of job satisfaction in community mental health programs, emerged with a similar finding. The factor most often cited as a source of satisfaction by their subjects was "doing something that gives one a sense of accomplishment." However, to achieve a sense of accomplishment in professional work, one must be competent.

A new public health nurse, Sarah Prentiss, conveyed well what the burden of responsibility is like for the new professional. She had become a staff nurse in a county health department four months before we began our interviews with her. She was responsible for the home care of all patients in a particular geographic area. At one point during our initial interview, she said:

> There are a lot of concerns about this job, thinking about all these people in the community that are kind of your responsibility. And I think about it. Like just this weekend, I had this woman who was having some problems, and I thought about her all weekend, just thinking about what I can do and what I should do. There's a little bit of pressure there, I'd say.

A new high school teacher, Alice Harris, expressed the same idea when she said:

> I really feel that I have a responsibility to be prepared for the students. I'm not just in a job. What I teach these kids is going to be important to them some day, I think—I hope. I don't feel I have a right to toy with them. They expect certain things from me as I expect certain things from them, and that gives me the get-up-and-go.

For at least one new professional we interviewed, the responsibility for others was so awesome that she shaped her career to initially lessen the burden and thus reduce the "need" to be competent. Shana Phillips was a new lawyer working in an agency that handled criminal appeals for indigent clients. During her interview, she said, "I was hesitant, coming right out of law school, to represent people charged with crimes where they could serve up to life. That's a very heavy trip, and my ego wasn't that strong." She avoided this precarious situation by going to work in the agency that handled only appeals. By working on the appellate level, she believed that she could learn criminal law and increase her self-confidence without jeopardizing her clients as much as if she were representing them at the trial level.

As students, the new professionals had not been as personally responsible if they made mistakes. They could often count on supervisors to intervene and prevent them from doing too much harm when they were in direct contact with clients or students. For instance, a new high school science teacher, Calvin Miller, said, "I didn't feel that much pressure as a student-teacher. I had a really good supervising teacher to work with, and it still was a learning situation. I knew he was always there to back me up if I did make a mistake." However, as an independent, certified teacher, Calvin was suddenly on his own. There was no supervisor looking over his shoulder, checking his work, ready to intervene at the slightest sign of misjudgment or inadequacy. The new teacher could really make mistakes now, and he would be solely responsible if he did. For Calvin Miller and the other new public professionals, the burden of being responsible for others made the quest for competence especially critical.

ESTABLISHING A REPUTATION

The new public professional's concern about competence was further exacerbated by pressure that came from colleagues and clients. Soon after starting their new jobs, the professionals found that one's reputation with colleagues and clients was based almost entirely on one's perceived effectiveness. Also, the expectations and standards for professional skill and knowledge at first seemed to be extremely high, far higher than the new professionals felt they could reach. The problem of establishing a reputation thus became another source of stress.

For instance, Shana Phillips, the new lawyer working in a public agency that handled criminal appeals for indigent clients, said that she felt tremendous pressure to perform well. The staff attorneys tried in every way possible to impress each other with their knowledge of the law and their successes in the courtroom. Proving one's competence to one's colleagues seemed to be a major preoccupation of the lawyers with whom Shana worked. One's social standing in the office seemed very much based on competence. When a lawyer could recite from memory a string of legal precedents in a conversation with a colleague, he or she was, to use Shana's term, "hot." And when one won a case, one was "superhot." For Shana, this emphasis on making a good showing increased her desire to be competent. Her standing with her peers seemed to depend on it.

Another new lawyer, Jean Chalmers, worked in a different agency, one that engaged in reform law. But she expressed the same idea. After describing her anxieties concerning her competence and the self-doubt she often felt, she said:

> You know, when you talk to lawyers, the first thing they say is, "She's a bad lawyer, she's a good lawyer. He's a bad lawyer, he's a good lawyer." I mean, they lose sight of ... "a nice person but doesn't know noodles about law." They want to know, are you good at what you do? "Nice person, but I'd never have her as a lawyer."

In professional circles, people tend to be judged not on how "nice" they are, but on the basis of how much they seem to *know*. The evaluation process goes on continually—in the office, after work over a beer, at cocktail parties—and the new professional observes what occurs and concludes that acceptance and self-respect depend primarily on one's competence.

Although law, as seen through the eyes of the new lawyers we interviewed, seemed to be more competitive and more reputation-conscious than the other professional groups, the same phenomenon occurs in all professions to some extent. For instance, high school teachers also seem to evaluate one another on the basis of perceived competence, and these evaluations appear to be taken seriously, at least by the new teachers. In the case of high school teachers, competence in maintaining class control seemed to be especially important.

The comments of Calvin Miller, the new science teacher, were particularly revealing. When we interviewed him, Calvin's teaching was going well in most respects. But in one class, there was a student whose behavior was disruptive, and Calvin had not been successful in controlling it. He was concerned about the effect of this student on other students, but he was also concerned about the effect on his "reputation":

> This is where I feel I fail. If I let his behavior interfere with the learning of anyone else in the class, then I've failed because my job is to try to deal with this kid and get him to learn. But most importantly, it's that he doesn't interrupt the other people in that class. It has really upset me when he's disrupted the class because there are a couple of people in that class who really want to learn and then they get upset. And then they go home and say something about how the class was just in an uproar today and Mr. Miller couldn't keep John settled down. So I get a reputation as not being able to keep control of the class.

When a new professional's colleagues seemed to expect a higher level of skill or knowledge than he or she actually possessed, the concern about competence became especially acute. For instance, nurse Sarah Prentiss said with some exasperation, "I don't know what they think I am because I just got out of school. But they think, 'Well, you just got out of school, you should know this disease.' And half the time, I don't know what it is."

Even when co-workers did not explicitly demand it, they often set high standards of competence for the new professional simply through their own performance, credentials, and experience. Consider, for instance, these comments of public health nurse Sarah Prentiss:

> There are nurses here that have been public health nurses for years, and this agency is really unique because everyone here is a B.S.N. A lot of the women are working on their master's degrees. These women are really up on current nursing practice, and that's really good. I'm really glad to see that, but you have to keep on your toes.

As did other new professionals, Sarah valued the opportunity to work with highly trained, experienced, competent colleagues. However, by their example, they increased the pressure to perform competently. As Sarah put it, they kept her "on her toes."

Clients, too, expected the new professionals to perform competently and provided one further source of pressure. For instance, several of the new lawyers complained that their clients expected too much from them. Many clients seemed to think that if they had an attorney representing them they were sure to win. Even though the attorneys knew that these expectations were unrealistic, they felt the pressure to do well. Sometimes when they lost a case their clients would ask, "Why didn't you say anything? Why didn't you do something?" The clients were clearly evaluating the professional's behavior and seemed to have "great expectations" concerning the professional's competence.

For high school teacher Cynthia Noble, the pressure came from parents as well as students. She felt that parents were constantly watching the performance of teachers and were ready to intervene whenever they believed a teacher had made a mistake. She said, "There's a lot of parents sticking up for their kids from what I've heard. When kids do something wrong and you reprimand them for it, they'll go home and tell Mom and Dad. And the next thing you know, parents are coming in and saying, 'Why? Why did you do that to him? That was embarrassing for him.'" Cynthia went on to say that teachers do not really have to justify their actions to parents and that usually the principal supports teachers. However, she also said that she did have to respond to parental criticism at least once during her first year, and she clearly felt the pressure of parental expectations. Clients and their families, like colleagues and the larger society, expect the new professionals to be effective. And the wish to meet these expectations, to be viewed as competent by peers and clients, becomes a major concern for the new professionals, an urgent priority in their personal agenda for work, and a source of self-doubt and stress.

THE PSYCHOLOGY OF "FALLING SHORT"

As previously described, establishing one's competence was, for a number of reasons, a critical concern of the new professionals we interviewed. In fact, virtually all of the individuals interviewed expressed doubt about their competence at some point during the initial phase of their careers, and they did so in a variety of ways. Not only did they *fear* failing; at some time, all believed they *were* failing, that they were not measuring up to the standards of performance established by their profession. Feeling inadequate and ineffective seemed to be part of being a new public service professional—an especially painful part.

A major cause of the sense of inadequacy in new public service professionals was "falling short." Falling short refers to a situation in which the professional cannot respond adequately to a client's problems and needs. In all of the fields included in our study, the professionals repeatedly confronted situations of this nature. As one subject put it, "What you can do for a client and what you should do are two different things." Sometimes they were limited by their own skill and knowledge. Sometimes they were prevented from fully solving a client's problem by constraints imposed by the social systems within which they had to work. And sometimes they were stymied by the client's lack of motivation, suspiciousness, or extreme deprivation. Whatever the cause, most new helping professionals in public service jobs constantly fell short in their efforts to solve their clients' problems. Each time this occurred, their sense of competence was shaken.

For even when the source of failure was clearly not in themselves, falling short prevented the new professionals from succeeding and thus also prevented them from experiencing a sense of mastery in their work.

Falling short obviously poses the greatest threat to the new professional's sense of competence when the cause seems to be located in the professional. Unfortunately, the new professionals frequently found that their skill and knowledge could not carry them far enough. For instance, Constance Simmel, a public health nurse working in a county health department, complained that she did not possess the skill necessary to work with the psychological aspects of patients' problems and that these aspects frequently played a major role in the nursing process. She felt that she could help people to "work through their experiences and frustrations up to a point," but that she was "inadequate to help them any further." Too often, she believed, she had no choice but to refer her patients to mental health specialists. Eventually, Constance decided to leave nursing and return to graduate school for training in psychiatric social work.

In many cases, it was not clear whether falling short was caused by gaps in the new professional's knowledge or by the intransigence of clients and their problems. Sometimes it seemed that the clients just did not *want* to be helped and were preventing the professional from helping them. For instance, public health nurse Sarah Prentiss described a case that had greatly troubled her. An elderly woman was suffering from a number of medical problems as well as the loneliness and impoverishment that too often accompany old age. Sarah had put a great deal of time and effort into this case, one of the first assigned to her. She had made several visits to the home, she had brought in a physician to examine some skin problems, and she had arranged for a senior citizens group to become involved. However, despite all of Sarah's efforts, the woman resisted help and became increasingly depressed and apathetic. During her last visit to this woman, the woman said to Sarah, "I don't know why you're bothering with me. I just want to die." After Sarah had related this story, she went on to say:

> You know, I think about her. I can't help it. She's in this big house, her plumbing doesn't work, no hot water; but she's been seen by a doctor, and the neighbors are aware of the problem, so I guess that's all we can do right now. She'll probably just stay in her house and die.

The interviewer asked Sarah how she felt personally when this incident occurred. She responded:

> It was kind of like a rejection sort of thing. It was, it was. I thought, "Gee, what's wrong with me?" or "What did I do?" And, you know, I might have done something. Maybe I just turned her off. Maybe it was just a personality conflict. But I didn't see it, and that's the thing that bothered me, that I didn't have enough insight to see the problem. So, yeah, it bothered me.

For this new professional and for many others we interviewed, falling short was a painful experience, not only because it meant continued suffering, and perhaps even the death of another human being, but also because it suggested to this professional the possibility that she was not as competent as she should be, that there were critical gaps in her knowledge and skill. Even though the client was the one who had refused and thus determined the outcome, this new nurse could not stop thinking that greater skill in working with the woman may have helped change her attitude and altered the outcome.

In other instances, the professional seemed to feel less personally responsible for the obstacles encountered in a case and therefore experienced less guilt. However, even then there was considerable disappointment, remorse, and frustration because falling short prevented the professional from achieving a sense of efficacy.

Sarah Prentiss described particularly well the kind of frustration that occurs in working with clients whose apathy makes falling short inevitable. She said:

> I've gone into homes where the husband's unemployed; he doesn't really care if he ever works again. And the woman is 10 feet across. She sits around and smokes cigarettes all day, and her house is a mess; her kids are all messed up, and she could care less. And that's really frustrating for me to go into that because I'm most concerned about the kids. The kids don't choose to be born into that, but they're in it because these people are their parents. I have a woman that I talked to today that's like that. I haven't visited her in probably three weeks, but I'm going out there tomorrow. It's frustrating for me because I don't know if I'm going to get anywhere with these people. They're keeping their clinic appointments at the hospital because there are some medical problems, and that was a big deal to have them even do that. But getting her to take a bath—I don't know.

There is nothing positive in this nurse's description of a particularly difficult family in her caseload, a family impoverished in just about every possible way. She did seem to be struggling to maintain some objectivity, if not sympathy, for the mother and her family's plight. However, the frustration of "not getting anywhere" in her work with them and the implicit assumption that it was *their* fault made it particularly difficult to maintain a positive or even neutral attitude. Falling short with this family prevented the nurse from feeling competent, something she sorely wanted at this stage in her career. She had become frustrated, and her frustration seemed to be influencing her perceptions and attitudes in ways that may have been detrimental to her work, at least with this particular family. Unfortunately, there were many similar situations reported to us by the new professionals we interviewed. In these situations, the professional's sense of competence was shaken, and the psychological stress level increased perceptibly for them.

Often, falling short seemed to occur because of systemic factors that had little to do with either the professional or the client. For instance, one new high school teacher spoke for all when she complained that the larger number of students she was forced to teach made it inevitable that she would fall short with many. She said:

> I've sort of lost some of the kids that had been getting more of my attention before. I'm not exactly sure how many students I have, but it's around 120 or so through the course of the day. It's really hard to give them the attention they need. With all the kids I have, there's just no way I can keep up with all of them. You're always slighting someone.

A similar theme was voiced by Perry Curtis, a new poverty lawyer working in a neighborhood legal aid office. The office had a six-month waiting list. Unless a new case involved a "dire emergency," there was simply nothing he could do to help a client. Eligibility was also a problem. Legal aid had clear guidelines that prevented the staff from helping individuals whose financial situation put them just above the cut-off point. In fact, the welfare system often seemed designed to thwart the attorney's efforts to help the needy. He gave us an example:

> You get very frustrated with a case like this. A woman had five or six children living in her house. The husband had moved out and was living in the garage. He was working and not giving the wife a cent to buy food, to heat the house, or anything for the kids. According to the Department of Social Services, he was living on the premises; he was working; therefore, they did not qualify for welfare and there was nothing they would do.

He went on to say that, as a legal aid staff attorney, he also could do nothing because the family's income made the woman ineligible for legal aid. Although he had the legal skills necessary to help this woman, the system prevented him from doing so, and he experienced this as falling short of his own expectations to meet the needs of those seeking his help.

Even when poverty lawyers are able to take on a case, the legal system does not always provide an adequate solution to people's problems. For instance, several of the lawyers we interviewed complained that court injunctions often fell short. In one case, a lawyer secured an injunction against harrassment for a client in a divorce case. However, the police refused to enforce the injunction, and so the estranged spouse continued to harrass the lawyer's client. All he could do was return to court for another, stronger injunction, but that, too, could be ignored. Also, the pressure of a large caseload made it difficult for him to take the additional time. As he put it, if he went into court every time an injunction was not enforced, he would be spending so much time preparing that none of his

clients would ever obtain the final divorce. The system seemed to make it inevitable that he would fall short with many clients. Like the classroom teachers
with too many students, the poverty lawyers always seemed to be "slighting
someone." When this occurred, their sense of personal inadequacy was heightened,
even if the cause seemed to be the "system" rather than their own lack of
knowledge or skill. In fact, "blaming the system" often seemed to be a coping
strategy used by the new professionals to lessen their sense of inadequacy when
they did fall short, and it was a characteristic symptom of burnout (see Chapter
6). No matter what the cause, falling short occurs frequently in the human services. For new professionals who had not yet had their professional competence
affirmed, falling short was a major source of stress and thus a potential cause of
burnout.

IMMEDIATE EFFECTS OF THE
SENSE OF INADEQUACY AND SELF-DOUBT

For all the new professionals we interviewed, achieving a sense of competence was a major goal, but, for many, attempts to achieve competence were
often frustrated by the nature of their work. The stress and strain created by this
predicament began to affect the new professionals almost immediately. Their
feelings of inadequacy and uncertainty were expressed in many different ways.
Some developed a strong need for reassurance from others. Some experienced a
need for more structure and clear guidelines. Others attempted to cope with the
situation by being overly scrupulous in their work. When things did not go quite
right, they easily became embarrassed, confused, and perplexed.

The first response of many new professionals to the crisis of competence
was to seek reassurance from others. For instance, Cynthia Noble indicated that
one of her greatest needs as a new teacher was reassurance to combat the bad
days. A "bad" day was a day when something happened that shook her self-
confidence, such as a parent calling to complain. When assaults on her precarious
sense of competence occurred, she wanted someone to counteract them by
telling her that she really was competent, that she was doing a good job and need
not worry about failing. During one of these periods, Cynthia confessed, "Right
now, I need some reassurance. Right now, I could use a pat on the back, somebody saying, 'Yeah, you're doing a good job.'" Although Cynthia had fewer
problems in the classroom than most of the other new teachers, she too had
doubts about her professional competence and wished for reassurance from
others to counteract them.

Another new professional used almost the same words to describe the
importance of reassurance. Gloria Bennet, the public health nurse, said that
receiving positive feedback from her supervisor and co-workers was essential.
"Hopefully, you get some of it from within yourself, except sometimes you

need a 'pat on the back.'" Apparently, the need for reassurance, a "pat on the back," does not disappear when one receives one's degree and becomes a credentialed professional. In fact, the uncertainty of "success" and "failure" in teaching, nursing, psychological counseling, and other fields probably makes professionals susceptible to self-doubt at every stage of their careers. However, feelings of self-doubt seem to be especially strong during the earliest stages of the career, and it is then that professionals are most likely to need and seek reassurance from others.

Related to the desire for reassurance was a concern about being taken seriously. Because the new professionals doubted themselves and often felt unworthy of the status they had suddenly achieved, they seemed to be especially sensitive to doubts others may have had about their competence. It was important at this time in their careers that they received validation as competent professionals. Thus, when they believed others did not see them as true professionals, they became deeply chagrined. It is ironic in a sense. The new professionals often could not view *themselves* as totally prepared to be effective in every instance, yet it was precisely because they doubted their own abilities that they found it difficult to be denied recognition and respect by others.

A good example of the novice's sensitivity about being taken seriously was provided by Nick Fisher. In his role as a counselor and psychotherapist, it was not easy to know how well he was doing from day to day. Thus, he had doubts about his professional ability, and it was important to him that his supervisor take him seriously, as the following quote suggests:

> One of the hardest things at first was to be taken seriously. First of all, I couldn't get very many referrals because we didn't have very many cases coming in, so I went to a lot of conferences and read a lot and stuff like that. My supervisor kept coming down and telling me this and that, real simplistic stuff. I felt that I just didn't like to be assumed to be real young or green.

The supervisor seemed to misjudge Nick's level of knowledge and preparedness. In telling Nick "real simplistic stuff," the supervisor seemed to be saying that Nick was less competent. For Nick Fisher and many other new professionals, not to be taken seriously seemed like a vote of "no confidence," so they became especially sensitive about the way others treated them.

Another effect of the new professionals' insecurity was that small problems and mishaps were more disruptive than they would have been if the individual were more secure. Similarly, victories, no matter how small, were often relished as signs of competence and mastery. Poverty lawyer Margaret Williams described how much her self-esteem was affected by what happened at work:

> My self-esteem varies from day to day. I don't really know anything specific it depends on. If I'm having a lot of trouble getting some-

thing done in a case or if I lose something bad that I should have won, then I feel pretty bad. If I win something . . . I won a big case. It was an auto negligence case, and I had a big-deal ambulance chaser that had been hired by the other side; I mean a real hot-shot. And I said to myself, "I don't have a prayer." We went through a two day trial on the thing, and I won everything. The judge kept hoping for me. I felt awfully good then.

[Interviewer: "So really, it depends a lot on how your work goes?"]

A lot depends on how my work goes. I'd say probably all depends on how my work goes.

Undoubtedly, any lawyer at any stage of her career would feel good about winning the sort of case Margaret described. However, for a lawyer who had been practicing for only a year, winning—and losing—such a case took on special meaning. Her self-respect seemed to be much more affected by the outcomes of specific cases than would have been true for a more experienced member of her profession.

Winning or losing at work was important for new professionals in other fields as well. In law, winning or losing is usually just that—one wins cases or one loses them. Of course, it is sometimes hard to determine whether one is a loser or winner when there is an out-of-court settlement or routine plea bargaining has produced a compromise. New lawyers found that the practice of law is often more ambiguous in its results than they had initially expected, and this discovery can also complicate the quest for competence. In other professions, winning and losing tend to be even more ambiguous and symbolic. Nevertheless, new professionals defined many incidents as either winning or losing, and these individual, seemingly trivial occurrences were important because they were measurements of competence.

For instance, Cynthia Noble was easily flustered by clumsiness or mishaps in the classroom that seemed relatively unrelated to the business of teaching, especially when these occurred in the classes that most threatened her sense of professional competence. In fact, one of these mishaps could ruin a whole day for Cynthia. "I had a bad day on Tuesday. A visual aid fell on my head, and the class finds that great fun. I get so embarrassed. I think I handled it pretty well, but it still makes me flustered for the rest of the day and makes me feel that I'm too uncoordinated or something to be up there teaching." A few moments later, after the interview had moved on to other topics, Cynthia returned to this theme and described another disturbing mishap:

I sat on my glasses one day. I took them off and put them on the desk. I was going through homework, and I sat down at my desk, on top of my glasses. That was a charge for everyone. The glasses didn't break, but the kids got a big chuckle out of that. That's the only real feedback I get from the kids. I know they think I'm not all together all the time when I do things like that. It always seems to happen during my senior class, which is the one that's the most touch-and-go for me, anyway, because most of the kids are very close to my age.

For Cynthia Noble and many other new professionals, to lose face in front of clients or students was "losing" To maintain one's composure, to be coordinated and smooth in one's actions, to maintain firm control, was "winning." With their sense of competence on the line, new professionals tended to over-evaluate relatively minor aspects of their performance. Deviations from the norm of cool, collected, competent professionalism often seemed to be threatening, for they suggested failure in a situation in which other indicators of success and failure were too ambiguous to decipher. Thus, for many new professionals, self-image seemed to become extremely important. Events that detracted from a "professional image"—such as sitting on one's glasses—were almost as disturbing as losing an important trial. In fact, most new professionals seemed to regard *themselves* as the ones "on trial," and relatively insignificant mishaps seemed to be interpreted as signs that the trial was going badly.

Because mistakes and mishaps could be so devastating to new professionals' fragile sense of competence, many initially sought a high degree of structure and explicit guidelines from others. They were bothered by apparent freedom and lack of guidance in their work. Lack of structure during this initial stage became yet another source of stress.

For instance, Cynthia Noble said:

When I student-taught, everything was pretty laid out for you, what you were to do, and you didn't have much freedom. And I got to feeling that that would be pretty much the norm—that wherever you go people would say, "Well, this is the course you're supposed to teach and you're supposed to cover this, this, and this, and you should do it in this length of time." And I got to the school district where I am now, and everyone said, "Well, here's the course you're teaching." That's it! I like the freedom, but I don't know if I was really prepared for it. I still feel like I need some guidelines. They're so relaxed out there, which in a way is good because I'm free to make changes that I want to make. But I also don't have anything too much to follow, and sometimes I'm not sure if I'm really teaching the kids everything they should know or if I'm making it too hard for them or too easy.

This illustrates well a major dilemma faced by all new public professionals. They were attracted to a profession initially because of the greater freedom and autonomy they believed it would provide compared to other work, and they continued to value these aspects. However, at the same time, they wanted very much to feel competent, and they confronted many situations in which they felt unprepared. At these moments, they preferred more structure, more guidelines, and fewer options. We shall see in Chapter 7 that these feelings changed over time. As the new professionals felt more secure and confident, their desire for autonomy and freedom became stronger. Many who initially preferred less freedom and responsibility came to desire more than they had and to resent limitations and constraints. However, during the initial stage of transition from student to professional, the lack of specific rules and guidelines was more often experienced as a burden than a blessing.

Insecurity and self-doubt affected many new professionals in at least one more important way. They initially worked harder than seemed necessary to be sure that they would not "fail." It was not unusual for them to work six or even seven days a week, eight, ten, or twelve hours a day, during their first months on the job. They felt there was so much to learn and that it had to be learned so quickly that there seemed to be no alternative. Self-respect was on the line. They had to succeed. So they pushed themselves, attempting to gain a sense of competence through sheer effort. When they began to feel more competent, more "on top of things," many eased off and became less intensely involved in work. However, most new professionals did not feel they could do so until they had proven to themselves and others that they were competent and could handle the job.

Cynthia Noble described this process of intense effort in work particularly well. When the interviewer asked her how much time her teaching job required, she answered:

> It's getting better. The first two weeks it was like I'd come home from school and start preparing. And I'd go to bed and get up in the morning and go to school. Everything I did was around that. Now I've got it down to where I kind of know . . . I can feel the kids better so I know how much they can absorb in a day and how much I can give them to do at night. I just have a better feeling for it. When I first walked in there, I wasn't sure, and I was doing a lot more than I needed to. I was not really over-planning, but I was working out every single homework problem for all my classes to make sure they were really appropriate. Now, I don't work them all. I just sort of glance over them, and I don't care if I read the answer out of the answer book.

Initially, Cynthia was overly scrupulous, doing things that were not really necessary, such as working out every homework problem herself. Although it was not necessary for her to do this, it may have helped reduce some of the anxiety she felt about her own performance. She was, in effect, keeping herself busy so she could not worry as much. She was being overly conscientious, perhaps as a way of protecting herself from the accusation that she was not performing adequately. How could she be accused of being a poor teacher when every waking hour was devoted to preparation and planning, when she did every problem herself before assigning it to her students? However, as she became more confident, more sure of herself and relaxed, she no longer needed to work so hard. The need for excessive absorption in her work had passed.

Cynthia was unusual in how quickly she felt comfortable enough to ease up, less than one month after school began. Many other new professionals continued to work six and a half days a week during their first eight months or more. In fact, the intensity of work involvement seemed to vary with the field and the nature of the job. Public health nurses and mental health professionals seemed to work less overtime initially than did teachers and poverty lawyers. New professionals with larger caseloads were more likely to devote many extra hours to their work. However, new professionals in general worked much overtime during the initial phase of their careers. Doing so seemed in part a way of compensating for feelings of insecurity and self-doubt. They hoped that by putting in extra time they would achieve the elusive sense of mastery they so much desired.

CONCLUSION: THE MYTH
OF PROFESSIONAL COMPETENCE

The struggle to achieve a sense of competence is a central theme in the life of a new public professional. There seems to be a strong "need" to do well and to succeed. Further, despite the lengthy and expensive professional training in this society, virtually all of the subjects interviewed felt inadequate at times, precipitating what we have come to call the "crisis of competence."

To some extent, a concern about competence can probably be found in any worker in a new job; public service professionals clearly are not unique in this respect. Anyone who is asked to be responsible for work in a way she has never been before will probably experience many of the same feelings—the anxiety, the self-doubt, and the insecurity—that were experienced by the new professionals. In fact, what may distinguish new professionals from other new workers is not their anxiety and worry about performance, but rather the widely shared myth that they do not feel this way and should not feel this way because they are, unlike other workers, "finished products." As Cherniss, Egnatios, Wacker, and O'Dowd (1979) suggested, a popular misconception about professionals is the assumption that "credentials" automatically imply "competence." There is the expectation that new professionals will be competent and feel competent when they begin their first jobs. They have received the training necessary to assume professional duties and responsibilities. Their credentials signify to all the world that they are ready. With added experience, they may become still more competent and effective. However, when they receive their degrees, it is assumed that they are relatively complete. It is in this way that professionals are most unlike other types of workers in the public view.

The one consolation for new professionals is that the crisis of competence does not seem to continue indefinitely. Perhaps the most consistent trend in the study was that over time the new professionals felt more confident. They learned and grew relatively quickly during their first year or two as practicing professionals. As they did so, the expected sense of competence and mastery gradually emerged. When it did, the feeling of accomplishment was especially sweet.

However, a lingering sense of inadequacy probably remains. For many helping professionals, concern over personal competence and a sense of self-doubt apparently persist. Theirs is an uncertain, complex world in which the techniques, skills, and even goals of practice are ambiguous. There is so much controversy over the efficacy of different models of psychotherapy, or different philosophies of instruction, or even different medical procedures, that practitioners can never be sure their performance is adequate. Often, they must choose the approach that seems most likely to succeed and hope for the best. Such a situation is hardly one in which mastery and self-confidence can flourish.

Unfortunately, new professionals are rarely prepared to accept the existential limitations of professional practice. The great expectations created by the myths surrounding professionalism in our society persist and continue to guide thought and action. And new professionals working in public institutions are among the victims.

3

COMING TO TERMS WITH CLIENTS

For the new professional working in a public human service agency, clients are a major source of both gratification and strain. They can provide the new professional with the appreciation and confirmation that is sorely needed at this point in the career, but they can also criticize, complain, and question. When clients are motivated and responsive, they can facilitate the helping process and make work more stimulating and fulfilling for the professional. But when the client is resistant or apathetic, the professional's task becomes more difficult and there is a feeling of resentment that the client is not keeping his or her side of the "contract."

It is not surprising that much of the strain experienced during the initial phase of a public professional's career relates in some way to the client-professional interaction, for the focus of work in the helping professions is contact with and service to clients. The ultimate goal is to help people. Initially, new professionals tend to be "client-oriented": they place client needs above all others which demand their attention (Kramer, 1974). Over time, this exclusive commitment to clients may weaken in the face of competing commitments to self, co-workers, agency, and profession. But in the beginning, much of their attention and concern is focused on clients. Relations with clients will thus tend to be a major source of gratification or strain, depending on what occurs.

The importance of client relations is further enhanced by the professional isolation characteristic of the early phase of the public professional's career (see Chapter 5). Although the degree of social interaction with one's co-workers and supervisor varies with the work setting and professional group, most new public professionals we studied found support, guidance, and evaluative feedback from peers to be scant. They are, in a sense, "thrown together" with their clients in a way that makes them even more dependent on the fate of client relations. Therefore, difficulties encountered in working with clients often become a major source of psychological stress and strain for the new public professional and an important contributor to burnout.

CLIENTS AS CRITICS

In a sense, professionals, like actors on a stage, are playing a role, with the clients as the primary audience; and, like actors, the professionals are concerned about audience response. In some cases, new professionals as well as stage actors may want more than anything else to be accepted and liked by the "audience." When this occurs, it can seriously interfere with the performance, whether it is on the stage or in the helping relationship. However, even when the desire to be liked by clients is controlled so that it does not interfere, being trusted and appreciated by clients is still a major source of gratification for most professionals, especially new ones.

There are many subtle and not so subtle ways in which clients gratified the new professionals in our study. For instance, one young school social worker was deeply moved when a high school student with whom he was meeting weekly for counseling brought him her diary to read one day. She said that he was the first person to ever see these most cherished and private thoughts. A new public health nurse was clearly gratified when grateful patients gave her fresh vegetables they had grown in their gardens. These gifts signified to the new professionals that their clients appreciated what they were trying to do for them. They were gestures of human gratitude to which all new professionals responded.

Clients could gratify the new professionals in less direct ways as well. During one interview, new high school teacher Cynthia Noble was asked, "What are the greatest sources of satisfaction in your job?" She immediately responded:

> Individual students, things they say, such as, "I got it all last night, I understand it now." That makes me feel good. Or it makes me feel good when kids come in for help, and they're really trying, and they bother to come in for help. Some kid came in today and he said to me, "I know you think I'm a moron because I come in every day for help," and I said, "No, I think the morons are kids who are not coming in for help and need it." He kind of looked at me really funny and he said, "Oh, then I can keep coming in." It upsets me when I have kids who won't come in for help and just sit there in class. Trying, I like to see that because it gives me new faith in the attitudes.

For this teacher, the greatest source of satisfaction in her job was to see a student suddenly understand or really try and come in for help. It was through these acts that students indicated that the teacher was reaching them, involving them actively and meaningfully in the learning process or, in a word, succeeding. Unfortunately, students and clients have the power to frustrate and annoy as well as to gratify. As teacher Calvin Miller said, it seems to be easier to get negative feedback from students than positive feedback, especially on a day-to-day basis.

In their role as critics, clients contributed to strain in the new public professionals in three different ways: by questioning the professional's competence, by complaining about the service they received, and by expecting or demanding more than the professionals could deliver. Clients who became disgruntled critics of the professional in any of these ways were often seen as "troublemakers" by the targets of their criticism. For instance, a new poverty lawyer, Perry Curtis, said:

> It's the minority that are troublemakers. Those few minorities can really make life miserable.
> [Interviewer: "What would someone do? Can you give me an example?"]
> Just harrass you and make impossible demands upon you, will not follow your advice. "Are you a real attorney?" I've had that asked. They think they know more than you do. "Well, my neighbor told me I could do this." And then there's the person who, because you're not there holding his or her hand every minute, they're calling everyone and complaining about the service and the attorney isn't doing this for them or that for them.

When clients criticize and complain, they are attacking the new public professionals in their most vulnerable spot. As stated in Chapter 2, the professionals want to feel competent, and client response is a major measure of effectiveness. However, displeased clients represent a more concrete threat as well; they can get the novice professionals into real trouble with their superiors.

To protect themselves from unhappy clients, the new professionals had to be careful about what they did. These precautions could require extra time and effort, imposing further strain on an already heavy workload. Poverty lawyer Perry Curtis offered the following example:

> I've been madder than hell a couple of times. I've gotten some complaints lately from clients. All of them were unfounded, but you have a chance to get defensive. People get mad. They can't understand why they can't get the individual service they would going to a private attorney.
> [Interviewer: "What does that do in terms of your own attitude toward your job and the kinds of things you see coming out of it?"]
> I don't think it has affected me that much. The only thing I do find is looking at a client and saying, "Is this one going to be a troublemaker? Am I going to have to keep extensive records on the file in case something comes up?"

means extra work. It means a confrontation with a client and the director of the legal aid society and a possible confrontation with the client, myself, the director, and the grievance board.

As this suggests, dissatisfied clients who complain are a source of strain not only because of the extra work they require of an already overworked professional, but also because of the personal "confrontations" involved. Even when the new professional appears to feel confident that he or she will ultimately be vindicated, the prospect of such confrontations is not pleasant to contemplate. Conflict and confrontation with displeased clients is a source of emotional stress for new public professionals; most novices seem to feel vulnerable and threatened in these situations.

The quote also suggests that professionals working in public agencies are especially likely to encounter displeasure in clients. The frequently large caseloads and personnel shortages mean that delays and errors are more likely to occur. When they do, it is the professional who is blamed by the clients. Also, clients who must go to a public agency for service because they cannot afford a private professional, as is the case with legal aid agencies, are likely to feel more powerless and unhappy from the start. They know that they are not in "the driver's seat" as they probably would be if they could afford to retain their own counsel. They do not believe they have as much claim to the time of the professional as they would if they were paying directly. Thus, they are especially sensitive to any sign that they have been slighted (and slighted they often are). The same phenomenon tends to occur in the public schools, in publicly funded mental health programs, and any other public human service agency to which clients do not come on a fee-for-service basis. The client's sense of impotence in dealing with the large, human service bureaucracy ultimately means that the new public professional is a likely target for complaints, grievances, and similar forms of "trouble." Both professional and client become victims of a bigness they can neither control nor escape.

At the same time that clients worry about being slighted, many seem to expect a great deal from the professional. The new attorneys seemed especially vulnerable to this problem. One of them, Reginald Smith, who worked in a juvenile defender agency, put it this way:

> There's this notion that attorneys are supposed to perform miracles and be magical; and, a lot of times, kids who end up getting convicted, even right after being represented, say, "Why didn't you say anything? Why didn't you do something?" You know, a lot of times they don't understand. Like one guy last week I saw over at the court. He asked for an attorney, and I represented him for a preliminary hearing. The referee decided to set a $300 bond, and there really wasn't much I could say in terms of argument. He does have the right to set any bond he wants as long as it's reasonable. There's

really not too much you can say; it's really a discretionary decision on the part of the referee. And the client didn't understand. He thought I was immediately supposed to say something, anything, you know. Object or something, even though it would have done no good. He would have felt he'd been represented, you see, if I'd said something to the court [which only would have succeeded in getting him in more trouble]. But he didn't understand. He felt that he hadn't gotten adequate representation. Like I said, a lot of those kids equate being represented by an attorney with getting off, because an attorney is supposed to get you off, even if the evidence is overwhelming and you in fact did commit the crime.

When clients' expectations are unrealistic, they will inevitably be disappointed. When this occurs, they naturally direct their anger and dismay at the professional who seems to have failed them. They become harsh critics and create further strain for the new professional who has not yet established a sense of competence. For even if the new professional recognizes that the client's expectations are "magical" and unrealistic, there is always the possibility that the professional could have done more or been more skillful.

Unfortunately, the new professionals who find themselves enmeshed in this situation cannot always put client criticism into perspective. For them, client complaints or even questions tend to be seen as a "slap in the face," to use the phrase of high school teacher Cynthia Noble. In her case, it was the parents whose criticism she feared. She said, "In this town, how the parents feel about you is really important, at least at this point in the game. Everything points to that. If most parents don't like you, you're going to be out."

Like lawyer Perry Curtis, Cynthia Noble was in part bothered by the extra work and care that the threat of client displeasure required. She said that grades were an expecially sensitive issue. She thought that it was necessary to justify every grade she gave because, "It's such a small district, and everyone seems to know everything." If two students in a class got different grades, one of the parents might call her and ask, "Why didn't Sally get the same grade her best friend Laurie did?" As a result of this concern about parental vigilance and potential criticism, Cynthia believed that grading became more time-consuming than was necessary.

It should be noted that the new professionals varied in how concerned they were about their client's evaluations of them. For some, it was extremely important. As did the new teachers studied by Ryan (1970), they seemed to have a strong need to be liked. An example was a new high school teacher we interviewed who admitted that she felt it was important that her students like her as a person as well as a teacher and who said she would "love to hear" what her students said about her when she was not present. But many others whom we interviewed seemed less concerned about whether their clients liked them as people. Paradoxically, those who most wanted to be liked and were concerned about their clients' reactions tended to be the most eager and committed. Because their clients often proved to be harsh critics, these more committed novices tended to experience more stress in their contacts with clients and were thus more likely to burn out. As Ryan (1970) observed of new teachers, when the professional wants appreciation and approval from the client and the client does not "come through," the disappointed professional is likely to turn against the client and retaliate. The client, seen as the cause of the disappointment, becomes the target of professional displeasure. Over time, annoyance toward individual clients may harden into a more general attitude of distrust and dislike toward all clients.

INSUFFICIENT CLIENT MOTIVATION AND ABILITY

Client motivation and ability is another major source of gratification or strain for the new professional working in a public agency. For a number of reasons, the professionals want to work with clients who are actively engaged in the effort to help themselves. First, client motivation and ability strongly influence the professional's sense of effectiveness in many helping situations. Motivated and able clients contribute to professional gratification because they make success more likely. Second, more motivated and able clients tend to be more stimulating with whom to work. Third, motivated and able clients are easier; they require less effort of a busy and tired new professional. Finally, there is a moral dimension involved: new professionals tend to feel more sympathy toward clients who are really trying. Those who are apathetic, who do not seem to care about their problems, and who do nothing to help themselves generate a negative moral reaction. They tend to be seen as less deserving, and working with them is a source of strain.

We have already seen that the student or client who tries, who comes in for extra help in the case of a high school student or who diligently furnishes required information in the case of a legal client or mental health patient, is especially gratifying for new professionals. We also saw, in the previous chapter, that new public health nurse Sarah Prentiss was especially upset by a patient who had given up and just wanted to die. Through their motivation or lack of it, these clients seemed to greatly influence how successful the professional was.

Merton Douglas, a new high school business teacher, represented a good example of how disturbing a lack of motivation in students can be in the classroom. Early in the first interview, he talked of his frustration:

> I think I would enjoy teaching college more than I would enjoy teaching high school because you don't have to put up with the garbage. I've got a service to perform for someone, okay? I think I know a little bit about the business field because my experience and

education have qualified me to teach. So I just don't feel that I want
to put any time in with a student who doesn't want to at least
give . . . you know, I'm not even asking to come half way. Just come
a little bit.

He went on to describe how a particular lesson took much longer than was
necessary because of the lack of student motivation:

They don't care. All they care about is they want to get in at 12:45
and leave at 1:45. For the last three days we've been doing tax problems that should have been done in one day. With the time I spend
introducing the 1040 and the itemized deduction sheet, and explain-
ing just how it's done, and just jumping up and down and saying,
"Pay attention," and answering questions, putting examples on the
board, putting numbers up . . . With the time I spend on that, it's
ridiculous that we should have to spend three days. There are a
couple of kids who still haven't finished, and there are a couple of
kids who haven't started because they don't want to.
[Interviewer: "It must be pretty frustrating."]
Yeah, it is. But you just write it off.

This suggests how lack of student motivation frustrates the new teacher because
it impedes completion of teaching tasks. It also shows how the strain associated
with this frustration may already have led to the beginning of burnout; he had
reached the point at which he "just wrote it off."

Low ability in clients can also interfere with the professional's efforts. For
instance, Gloria Bennet, the new public health nurse, said:

I get impatient with my clients, sometimes. This job involves a lot of
teaching, a lot of patience, a lot of people doing for themselves. I do
get impatient with them, and it takes awhile to tone myself down. I
want them to catch on quicker, or I can't understand why they can't
do it. I mean, I know I'm doing this, and I'm aware that it's not the
right thing to do. But I can feel myself doing it sometimes.

Although lack of ability in clients was an impediment in all fields studied,
the problem was probably most frustrating for the high school teachers, especially
when their expectations of student ability were unrealistically high, as was often
the case. The following quote from an interview with Merton Douglas clearly
illustrates the frustration and tension that low ability in students created for new
teachers:

I've got a girl in that class whom I worked with yesterday on the
problem. She's very, very poor in math. I'm sorry, let me correct
myself: she's very, very poor in arithmetic. She knows how to add

and subtract—sometimes. You get to four times nine and she doesn't know it. Now, this is a 10th grader.

[Interviewer: "How does this affect your satisfaction with teaching? Did you expect to have this kind of situation?"]

Well when I first started teaching, I never expected it to be this bad, where the students were just so out of it. Like I said, I came from a college prep school, and my senior year in high school was just like my freshman year in college. There was no difference. Then, of course, after student-teaching, you see the other side of the coin. I don't know. You live with it.

Although all of the new professionals interviewed "lived with" the frustration caused by unexpected deficits in client ability, they certainly did not like it or find it easy to "live with." Lack of ability in clients, like lack of motivation, was a source of strain in the work lives of new public professionals, part of the job they did not expect or think they were "buying into," and a major cause of estrangement between client and professional during the early part of the professional's career.

The motivational and ability levels of clients also influence the amount of stimulation obtained from the work. Eager, interested clients who actively participate in the helping process allow the professional to fully utilize his or her skills and to apply the knowledge gained through many years of advanced training. When clients do not cooperate, much of the work with them seems more like "babysitting" or "hand-holding." For most new public professionals, the work of trying to get clients motivated and involved is much less interesting and seems much less meaningful than the more technical aspects of their work. Working with the motivated and able is stimulating; working with the unmotivated and less able is boring.

Working with the unmotivated and less able can also be harder. Several of the new professionals we interviewed said that trying to get students or clients involved, or dealing with the problems that develop when they are not involved, proved to be difficult, tiring work. A good example came from high school teacher Calvin Miller. He believed that lecturing was the easiest teaching method to use and wished he could use it more. But he thought that the limited attention spans of his students made lecturing impossible. He had to use different methods, methods that more actively engaged the students in the learning process and that took more time and effort on his part. "Their attention spans are shorter. This is part of the problem—why you can't use the lecture method at the high school level. Their attention span is just so short, and it gets shorter as you go down. It just drives you bananas yourself. You have to do something different for them every 10 minutes." Calvin went on to say that his "bad class" was bad because the students "make me work harder to keep their attention on the subject." For Calvin and the other new high school teachers, the arduous task of getting and keeping their students' interest added much pressure and strain. While many of the previous quotes came from interviews with high school teachers—they seemed to be the group most adversely affected by the "motivation problem"—professionals from the other groups encountered similar difficulties and frustrations. All professionals working in public agencies must come in contact with apathetic, unmotivated, less able clients who are less stimulating and require much time and effort. For the novice, this can produce enough strain to lead to early burnout.

Many of the new public professionals we interviewed seemed to have an implicit, "contractual" conception of the helping relationship. They seemed to believe that they were not obligated to put forth much time or effort for a client if the client did not reciprocate by putting forth some time and effort on his own. As high school teacher Merton Douglas said, "I just don't feel that I want to put any time in with a student who doesn't want to at least give . . . you know, I'm not even asking him to come half way. Just come a little bit." Another high school teacher, Alice Harris, was even more explicit when she said, "Why should I spend my time writing lengthy comments on their paper when it's obvious that they didn't put forth any effort? They could do well if they studied."

Of course, there is a very different point of view concerning professional effort and client motivation: the less motivated (and able) clients are the ones who *most* deserve the attention and skill of the professional because they are the ones who most need outside help. With the right kind of help, these less motivated clients might break out of their apathy and overcome their problems. The more motivated and engaged clients should not be ignored, but their needs are less strong.

For understandable reasons, there are few if any new public professionals who adhered to this second point of view. It is understandable because the less motivated clients are less successful and thus provide less confirmation of competence to the new professionals. Further, the new public professionals (with the exception of the mental health group) did not typically receive training in the interpersonal and psychological dynamics involved in the helping relationship and thus often did not possess the tools necessary to motivate apathetic or resistant clients (see Chapter 13). Perhaps with greater skill and knowledge in these areas, the struggle to engage clients meaningfully in the helping process would be more stimulating, meaningful, and rewarding.

Finally, there is the attitude that the apathetic, resistant client does not really deserve the professional's help. The lack of motivation in clients is stressful for new professionals not only because it means less stimulation, less success, and more work; there is also a tendency to see apathetic clients as morally "bad" and not "deserving" of help. Having to help those who are "undeserving" because of their apathy becomes a particularly annoying part of the job and another source of strain. Clients who receive professional help without putting forth much time or effort on their own behalfves are seen as getting a "free ride." They generate a moral reaction in most new professionals that is difficult to repress. Yet often the professionals must repress it. The rules of their employing institution and of their profession require that they provide service to such clients. They thus find themselves working with people whom they do not believe deserve the time, effort, and skill expended on their behalf. This moral indignation probably contributes as much to the problem as does anything else. As long as professionals working in public agencies believe that unmotivated clients are somehow less deserving of assistance, the requirement that they attempt to help these clients will create considerable internal conflict and strain.

BEING ABUSED AND MANIPULATED BY CLIENTS

Part of the "shock" of being a new professional is discovering that some clients lie and attempt to manipulate those who want to help them. Also distressing is the actual abuse that is directed at professionals by clients. Usually this abuse is verbal or symbolic, but we found instances in which professionals were physically abused as well. Abuse and manipulation directed at them by clients is yet another source of strain for many new professionals in public agencies.

One of the most distressing aspects of the client for new professionals is his or her tendency to lie. To be lied to or otherwise taken advantage of by a client was called "being chumped" by several of those we interviewed. To be chumped by a client is to be made a fool, and for the new professional who is struggling to attain a sense of self-respect and competence, appearing foolish is particularly unpleasant. As a result, many new professionals were greatly angered when clients occasionally lied. A particularly strong statement concerning this experience came from Margaret Williams, the new lawyer who worked in a neighborhood legal aid office. "Oh, let me tell you about clients lying to you. They lie like crazy. I can't stand anything more than clients who lie to you." [Interviewer: "Did you expect that? Did you have any idea. . . ?] "I had no idea that I was going to be lied to as badly as I have been." Margaret went on to describe a client who lied about his income in order to obtain public assistance (she also said that the income came from "nefarious activities"). She described a couple she represented who were being sued by a former landlord for damages they allegedly inflicted on their apartment. They swore that they left the apartment spotless. Margaret described the case in great detail:

> I was just thinking of a landlord-tenant thing that I really busted my ass for. It was a landlord suing a former tenant for damages. A young couple, black, allegedly not working; the guy's out of work. I don't know about that. They seem like nice people, and the landlord was suing them for damages to the place after they had moved out. I was kind of annoyed because I had dealt with that lawyer before, and I thought he was "flim-flamming" them. I counterclaimed for breeches

of the housing code and was doing all kinds of interesting things with the case. I thought it was up for grabs, and I was going to give it a run for the money. And eventually I was getting ready to go to court, and he'd been threatening me that they had some pictures of how bad the place looked. And I said, "Yeah, sure," because they always say that. Well, I went into his office one day, and he pulled out the pictures. It looked like a tornado had been through the place. My people had sworn up and down. So I thought one of two things: either my people lied like hell or those are pictures that they show everybody, and they're not really of my people's apartment. So I called up my people and said in these exact words, "I just went over to the other attorney's office and saw these pictures he was screaming about before, and I'll tell you frankly, if the jury takes a look at them, they're gonna kick the shit out of you. So I think you better start thinking about cutting a deal." And I figures if, in fact, they had been telling me the truth before, or . . . I don't know, truth or not truth, it might be just a matter of exaggerating . . . I figured if, in fact, this weren't their apartment, they would be very indignant with me and say, "Well, I don't know what pictures those are because I know that we didn't do that." They said, "Well, ahhh, let me think about it. How much do you think he's going to settle for?"

[Interviewer: "So it bothers you that you found out that the clients lied to you?"]

Yeah, it bothers me when they lie to me to the extent that I don't have a good case anymore. If they lie to me about something that doesn't go to the essence of the case, it's one thing, but when they really have a loser and from what they're telling me they've got a winner, and I break my neck on something, and it turns out that I've made a fool of myself, that's something different.

Margaret suggested that she resented "being chumped" because it meant that she worked harder on a case than was useful, wasting valuable time and effort, and she also "made a fool" of herself. As a result, she had little sympathy for a client when she found that the client had lied to her, and, over time, she became increasingly suspicious of all clients.

Other new poverty lawyers reacted in much the same way. For instance, Shana Phillips said, "You'll start off a hearing, you'll subpoena people in, and you'll be a real adversary and pursue the matter to the best of your ability, and then it turns out that the client was lying to you, and you feel 'taken.' That was one of the things that discouraged me."

Poverty lawyers were not the only ones who experienced this. According to high school teacher Merton Douglas, students frequently lied and tried to "con" him and other teachers:

First of all, when you come in there and student-teach, they know that you're new, and they know that you're not "the man." They know that the critic-teacher is "the man." Last year, they pulled everything on me. Three chicks from the area there would each come up and get a pass to go to the bathroom, and they'd go out there for a cigarette. I had the whole ball of wax pulled on me. This year I'm wise to that stuff. They just don't get away with a whole lot in my class. I don't like being "chumped" by students, I really don't. You know, I used to "chump" teachers every once in a while myself. That's one of my pet peeves, I think, not only with my students, but in associations with people in general. I don't like being taken, and I don't think anybody really does.

Although "being chumped" is sometimes annoying because it interferes with the professional's attempts to do his or her work effectively, as when a lawyer receives inaccurate information from a client about a crucial aspect of a case, the negative reaction by the new professionals we interviewed seemed to have a strong moral cast to it. On principle, they did not like being lied to fooled. They believed it was wrong and resented being the victims. And, of course, there was also the effect it had on their precarious sense of professional self-esteem: to look foolish was to appear less competent, less *professional*, to others and to oneself.

However, not all of the new professionals interviewed reacted as strongly to the experience. Some of the subjects were not bothered by clients who lied or otherwise tried to manipulate them. They regarded such behavior as more symptomatic of the conditions under which their clients had to live. Rather than blame the clients, these professionals blamed social systems affecting the clients or they just accepted it and blamed nothing. They recognized that clients sometimes lie, they knew that they were "chumped" by their clients from time to time, but they were not bothered by it. An example of this more charitable response was found in lawyer Jean Chalmers, who said:

Sometimes clients do lie. One guy wrote to me, "My ankle is hemorrhaging and they won't give me medical assistance." Now, his situation wasn't that bad, but it was some way of getting attention. That kind of stuff I can deal with because prison makes people crazy, and I can understand why people lie because the standard for prison brutality is that if the guy still has his kidneys, the court won't look at it, so they really have to exaggerate to get some attention. The level of abuse is so constant, the way that they just constantly play with your mind, it means that you really have to say something outrageous before you're going to get someone's attention. The kind of harrassment is subtle; it goes on all the time. I can understand how people get like that. People are frightened. They don't know what their rights are, and they think if they really lie, they're going to have more rights. But then, lots of attorneys lie.

Although other new lawyers whom we interviewed occasionally referred to the oppressive conditions in which their clients lived and conceded that their clients' situations contributed to how they behaved, they would nevertheless become frustrated and "forget" what they had said earlier about the influence of environment on their clients. Few of the new professionals whom we interviewed were able to maintain a composed attitude toward clients who "chumped" them. Usually, they took it personally and became angry at the client. Over time, their attitude generalized to the point that they were angry at *all* clients.

In addition to manipulative behavior, psychologically and physically abusive behavior of certain clients also bothered many new professionals and contributed to a decline in their general sympathy for clients. For instance, one new poverty lawyer, Margaret Williams, told us that she had been robbed twice in her inner-city office by clients, and, consequently, she had become much less sympathetic toward clients in general. High school chemistry teacher Calvin Miller also complained of stealing by students and the problems it created for him. When he began teaching, he found that lab equipment of all sorts just disappeared unless it was put away or watched. The need for constant vigilance became a real source of strain, a "hassle" that greatly detracted from the teaching process for Calvin. Not surprisingly, he increasingly came to resent the students.

For high school teachers, "discipline problems" could be a particularly stressful part of their experience during the first year of teaching. Those who experienced these problems were particularly tense, anxious, and close to burning out. By "discipline problems," the teachers meant behavior such as defiant comments and gestures by students; throwing papers, snowballs, or other objects in class; writing on the desks; misusing equipment; and so on. The new teachers seemed to be bothered by this kind of behavior in part because they perceived it as a challenge to their authority and competence. It also disrupted the positive and sympathetic bond that the teachers generally hoped to create between themselves and their students. Discipline problems, such as lying, contributed to estrangement between professional and client and created additional psychological stress in the novice.

Even when the client's abusive behavior had occurred at another time and place and was not directed at the professional, it could still be a source of strain. For instance, the new lawyers were especially bothered by certain behavior in which their clients might have previously engaged. Shana Phillips described what it was like for her to represent murderers:

> It's also frightening when you talk to some of these people, and they show no remorse for having killed someone, or mutilated someone, or beaten someone up very maliciously. It's scary. I mean, we have clients who have done nothing other than stolen something out of a supermarket to clients who have raped a woman and then set her on fire afterwards. It's hard to relate.

Another lawyer, Reginald Smith, admitted that he had "some qualms" about defending a client who was charged with raping a seven year old girl, especially when he realized that it was the second time he had represented the client on the same kind of charge.

Of course, few of the new professionals we interviewed had to work with clients who were remorseless killers or chronic child molesters. However, all of the new professionals had to work with some clients whose past and/or present behavior was so morally distasteful, if not heinous, that it was difficult to provide service without experiencing some conflict and ambivalence. Because they worked in public agencies that were required to serve all clients who met standard eligibility requirements, the new public professionals had little control over the kinds of clients with whom they worked. As a result, there were times when they had to try to help an individual whose behavior made it difficult to even be in the same room with him or her.

One other type of client behavior with which it was difficult for some new public professionals to cope was extreme dependency. Some clients made constant demands on the professionals' time, repeatedly asking for help with problems that were either not very serious and could have been attended to by the clients themselves or were not even the professional's responsibility. Given the large caseloads and other emotional demands being made of them, the new professionals sometimes became frustrated and angry with such clients. Again, there seemed to be an implicit "contract" between client and professional in the mind of the professional, and the dependent client who needed much reassurance and "hand-holding" violated that contract. When this occurred, the professionals might well respond with the anger of moral indignation. Public health nurse Gloria Bennet was one of the new professionals who found excessive dependency in clients especially hard to tolerate. "I felt kind of impatient sometimes, I think, with some elderly people who, if I can't make it one day, just get really naggy and whiney. They get on my nerves, and yet I understand why they're doing that: they're very lonely."

Poverty lawyer Margaret Williams, after eight months of working in a neighborhood legal aid office, was even less sympathetic about these types of clients. She said:

> Some of them are cranks. Some of them have little bullshit cases and call you up, and you say, "Listen, I've got people here getting evicted . . . you know, I'll work on your case, but you know it isn't urgent. I'll do what I can when I get a chance; just sit tight, and if you don't like it, cram. . . ." Well, I don't say, "If you don't like it, cram it," but that's what I feel like saying. It isn't that I'm saying, "Go to hell." I promised them I'd do some work for them. But, you know, a lot of our work is really reactive. We work with things when emergencies come up.

In Margaret's case, clients who were demanding and dependent were a source of strain primarily because of all the competing demands being made on Margaret's time. However, in the cases of other new professionals interviewed in the study, such clients were a source of dissatisfaction even when the professional *had* the time and resources, because the clients' dependency was seen as *wrong*. One example came from public health nurse Sarah Prentiss who felt that she had reached the point at which the client was becoming too dependent:

> I visited her for so long, and finally I got to the point where I felt like I was using all my time, and I was really working a lot harder than she was. She was getting really kind of dependent on me. She'd call me every day and she'd ask me if I'd call the attorney, which I didn't mind doing, but she wasn't doing it either. But this woman has a lot of problems herself.

In her last sentence, Sarah reveals part of the dilemma faced by new public professionals in working with especially dependent clients: excessive dependency or neediness seems to be wrong, *but the professional and his or her agency are there to help needy people.* When clients are especially needy, they will be more dependent, and that may be permissible, according to the vague client-professional contract that the new professionals seem to follow. Because it is difficult to determine exactly when the client crosses the line between reasonable and unreasonable dependency, the dependent client becomes a source of ambiguity, uncertainty, and added psychological stress for some new professionals. Thus, like abusiveness and manipulativeness, excessive dependency in clients can be a source of strain for the novice professional working in a public human service agency.

THE "PERSONAL INVOLVEMENT" DILEMMA

One of the most difficult conflicts with which new professionals grappled during the first phase of their careers concerned the question of personal involvement versus detachment with their clients. As we have seen, many of the new professionals we interviewed wanted to be liked by their clients. Also, many felt that a close, warm, friendly relationship with clients would facilitate the helping process. For instance, lawyers might believe that by being more friendly and sympathetic, they would put clients at ease and get necessary facts about a case more easily. Teachers might believe that by being more involved with students on a personal level, they could more effectively motivate them and see more progress in the students' learning.

However, developing more personal relationships with clients was also seen as risky for at least two reasons. First, several professionals indicated that if one becomes too friendly with clients, it is easier for clients to take advantage. In other words, if one develops a closer, more personal relationship with clients, one is more vulnerable to being chumped by them. Second, a professional who becomes friendly with a particular client and relates to the client on a more personal level may be charged with "favoritism" or even worse improprieties. Thus, the new professional is pulled in two different directions, and there is often little in the professional's previous experience or training that helps in determining how close or distant to be with any particular client or with clients in general. And, for many, the issue of personal involvement becomes a source of strain that is only resolved after much soul searching and trial-and-error learning.

Of all the groups studied, the teachers seemed most perplexed about how personally involved to become with clients. For instance, teacher Cynthia Noble found that many of her students responded well to individual attention, warmth, and support. But she was afraid of getting too close to them because of the jealousy it might create among other students. When asked if she thought that she should get to know students personally, she responded:

> I think that's a very important part of the role. I've noticed that some of the kids that I've taken a lot of time out with to really work with them individually and really care about them have changed so completely in class, and their grades have just shot right up. One of them in particular seemed to be the type of guy that was always looking for attention by disturbing the class. I got upset with him because of his grades and started giving him individual attention outside of class to get him to do the work. And he's gone from a "E" to a "B+" on his last test. Then again, at the same time, I'm really getting involved with these kids because I've kind of taken them on as my special cases. I like to talk, and most of the kids do, too. We always get off on what they do outside of school and things like that. I don't know . . . A lot of kids need a friend, and I'd like to be able to be their friend, but I don't want to get too chummy with them because then you get other kids being jealous, saying, "So-and-so is teacher's pet," and then you can run into all kinds of troubles.

Cynthia went on to describe a male teacher who got into trouble when he became very friendly with two female students. Although there was nothing improper going on, other teachers and parents in the community became concerned about the relationships, and he was advised to "back off." Cynthia was clearly concerned that if she showed certain students too much individual attention, the same might happen to her. Thus, while a closer personal relationship with certain students seemed to greatly enhance student learning and motivation, this new professional perceived real risks in taking such an approach with her students.

Other new teachers were concerned about how personal involvement and informality with students would affect control and discipline. Merton Douglas was concerned that if he were too nice to the students, they would take advantage and be more likely to "chump" him. In our second interview with him, he said, "There's an old axiom among teachers, I guess, and you've probably heard it: 'Don't smile 'til Christmas.' Well, I can't say I'm an advocate of that, but there's a lot to be said about that old saying because if you're too nice at first, they're going to walk on you." But, like many other new professionals, Merton liked developing a closer, more personal relationship with students. In fact, the development of positive personal relationships with students was one of the primary gratifications of teaching. He told of one incident that revealed the importance of positive interaction with students:

> That's how come I've come to like my job so much—because I've gotten to know more kids. You see kids in the hall: "Hi Mr. Douglas, how are you doing?" Kids come to you with problems. Today in class I mentioned that it's my father's birthday. So we finished class, and one girl comes up to me with a homemade envelope addressed to Mr. Douglas' father. She says, "Now, you give this to him and don't peek in it." Well, she left so I had to peek; I had to see what she wrote to my dad, so I peek in there and pull it out and it said, "Roses are red, violets are blue, some poems rhyme, but this one don't. Happy Birthday, Mr. Douglas' father," and, in parentheses, "Your son gave us a test on your birthday." And then it had a little piece of candy in there for my dad for his birthday. You know, that's cool stuff. I like that.

So, despite his concern about being "chumped" by students if he became too friendly with them, Merton found it difficult to resist the gratifications involved in developing warm and friendly relations with students. The dilemma was how to develop such relationships without suffering the potentially negative consequences.

The dilemma of personal involvement with clients is one with which all professionals must deal, and most professionals have developed certain ethical standards concerning the issue. Public institutions that hire public professionals, such as schools, also develop standards. However, there are still ambiguous situations that require the professionals to work out their own resolutions. Experienced professionals probably have done so; they have developed certain rules of thumb or personal policies for dealing with the issue of personal involvement with clients, based on repeated experience. But most *new* professionals do not yet have a standard response for dealing with the issue, and it remains an inner conflict and source of strain until they have had more experience.

CONCLUSION: LOCATING THE SOURCES OF STRAIN
IN PROFESSIONAL-CLIENT RELATIONS

We have seen that considerable strain is generated by the professional-client relationship. In discussing the strain, the focus has been on client behavior:

low levels of motivation and ability, manipulativeness, criticisms of the professional's work, and so on. However, it would be wrong to "blame the clients" for the strains experienced by new professionals working in public human service agencies. Of course, clients do differ, and there are some whose behavior creates considerable difficulty for the professionals who must serve them. But the extent to which this problematic behavior becomes stressful and a source of burnout for the new professional depends on the work setting. Both the professional and client are captives of an institutional structure they can do little to control. Much of the strain experienced by the new professional can be traced to that structure.

One underlying cause of strain in professional-client relations is the great social distance that separates professional and client. Like a wide chasm, it can be difficult, even impossible, to cross. The professional and the client tend to come from different social worlds, especially in the case of public human service agencies to which many clients come from working and lower class backgrounds. Long training and controlled access to the professions set professionals apart from others. They become an isolated elite. Even if the professional comes from a background similar to that of the client, the professional tends to become alienated from those roots during his or her training. The great differences in values, language, and, most of all, experience, lead to a cultural clash of great proportion, a clash that makes effective communication and trust between professional and client difficult.

Another underlying cause of strain in professional-client relations was discussed in Chapter 2: the crisis of competence. The new professionals want very much to prove to themselves and others that they are professionally competent. They frequently fail to do so, at least in the way they initially believed they should, and the clients seem to be the cause in many instances. When a client lacks motivation, it is more difficult for the professional to be effective. When a client "chumps" the professional, he seems to be ridiculing the professional and demonstrating for all the world that the professional is clumsy, inept, and incompetent. Chumping by clients affects the new professionals where they are weakest: their professional self-esteem. When clients complain about the service they are receiving or act as though they know more than the professionals, they are again suggesting what the new professionals themselves fear most. If new professionals felt more secure about their competence, the problematic behavior of clients would not be as stressful. Coming to terms with clients becomes especially stressful for new public professionals because it occurs in the context of personal self-doubt and uncertainty.

A third important cause of strain is the unrealistic expectations that new professionals bring to their first jobs. Even when they had gone through clinical law programs or student-teaching or other types of field placements prior to becoming professionals, most of the novices interviewed thought that their expectations regarding clients were too positive, too idealistic, and too romantic. They began with the implicit belief that the typical client would be grateful and pliable. They expected the typical client to know that the professional is concerned with the client's best interests. The typical client was supposed to be honest and cooperative, recognizing that the professional cannot be helpful unless the client provides the necessary information and faithfully carries out the professional's prescriptions. When the new professionals found that a disturbingly high percentage of their clients failed to fit the stereotype, they experienced an unsettling "reality shock."

It is not that the new professionals did not expect to work with some clients who were apathetic, distrustful, nasty, or manipulative. They simply were not prepared for so many of them. They seemed to expect that most clients would be "good" clients. Also, new professionals often seemed to expect that they would be more successful in overcoming these problems in clients than they actually were. The new teachers in our study believed that their compassion and skill would overcome discipline problems or prevent them from ever occurring. The new mental health professionals believed that they would overcome client resistance or apathy and help the clients to achieve new insight and growth. The new lawyers expected that, because they were dedicated defenders of the oppressed and dispossessed, their clients would trust and appreciate them. Unfortunately, their work experiences did not conform to these expectations.

The client's expectations also contribute to strain, and there are underlying sources here as well. The client who comes to a poverty law agency or public health department for service has usually had many previous contacts with public agencies whose conflicting goals, large caseloads, and lack of resources have made them woefully unresponsive and ineffective. Over time, many clients of these agencies come to adopt cynical, manipulative orientations toward *all* public agencies and professionals. They *expect* to be lied to, shortchanged, put off, and misunderstood. They have come to see the "helping relationship" as an adversarial situation in which one must use whatever tactics available to gain whatever advantage one can. Also, the clients have come to believe that, in this contest, they are at a relative disadvantage. They feel powerless, and consequently they are ready to strike out against any professional with whom they must deal.

But perhaps the greatest underlying source of strain is the structure of the professional's job and work setting. As we shall see in the next chapter, public service bureaucracies create many obstacles and frustrations for the professional. Their ambiguous and conflicting goals, their sometimes excessive concern with the politics of survival and growth, their heavy caseloads, and their apparent insensitivity to the needs of both clients and staff make these institutions difficult places in which to work. Ultimately, the unmotivated or difficult client represents just one of many thorns in the new public professional's side. If much of the anger is directed at the client, it may simply be a function of the client's unenviable position: the client is an obvious cause of difficulty and failure. And the client is a factor against which one can retaliate to some degree. The work setting, however, is large, complex, and amorphous. Its influence is often less direct. Before it, the new public professional usually feels powerless. Thus, the client becomes the most convenient target.

To summarize, clients were a major source of stress and strain for new professionals working in public agencies. However, it is important to recognize that many of the problems that frustrated the new professionals were not simply the result of human perversity in clients. It is all too easy to blame clients for lack of motivation, for unfair criticism and suspiciousness, and for abusiveness. A more careful analysis of the context in which such behavior occurs forces us to recognize it—and the impact it has on professionals—as far more complex. There are institutional factors that make such client behavior as inevitable as the professionals' reactions to it. As long as these factors exist, new public professionals will experience great stress and strain in their interactions with clients.

4

BUREAUCRATIC INTERFERENCE AND PROFESSIONAL AUTONOMY

Enhanced social status is a weak base for continued satisfaction when daily reality confirms that you are not in control over your destiny, that decisions affecting your work and life are made elsewhere, often by people and forces unknown and unknowable to you. The creeping sense of impotence, strange to professionalism however defined, has made professional work more problematic than ever. (Sarason, 1977)

Bureaucracy is perhaps the greatest enemy of professionalism. In several respects, the "professional ideal" and the "bureaucratic ideal" are completely incompatible. They represent two very different modes of organizing human action. For instance, important decisions in bureaucratic systems are made by those near the top of the hierarchy. Subordinates wait for instructions from superiors and are expected to carry them out without question or hesitation. Furthermore, the personal characteristics of the subordinate are of no importance: one's responsibility, discretion, and obligations are determined by one's position on the organizational chart, not by one's educational background, credentials, or skills. In other words, many controls in the bureaucratic form of organization are *external.*

In the professional mode of organization, the controls are *internal.* The individual workers participate in a lengthy program of training and socialization before assuming their work roles. They are expected to internalize the norms necessary for moral and effective performance. Once they have completed their training, professional workers are only loosely supervised and monitored, and then only by their colleagues. The organization is collegial rather than hierarchical. Formal controls are minimal.

Because the professional and bureaucratic modes of organization are so different, it should not be surprising that the new professional working in a public human service institution organized along bureaucratic lines often finds the formal rules and procedures a "hassle." The organization infringes on one's autonomy and often does so in ways that seem to be harmful to one's clients. Many of those we interviewed gradually came to believe that it is simply impossible to provide effective, humane, and responsible service while adhering to the plethora of regulations and restrictions imposed by faceless and seemingly insensitive bureaucrats. Not only does the "managerial demi-urge" (to use C. Wright Mills' colorful phrase) consume much precious time in paperwork and meetings, it also frequently seems to be at odds with the needs of clients. Unexpected organizational constraints on the new public professional's autonomy and control thus represent another major source of strain early in the career.

ASSAULTS ON PROFESSIONAL AUTONOMY

The new public professionals in our study varied in their initial concern about their own status and autonomy within their work settings. Some were more sensitive about the issue than others. The novices also varied in the degree to which their jobs, supervisors, and co-workers gave them the autonomy and status they associated with being a professional. However, sooner or later all of the new public professionals confronted situations in which the "system" demeaned them and interfered with their work. Suddenly, they were no longer special people with special training and skill; instead, they were simple cogs in a wheel, with little say about important decisions affecting them or their work.

Clinical social worker Douglas Furth was particularly sensitive about the issue of autonomy and status. For him, the collision with the impersonal and arbitrary nature of the bureaucratic system occurred during his job interview. As a therapist in a mental health clinic, he had expected to have some say over his salary and working conditions and thus attempted to negotiate these during his job interview. He soon found that things were done differently in this setting:

> I was very surprised about how they brought me in. I had no say, almost, in what I would be doing. Like when it came to discussing salaries, they wouldn't talk about it. They said, "This is how much we'll give you for your past experience." Well, it's as if everyone's past experience is equal based on time, not the actual work or the quality of the work or what projects you were doing, and I thought mine were unusual. And already I felt discounted, like right off, at this place. They weren't seeing me as an individual. . . . It was almost as if you're a cog, you know, "If we hire you, this is what you will

do." So I was negotiating on what clients I would see, whether I would have families and children, and they would not promise me that. And they knew I was good at it, they had heard good things. They said, "Well, we distribute the kids evenly." Well, I thought, that's stupid. Like why should everyone see the same number of kids? And so far, I have one child under the age of 12 years old. Out of 14 cases, they've given me one of what I want. And I'm not satisfied with that. . .

In this example, what appeared normal and natural for the new professional was seen as deviant by the setting. Two very different conceptions of the autonomy due a professional came into collision. As a result, a new professional got off to a bad start in his first job, and his notions about being a professional in the public sector were roundly shaken.

The new professional's autonomy may also be restricted by settings other than her own. Public health nurse Sarah Prentiss described an incident involving a program she was coordinating in a public school. She was asked by the principal if she could set up a "growing up" program, and she agreed. After she had arranged to borrow a film and present the program on a certain date, the principal informed her that he wanted to change the date. Also, he told her that she could not have as much time with the students as she felt was necessary. She resented greatly his arbitrariness, his expectation that she would change the program simply because he had ordered her to, and his attempts to tell her how the program should be structured. She felt that he was infringing on her professional autonomy:

The principal mentioned to me about a growing up program, so I went down and talked to the teachers that were going to be involved in it, and I set up a date, and I told him the date. He wanted it the first week in May, so I went ahead and ordered the film. Okay, I walk in there last week and he ways to me, "Well, we set up the program for Wednesday evening at 7:30," just like, "Okay, you do this, this, and this." And I looked at him and I . . . First of all, fifth and sixth grade boys and girls in two hours? He's crazy! You know, there's no way. I said, "First of all, we need more time than that," and he says, "Well, we've gone for two years like that," and I said, "Well, I know how much time I spend with these people, because they have a lot of questions. Fifth and sixth grade kids know a lot; they're doing a lot of things that we weren't doing." And this man says to me, "Well, if they have questions, they can go home and ask their parents," and I said, "Well, what's the purpose of doing this? The reason that we do it is because parents don't do it at home." He said, "Well, I don't know if I agree with that," and I said, "Well, what's the whole philosophy education?" I got into a big discussion with him. We were out in the hall, and I was just burning. I just had

had it. He was putting me down . . . I guess he might have been in a lousy mood because he is kind of temperamental, kind of dictatorial. That school is run like the Army or something. He's really strict. His secretary jumps when he says something. You know, he likes to control people like that, so I understand that personality. But you know, here I am, I don't work for the Board of Education. I'm a resource person.

Like the director of Douglas Furth's agency, this principal's conception of Sarah Prentiss' role was very different from hers. She saw herself as a professional who was providing a service first and foremost to the students and only secondarily to the schools. On the other hand, the principal saw her as an employee who was under his jurisdiction when she was working in the school. Such clashes, therefore, are inevitable, and they occur most often to newer professionals who have not yet learned that their conceptions of professionalism are not valid in the public bureaucracies in which they work. Their anger, frustration, and disillusionment then add to the emotional stresses they are already experiencing as new professionals, increasing the likelihood of burnout.

New professionals also learn early that they have virtually no control over the political processes that affect many aspects of their work situations. For instance, they find that contrary to their expectations even their jobs can be eliminated with the stroke of a pen; an intricate process over which they have no influence and which they barely understand determines what they will be paid and even whether they will be paid at all. Their precarious status adds to the sense of powerlessness and helplessness they are already experiencing. For example, social worker Diane Peterson was hired to work as a therapist in an alcoholism program. She was hired as part of a grant that she was led to believe would run for three years. Gradually, however, she learned that there had been "administrative problems" and that the grant might be terminated in the very near future—and with it, her job. As a result, she and the other workers hired with her were experiencing considerable anxiety:

> They got a special grant for three years, and so they hired us. I think the plan is that, hopefully, maybe at the end of three years, the agencies that we're placed in could absorb us. They would see our use by that time. Except, they're coming up for our first year's renewal next fall, and we're not quite sure we're going to get it because, first of all, they were very slow in getting their staff together. I hear they went through about four directors in the first six months. They were supposed to have all their staff hired, trained, and ready to go by January 1, and I was the last person hired, in the middle of March, and not fulltime until May, so we're way behind where we're supposed to be, and so there's a little bit of anxiety—there's a *great deal* of anxiety.
> [Interviewer: "Not a little bit?"]

Tremendous, because we hear of other jobs opening up, and everyone's bounding in to the personnel director. You know, like one day we hear we're a sinking ship, and the next day we hear there's funds through at least the end of the year.

Undoubtedly, waiting to hear from some unknown powers about whether they would have jobs in a few months was very different from what Diane and the professionals like her expected when they chose professional careers. They had worked hard for all of the benefits, such as security and autonomy, that they thought professional work would bring. "Running in to the personnel director" every day like frightened children must have been very different, indeed, from what they expected professional status to be like. But as *public* professionals, they were at the mercy of a large, impersonal, and distant bureaucratic apparatus. It is not surprising that professionals everywhere are beginning to unionize in an effort to regain some of the control they believe they have lost to the bureaucratic machinery of their work places.

Not all of the new public professionals we interviewed complained about lack of autonomy and control in their work. In fact, five of the 28 subjects did not mention this as a problem.* Also, even those whose autonomy was limited in some situations enjoyed considerable autonomy in others. For instance, public health nurse Sarah Prentiss said she especially liked public health nursing because of the greater autonomy one had in comparison to hospital nursing. In hospital nursing, according to Sarah, there are physicians and nurse supervisors "telling you what you can and can't do all the time." New public defender Reginald Smith struck a similar chord, saying that he liked the job because there was much more autonomy than he would have had working as a lawyer for the government or a large firm in which "you have to run out to get cigars for the senior partners all the time." Interestingly, in both these examples, autonomy in the job was seen as satisfactory because it was being compared with another type of job in the same field. Autonomy in public health nursing was high compared to hospital nursing. Thus, although there were situations in which new public professionals could find some degree of autonomy, and certainly their autonomy was greater than would be found on the assembly line in an automobile factory, the lack of autonomy and control over their work life, compared to what they had initially expected and wanted, was a major source of dissatisfaction and frustration for many of them.

---

*This included one mental health professional, two public health nurses, and two lawyers.

BUREAUCRACY'S IMPACT
ON THE WELFARE OF CLIENTS

The bureaucratic system is distressing to many new public professionals not only because of the way it limits their own autonomy, control, and status, but also because of its impact on the welfare of their clients. When clients are involved, the bureaucratic mode of organization sometimes imposes priorities and values different from those the new professionals believed were right and proper. According to Warnath (1973), new professionals are indoctrinated to a social service value system that places the dignity, needs, and welfare of individual clients first. But the roles they assume in public institutions are oriented primarily to the needs of the institution. Success requires "business-bureaucratic skills and attitudes" rather than humanitarian commitment.

Kramer (1974) presents a good example of this conflict between bureaucratic norms and the professional service ideal. A new nurse starts talking to a patient recovering from major surgery. For the first time since the surgery several days before, the patient has begun to talk about the things that are bothering him. The nurse listens sympathetically, knowing that this patient's physical as well as mental health may be affected. But it is time to serve dinner to all of the patients on the ward. Organizational rules require that patients be fed at a specific time. The institutional machinery does not work smoothly if they are not fed within a few minutes of the appointed hour. Yet the depressed patient may need a sympathetic listener at that particular time, and there is no way of determining by administrative fiat the most opportune time to talk sympathetically and at length with any particular patient.

Thus, there is always the potential for conflict between the needs of an individual client and the established rules and procedures of the bureaucratic institution. In public settings, the professional practitioner stands in the middle, often torn between the demands of bureaucracy and client. Unfortunately, most new professionals working in the public sector are little prepared for this kind of conflict. They have been led to expect that they will have the autonomy and discretion to do whatever is best for the client. They are not prepared for the fact that skill and patience are necessary to mediate between bureaucratic demands and client needs. And they certainly are not ready for the limited options they are often given in such situations.

The situation is made even worse because of the way in which the system thwarts efforts by new professionals to prevent harm to clients and bring about change. New public defender Reginald Smith described the response he received whenever he attempted to make a motion in court to suppress evidence that he believed was gathered illegally by the police:

> It causes mass chaos over there if you file a motion to suppress illegally seized evidence. They're not set up or geared to deal with

that, and they don't even know how they should deal with it. They don't run suppression hearings over there and, consequently, when you shoot a motion to suppress, it just throws a monkey wrench in the whole situation. What they have a tendency to do is not to do anything, not even to set a court date. I imagine the rationale is, "The defendant will probably come back into court on another charge, and we'll deal with it then." They really need to have a motion calendar where these kinds of motions can be heard, but they don't do that, and there's no real system for doing that. So when you want to make a motion for anything, it causes chaos. . . . A lot of times they complain because we're balling up the system by simply asking them to allow kids constitutional rights.

In this example, the welfare of clients suffers because of the need for bureaucratic efficiency. Safeguarding constitutional rights slows down and disrupts the bureaucratic machinery of the court. Thus, defense attorneys like Reginald Smith are strongly discouraged from doing what their training and professional code of ethics directs them to do. They are, in other words, caught in the basic conflict between the bureaucratic imperative on the one hand and the professional concern with client rights and welfare on the other. Such role conflicts can generate much stress and strain for the new professional.

New professionals in other fields sometimes experience similar dilemmas. For instance, school social worker Nick Fisher said that he found himself working in and for a "totalitarian" system whose values and practices he abhorred but was expected to carry out. Of all the things that were wrong with his job (and he cited many), he said that this conflict was his main source of dissatisfaction. He described one situation in particular:

I get a lot of feeling from other people that my role is to handle discipline, which is something I don't want to do at all. I'll be walking through the office, and if there are a couple of kids that have just been brought in from a fight, the principal will say to me, "You'd better talk to these kids." And I'm supposed to solve their fights. I don't like that. I usually try to take that middle ground of sort of doing it my way. I still feel uncomfortable, like I've done nothing. It's hard because you have to pull off a lot of things. If you don't have the backing of the administration, you can't do anything anyway. The last social worker that was here got in a fight with the administration over one kid, and he just lost total effectiveness. It really is a trade-off. The demands put on you by the job mean that you have to be doing things that you're ideally opposed to, and yet, how do you do that and still remain idealistic? It's hard. Some of my feelings were the best thing to do with the schools is just blow them up. Start from scratch. That's hard. You have to make some concessions.

After discussing his frustrations, Nick went on to state that the conflicts were really bad at only one of the schools to which he was assigned; he was not always put in the position of defending the system to the detriment of his clients. But it was clear that he had to walk a tightrope, attempting to maintain his professional ideals while working in a destructive system on which he was totally dependent. The situation created considerable tension and stress for him.

In our follow-up interview with him, we found the situation had deteriorated as the year progressed, and the stress and strain for him had increased as it did so. The principal of the school had become increasingly displeased with Nick's performance and had called for a special meeting with him and his supervisor to discuss their "communication problems." Nick's anger and fear reached the surface during our interview when he said, "You know, I don't like to be put in a corner, but if I'm put in a corner, I can fight pretty good. I mean, I could dish it out to those assholes." He went on to say, "But I don't want to do it because these are people you have to work with." Still walking the tightrope. After some more discussion of the situation, the interviewer said, "It seems that that could be draining on you as a person who's trying to do his work." Nick answered:

> It makes me feel a lot like I'm in a battle zone with bullets whizzing over my head, always keeping my head low. And I really feel like I'm avoiding problems; I often find myself not wanting to talk to people, planning my day so that I don't have to be around the office, just trying to stay out of people's way where they're looking for somebody to be angry at.

In trying to mediate the conflict between the "system" and the client, it is difficult for the new public professional to "stay out of people's way." Although not all of the subjects in our study were "shot at" in the way Nick Fisher had been, most would probably agree there were times when they felt they were in a "battle zone with bullets whizzing" over their heads.

At other times, the new professionals had to watch and participate in a bureaucratic system that was not so much destructive as simply absurd and meaningless. These situations were clearly less stressful, and they even could be the source of a certain amount of comic relief. But being a part of a system that is irrational and wasteful was, for idealistic novices, a source of distress as well. A good example was provided by alcoholism therapist Diane Peterson:

> I went out on the request of the homemakers and saw a client at 4 p.m., and the public health nurse went out at 9 the next morning. She had gotten the referral through the health department. So we said, "Look this is ridiculous. First of all, neither of us should be seeing him because he's an 89-year-old chronic alcoholic; and the thing is, he's not going to come up here for his lectures [the kind of

service usually offered to alcoholics], and it's pretty hard to tell an 89-year-old man that the average age of the alcoholic at death is 53 because he's beaten it by 36 years!" The thing we decided to do was make sure that he does not die alone and ill. Make sure that someone stops in to make sure that he gets hospitalized if he needs it, make sure he has food, and probably he's not going to make any great changes in his drinking habits at 89.

Absurd or harmful, the bureaucratic organizations in which they worked intruded upon the new public professionals' autonomy. Excessive paper work, long and unproductive meetings, and rigid, seemingly senseless rules and regulations frequently hampered their efforts to help. The "managerial demi-urge" and the helping process often seemed to be at odds, and the new public professionals were the ones in the middle.

BUREAUCRATIC STRUCTURE
AND THE PROBLEM OF BOREDOM

Those who enter the professions tend to assume that their work will be varied, meaningful, and stimulating (Sarason, 1977). Unfortunately, the structure of work in public bureaucracies often limits job variety and meaning. The work that the new professionals find themselves doing tends to be routine, monotonous, and uninteresting. Opportunities for intellectual stimulation and personal growth are limited. Consequently, many novices become bored and restless.

As Kramer (1974) noted, routine and boredom tend to occur more often when work is bureaucratically organized. In the bureaucratic mode of organization, work is divided as much as possible into limited (and often meaningless) tasks with an emphasis on efficiency and fairness. Opportunity for individual discretion, creativity, and flexibility is minimized in an effort to maximize predictability and uniformity. Far from abhorring routine, the bureaucratic ethos and its associated form of organization seeks to increase it wherever possible. Order, rationality, and sameness are the goals. Providing variety, stimulation, and creative expression to the worker is seen as irrelevant at best; more typically, it is seen as potentially dangerous. As the Task Force to the Secretary of the Department of Health, Education and Welfare wrote in its report on work in America, "The organization acknowledges the presence of the worker only when he makes a mistake or fails to follow a rule, whether in factory or bureaucracy, whether under public or private control" (O'Toole, 1973, pp. 38-39).

For the new professionals in our study, the lack of variety and stimulation in work became a concern only gradually. During the first weeks and months of the new professional's first job, the many things that had to be learned and the uncertainties surrounding personal competence made the job anything but routine and unstimulating. However, this initial period of transition eventually ended. For most of the new high school teachers, it seemed to peak in the second and third months; by the late winter or early spring of their first academic year, at least three of the seven interviewed were already complaining about the monotony and lack of intellectual stimulation. For many new lawyers and mental health professionals, the excitement associated with newness faded even sooner. Gradually, most of the new professionals seemed to become somewhat disappointed with the lack of challenge and variety in their work. Being a professional simply was not as interesting as they had expected.

Margaret Williams, the new lawyer working in a neighborhood legal aid office, was fairly typical in this respect. To her surprise and dismay, she found that she spent much of her time at work on the phone, obtaining information for clients on matters that often were not even legal in nature. And the legal work she did was often simple and routine: name changes, guardianships, and so on. Not surprisingly, she soon tired of this daily fare:

> I spend more time on the phone than anything else. A lot of things we can straighten out with some phone calls, a lot of welfare and social security problems. A lot of times, the clients don't know what the hell is happening to them; they say "I didn't get my social security check and I think it's because of blah, blah, blah, blah," and you make some calls and find out there's been some red tape screwup and there's nothing about the person's eligibility or anything that's at all a legal question, but the person just doesn't know what's happening or doesn't know how to sit tight and wait . . . . So I spend a lot of time doing routine things like name changes and guardianships. At first, I was so happy that I got a job, I wasn't going to criticize anything at all. And I've had no criticisms whatsoever until very recently when I started getting sick of doing all of this real diddly shit and not getting into any big cases. What I'd like, best of all possible worlds, is to get to work on some big cases and not only this crap. That's what I'd like, but who wouldn't?

Contrary to what they had expected, many new public professionals find that they must perform the functions of the "street-level bureaucrat," an individual who, while providing service directly to the public, is also expected to perform a bureaucratic function (Prottas, 1979). They are the ones who categorize the clients and process the forms in ways that enable public bureaucracies to function. In the typical public bureaucracy, people cannot be provided with service until they are transformed into "clients." This is accomplished by matching certain client characteristics with the fixed categories of service defined by the bureaucratic system. To her surprise, Margaret Williams discovered that most of her work was of this nature. For instance, the procedures for name changes or guardianships are standardized and routine. In her role as street-level bureaucrat, Margaret had to merely transform what she learned about a client's situation into the basic information required to initiate the appropriate legal machinery. This work is essential; both the client and the organization depend on it. However, for new professionals like Margaret Williams, this kind of work quickly loses whatever interest it originally had, for it is monotonous and mundane.

The division of labor in legal aid offices further contributes to the high degree of routine and lack of stimulation. These agencies handle no criminal work, only civil actions. Also, there is usually specialization within the agency so that one attorney may handle primarily divorce cases, another may concentrate on landlord-tenant work, and so on. Thus, for the practicing lawyer, the range of legal work tends to be rather narrow. Over time, the work becomes oppressively routine, as one case follows another and each is relatively similar in the legal issues and procedures involved. Also, the intellectual and legal issues in these cases are usually clear cut; even when they are not, the legal aid attorney has neither the time nor the mandate to think through and act on the more intricate, problematic issues. Thus, the work proves to be more monotonous and less intellectual than the new lawyers expected.

Analysis of professional work in the other fields suggests a similar picture. For instance, public health nurse Gloria Bennet said, "When I first started, I was impatient because they were so busy showing me a lot of the paper work, and there's a lot to do with these insurance things. 'Make sure you have the correct Medicare number and the correct Blue Cross number. . . ,' this kind of thing, which is not something I find very exciting. So that kind of irritated me."

The complaints of new high school teachers were similar. Merton Douglas described the classroom as "confining." He feared that the routine soon would become deadening. Every hour was becoming like the last, with the pattern rarely varying. And his own role in the learning process seemed increasingly insignificant to him as time passed. "I just think that after awhile, I'm going to start to feel like a t.v. set spewing out information; I'm going to get to feel like my function isn't necessary. They could get a P.A. system to repeat what I repeat each day. Of course, the P.A. system couldn't answer the questions, but I just kind of feel like I'm a robot functioning as a program, in a sense." Merton's images of "t.v.'s" and "P.A. systems" and "robots" convey the sense of work being mechanical and routine. He clearly saw himself as a cog in the educational "machine," one that could easily be replaced. For him, there was little meaning or stimulation involved in teaching. Work was an unexpectedly poor vehicle for personal expression, growth, and fulfillment.

The mental health professionals were not exempt, either. Mark Canner, a school psychologist, complained that he spent most of his time administering psychological tests. His only other activity was a counseling group that met one hour a week. He had hoped that the "progressive" school system where he worked would define the school psychologist role more broadly. Thus, his disappointment with the lack of variety and meaning in his work was especially great.

It should be noted that not all of the new professionals interviewed presented such a bleak picture of the quality of work life. There were exceptions. Of the 28 people interviewed, eight (29 percent) indicated that they found their work interesting, varied, and stimulating. This included two subjects from each of the professional groups studied. For instance, public health nurse Sarah Prentiss said that she enjoyed considerable variety in her work, which helped make it interesting, and that her caseload allowed her to read and think about the work she was doing, which contributed to intellectual stimulation and learning on the job. High school teacher Cynthia Noble, although most of her classes were like Merton's, was able to teach one that was different: a class on computers with only six students. What she liked most about it was that, unlike her other classes, she became a learner herself. Thus, for some new professionals, there were opportunities for variety, challenge, meaning, and personal growth in their work. But these situations clearly stood out as the exceptions; most were disappointed and frustrated that the work lacked the stimulation and meaning they had expected.

Unfortunately, as long as new public professionals expect their work to be stimulating and fulfilling and find it to be otherwise, the potential for burnout in this group will remain great. The frustrated quest for meaning and fulfillment in work leads to the kind of psychological stress that increases the likelihood of burnout. Although we usually think of stress as being caused by a condition of "overload," research has suggested that understimulation may be as stressful as its reverse (McGrath, 1970). Stress is also produced because gratification of personal needs is blocked. When new public professionals expect and desire meaning, intellectual stimulation, and self-actualization through work and their efforts to fulfill this need are thwarted, the frequent result is frustration, discomfort, and even anxiety.

One form of self-protection is to reduce effort and involvement in one's work. But this strategy may simply make things worse, for the less effort one puts into one's work, the less fulfillment one is able to get out of it. A good example of this phenomenon was high school teacher Merton Douglas, who complained more than any other subject about being in a "rut" and feeling like a programmed "robot." After he had complained about the lack of variety in his work, the interviewer asked, "What if you had more variety? For instance, what if you had three preps, instead of only two? Then you would have three different kinds of classes." Merton responded, "I'd probably like that less because it would be more work, and I don't like to do a lot of work—the most output with as little input as possible. One prep [that is, teaching the same class all day long] wouldn't be bad, but then I'd get bored." By trying to do as little as possible, Merton actually increased the lack of variety and boredom. He was caught in a vicious circle in which the more bored he became, the less time and effort he put into his work, which in turn made the work even more boring. Of course, there is often little that a new professional working in a public agency can do to change the structure of the job to any significant degree. A poignant example was provided when Merton said that he tried to increase variety in his job by altering the order of quizzes and filmstrips in his classes. During the first two classes he taught, he would give the quiz and then show the filmstrip; for the third class, he showed the filmstrip and then gave the quiz. Although another teacher in his position might have found more creative—and effective—ways to increase variety and interest, most new public professionals are constrained in how much additional variety and fulfillment they can squeeze out of their jobs.

Thus, the structure of work in bureaucratic settings makes the quest for fulfillment and meaning in work a frustrating one for most new public professionals. The lack of variety, intellectual stimulation, and growth in their jobs generates much disillusionment and stress. Ultimately, the routine and mundane nature of the work contributes to a higher incidence of professional burnout in public agencies than would otherwise occur. Then pain and disappointment is felt not only by the professional, but by all who come into contact with the professional.

IS "BUREAUCRACY" BAD?

Much of what has been said here about bureaucracy's impact on professionals could be interpreted as an indictment of bureaucratic structure or any form of organizational control and authority. This was not the intent. Organizational structure, control, and accountability are necessary in the delivery of human services. Even if consumer groups and governing boards did not insist on a bureaucratic form of structure, some degree of organizational control would be necessary to ensure fairness and coordination in the delivery of service. In fact, to violate organizational policies created to ensure humane and responsive service would not be "professional" behavior. The professional's commitment to client needs and client welfare requires conformity to organizational authority in many situations. In other words, professionalism, client welfare, and bureaucratic organization are neither always nor necessarily incompatible.

However, professionals—especially new professionals still under the influence of an idealized conception of professional work—tend to *perceive* many conflicts between "appropriate" professional behavior and organizational rules. They see many organizational policies and structures as improper infringements on their autonomy. Further, they lack a conceptual understanding of their work situation and a set of skills that could help them overcome many of the obstacles the organization puts in their way (see Chapter 12). Finally, even if much of the organizational control structure is ultimately adaptive for all concerned, there are weaknesses and limitations associated with hierarchical, bureaucratic forms of organization that ensure that irrational and destructive organizational interference will occur at times.

Further, the central problem faced by new professionals—the crisis of competence—is affected by their limited autonomy and control in public work settings. When bureaucratic rules and regulations impede professional effectiveness, it is more difficult for a sense of competence to develop, especially when the individual feels powerless in removing or modifying those rules and regulations. A sense of competence can only develop when the individual is able to succeed—or fail—on the basis of her own efforts. When failure frequently occurs as the result of organizational and institutional factors over which the new professional has no control, the crisis of competence becomes especially difficult to resolve. Personal control and a sense of competence are inextricably linked.

Consequently, all professionals working in the public sector at times experience frustration, helplessness, and despair. The experience is strongest in new professionals, and without adequate support and guidance from colleagues, supervisors, friends, or family, the chances are great that this sense of helplessness and despair will become unbearable and that psychological withdrawal, that is, burnout, will occur. When this happens, the "blame" is neither the professional's nor the organization's. Each plays a part, and both are responding to historical forces and contemporary pressures.

To summarize, the irrational and sometimes destructive rules and policies of public service bureaucracies represented a major source of frustration and stress for many of the new professionals we studied. The bureaucratic machinery of their own agencies and other agencies often limited their autonomy, discretion, and effectiveness in unexpected ways. The bureaucracy often assaulted the dignity and welfare of their clients and prevented the professionals from helping them. Frequently, the bureaucratic organizations of which the new public professionals were a reluctant part treated both client and professional as though they were faceless abstractions—mere categories to be ordered, regimented, and processed. To make matters worse, the professionals often had to be the ones to impose the bureaucratic imperative against their own clients. In fact, it seemed that the real client was not the needy and/or suffering individual sitting before them asking for help, but the bureaucratic organization that paid their salaries and could hire—and fire—them. Of course, the subjects in our study varied in how much freedom, variety, and meaning they enjoyed in their jobs and in the degree to which their organizations were inimical to the welfare of their clients. As we shall see in later chapters, the new professionals also varied in their reactions to the conflict. However, for most of the new professionals we interviewed, there was less autonomy and control and more routine and boredom in their jobs than they had expected, and interference from bureaucratic rules and actions occurred often enough to become one of the most disillusioning aspects of their jobs and a major cause of burnout.

5

THE ELUSIVENESS OF COLLEGIALITY

The new public professional's sense of social and professional isolation at work was another dominant theme in our interviews. Although not every subject experienced this isolation for an extended period of time, almost all felt it initially, and the sense of isolation returned from time to time. When it occurred, it was a major strain for most new professionals. Some sort of contact and support from colleagues was valued and strongly desired by most new professionals, but it was frequently minimal or absent in their work situations.

As students, the new professionals had had considerable contact with their peers. Students would meet before and after classes to gossip, "compare notes," provide one another with support and corrective feedback, and contribute to one another's educations. In fact, it has been said that students in institutions for higher learning learn more from one another than they do from the faculty (Newcomb & Feldman, 1968). Whether this is true, fellow students are readily available. There is a common thread of shared experience and values among students that brings them together. And in most training programs, there is usually a large cohort of students from which one can select a small group of intimates with whom to share the student experience.

Unfortunately, the situation is quite different when one finally relinquishes the student status and goes to work as a new professional in a public human service organization. Not only are there many fewer peers available for contact and sharing of experience, but there are numerous barriers to collegial interaction that were not present in the student situation. The work setting, to state the obvious, is a very different culture, and the norms for social interaction among professionals in public institutions are quite different from the norms that governed interaction among students in the school setting. When new professionals most need the support and sharing that they took for granted as students, it is rarely available to them. They must face the trials and tribulations of being a new professional more or less on their own, and this makes coping more difficult. Further, their interactions with colleagues sometimes become another source of stress, adding to the burdens already considered. Thus, when the new professionals need and want it most, the collegiality they thought would characterize peer relations in their work is elusive at best.

THE BENEFITS OF PROFESSIONAL INTERACTION

The lack of collegial interaction in their work settings is a major deprivation for new public professionals because such interaction provides numerous psychological benefits. Colleagues can provide a sympathetic ear when one is concerned about a work problem; talking to colleagues can be a cathartic experience that reduces emotional tension and helps one acquire better perspective and understanding. Other professionals can also provide "moral support" and share the risks in conflicts with administrators or other groups in the organization. Professional colleagues are an invaluable source of not only technical information and practical advice, but also of feedback on one's performance, feedback that is critical for the development of a sense of competence (see Chapter 2). Finally, for all these reasons, colleagues can make one's work more interesting and stimulating; one's motivation tends to increase when there are liked and respected colleagues who care about one's work.

Emotional Support from Colleagues

Of all these benefits, emotional support is probably experienced as the most important by novice professionals working in public human service agencies.

The new professionals we interviewed frequently told us how helpful it was to "ventilate" their feelings to a co-worker when they were tense, worried, or frustrated. Although they could—and did—discuss their concerns with friends, family members, and others outside of work, co-workers seemed to be an especially desirable audience. Colleagues could understand and sympathize with the new professional's worries and frustrations in a way most others could not. Unfortunately, the structure of their jobs frequently prevented them from interacting with colleagues as much as they would have liked.

Public health nurse Sarah Prentiss spent most of her time in the field, making home visits and working in local schools. It was important for her to meet with her colleagues when she could, but the opportunities were limited:

You go from family to family or school to school, and you really aren't working with people as you are in an office. And you get kind of lonely, sometimes, or you want to talk about something because you're listening to all these problems people have, and just venting a few of your own feelings sometimes is really important. . . . It's nice to be able to communicate with people you work with, especially if there's a problem. But you're not in the office that much. You come here to do paper work or make phone calls, and then you just leave and get on your way.

This theme of loneliness in one's work and the need to interact with colleagues in order to reduce emotional tension was also expressed by new mental health professional Douglas Furth. Like Sarah Prentiss, he found that his work setting provided few real opportunities to receive emotional support from co-workers:

I really need them [colleagues]. It can be a very lonely place. For instance, after I see a couple of clients, maybe even one, I need to get some time for myself and talk about what happened and whether I was pleased or upset about something. And it's very easy to start feeling you're not doing well. Let me give you an example. Often, I find that clients will talk about certain things that restimulate feelings in me. Like somebody's wife is leaving him, and he gets into, "Why?" And I'll start thinking about my relationship with women or friends. I'm not always able to stand off from it, to keep my attention on them without some attention for me. And it's not built in to get attention for the worker here. I don't know any place that it is. I think it's really important for workers to have time with each other. And see, it doesn't happen at clinical staff meetings. It's not built in there, either. So you've got to create it, like everything else in this place. You've got to make it.

Although it was slow in coming, Douglas was gradually able to develop relationships with some co-workers from whom he received the emotional support and attention he desired:

I've been able to go to people now, like when I've been really upset. For instance, I had a supervision, I had two clients and a staff meeting, and I had just had it. I didn't want to see clients any more. I didn't want to give out attention. I was just pissed off in general, and I needed some time for *me*. And, if I didn't have these people there [colleagues], what the hell would I do? You know, I'd just freak out. And I feel that way sometimes there at work, as I'm finding many of them feel as we're getting closer over a few months.

In addition to helping reduce emotional tension simply by listening to a novice "ventilate," colleagues can help more actively. One way is by confirming the new professional's perceptions. For example, high school teacher Cynthia Noble was upset because the teachers' union at her school seemed to have little interest in her specific grievances as a new teacher. Sharing her feelings with another new teacher did nothing to change the situation, but she did feel better about it when the other teacher agreed with her. As Cynthia put it, "I thought it was just me, but the other new teacher, the one I talked to today, felt the same way."

Professional colleagues also help reduce some of the tension and stress experienced by the novices by "giving them permission" to adopt more modest goals and standards for themselves. For instance, Cynthia Noble, like most of the new high school teachers, was bothered because she could not seem to "reach" all of her students. When she finally discussed her concerns with some sympathetic older teachers, they encouraged her to stop trying so hard. "They said, 'This is your first year here. Just make it through and don't worry about what happens.'" Even if the novice chooses to disregard this kind of friendly advice, being told that one can do less is reassuring.

Helping a new professional understand and put feelings into perspective is another way in which colleagues can contribute to tension reduction. For instance, new public health nurse Sarah Prentiss had been upset by some things that had happened at work and had discussed her feelings with one of her colleagues:

> When this whole thing happened, I talked to one of the nurses here who's really done a lot, knows a lot, and she can really think. And she said, "Sarah, you're a new graduate . . . Everybody goes through this. There are problems here, and hopefully we'll do something about them. But the idealism of being a new graduate . . . the first few months are really hard. I went through the same thing." I was glad she told me that because she was really trying to be helpful. She told me that she admired the fact that we were trying to do something. I'm glad that she pointed it out because it helped me to understand why I was reacting to the whole thing, why I seem to be more upset about it than other people. I think I'm learning more about myself now. When I get into that situation now, I can think through it and realize why I'm feeling that way. So talking to this other nurse really has helped.

For Sarah and many other new public professionals, insights gained from talking to older colleagues often seemed to help reduce anxiety by making them feel that they now had the understanding that would help them deal with difficult situations better in the future. Thus, in numerous ways, professional colleagues' support and reassurance and their sharing of experiences can help the novices put their concerns and problems in perspective and reduce some of the anxiety and tension experienced at this stage of the career.

Colleagues as a Source
of Information and Advice

Most professional training programs prepare students by providing them with general principles of practice applicable in a wide variety of work situations. It is assumed that much of the specific information necessary to perform effectively will be provided on the job by more experienced colleagues and supervisors. Thus, in all of the fields studied, the new professionals found that they initially need an enormous amount of important information in order to do their work, and they soon realized that much of it could only be learned from their colleagues.

For instance, poverty lawyer Margaret Williams did not know the first thing about filing briefs or courtroom procedures. During her first week, she constantly had to go to colleagues in order to get the answers. High school teacher Cynthia Noble went to other teachers in her department to find out how realistic her pace and standards were for each class she taught. She also learned from colleagues the best approach to use with particular students whom her colleagues had taught before. Without this kind of information, she would have felt less secure about her effectiveness and the crisis of competence would have been even more difficult to resolve.

The critical role played by colleagues in the orientation and professional socialization of the novice becomes most apparent when access to knowledgeable colleagues is limited. For instance, Margaret Williams complained that the lawyers working in legal aid tended to be young and inexperienced like herself. Consequently, within six months she believed that she knew as much as anyone else in the office. However, she realized that there was much more to learn and that she could be more effective in handling many of her cases if she had better advice. She said:

> I think it's really important to have co-workers that you can get a lot from in terms of your own work, and I don't have that there. Why's Bill quitting and going over to work at the center? The only reason he's taking a three grand pay cut to go over there is because he wants to be able to work with certain people.
>
> [Interviewer: "And that's a value for you, too?"]
>
> Yeah. At this point, if I have a case I don't know what to do with, I want to go to somebody and say "What do you think about this or that?" ... If I have something like a housing fraud case or a landlord-tenant case, there's not one person in the office I could ask anything.
>
> [Interviewer: "You really want to learn from this job."]
>
> Yeah. I learned some things. I learn a lot just not having any direction, just being told, "Okay, kid. Here you are. Sink or swim." That's good for a while, but not when you really want to do competent, good work.

Evaluation and Feedback from Colleagues

Besides providing information and advice, interaction with colleagues contributes to the development of competence when the colleagues provide feedback on the novice's performance. As noted in Chapter 2, new professionals become especially sensitive to the importance of their "reputation" among their colleagues, and this reputation is primarily based on their perceived competence. Colleagues are an important source of confirmation, for they are able to evaluate the novice's performance. When they are not accessible, the crisis of competence is prolonged.

The importance of colleagues' views is increased because, as described in Chapter 3, the new professionals soon find that clients rarely give them positive feedback. Client dissatisfaction is expressed in a variety of ways while satisfaction and gratitude are communicated infrequently, if at all. Thus, it is often feedback from co-workers that provides new professionals with feelings of success and accomplishment, which are so important at this stage. As clinical social worker Douglas Furth put it, he felt as though he had been hired by the staff. What they thought of him, particularly his competence was important to him. "You know, I've been wondering what they [the rest of the staff] think of me. You see, it felt to me like the whole staff hired me, really. It wasn't as if only the director hired me. . . . And I feel they all know about me—or I'm wondering what they do know about me, what's been said behind my back." Not surprisingly, one of the most gratifying moments occurred for Douglas when a respected older worker said that she would like to lead a group with him. The confirmation he had sought had finally come.

Even when colleagues provide negative feedback, they may be contributing to the development of competence in the new professional. For instance, new high school teacher Alice Harris was fortunate to be placed in a special team-teaching situation during her first year. One of the benefits of this arrangement was the frequent opportunity it afforded for more experienced and accomplished colleagues to observe her performance and provide corrective feedback:

> I don't get depressed [about work] real easily. If I've had a bad day, I say that I've had a bad day, the lecture went terribly, the kids weren't picking it up, and that's the end of it. I don't sulk. It just doesn't pay. Most of the time, any real worries I have—let's say I didn't think the lecture went well. All I have to do is ask someone on the team and just say, "Hey, did that make sense to you?" And then they'll either say, "Yes," or they'll say, "No," and they'll make a suggestion. And the depression that I might have felt about that is lifted because now I know what to do about it the next time.

Even negative feedback on one's performance from colleagues can alleviate worry and depression because it can provide the means for positive change. Without that kind of feedback, the new professional may feel helpless, and it is this sense of helplessness in the face of failure that is the major contributor to burnout.

Colleagues as Allies
in Organizational Conflicts

In Chapter 4, we saw that new professionals in public institutions frequently find that the way they wish to do things conflicts with the bureaucratic structure of their work settings. Wanting or attempting to make changes in these situations can be overwhelming and threatening to the novice. When they can find colleagues who agree with them and are willing to join them in attempts to challenge the way things are, much of the pressure and strain of waging such battles is alleviated.

For instance, public health nurse Sarah Prentiss was frustrated with the staff meetings in her agency; she wanted them to be more stimulating exchanges of ideas and experiences in which everyone felt free to express themselves without being attacked. As a new staff person, it would have been difficult for her to find the courage necessary to express her concern openly before the group. However, when she found that two other members of the group shared her frustration and were willing to support her if she raised the issue, she was able to do so and some change occurred. Sarah also described how commiseration and moral support among colleagues had helped another new nurse in her group who had been having problems with her supervisor. "She really didn't want to talk to our supervisor, even though she was kind of upset about it. Ultimately she did, but at first she kind of shared those feelings with us and asked us how we were dealing with the problem."

Without the moral support and group solidarity that colleagues can provide, many new professionals would not make an active effort to resolve difficulties in their work situations. Instead, they would simply withdraw into a mindless conformity or apathy, arresting their professional development as a result.

Colleagues as a Source
of Stimulation and Encouragement

As described, a new professional's colleagues provide a strong impetus for sustained commitment to one's work. When the professional works in isolation, the work may not have the same sense of vitality and significance. The clients are there, and they provide some of the impetus. But one's colleagues are an important part of the "audience" that make the "role" worth acting—and acting well. Margaret Williams represented one of the clearest examples of professional burnout in our sample; in one statement made near the end of our final interview with her, she suggested that her commitment to her work might have been maintained longer if she had been working with colleagues whom she respected and liked:

> You know, a lot of times, when I'm depressed, I think the whole job is a pain in the ass and I say, "Shit! I don't know why I'm doing this. All my clients are running some crap line to me, and my boss is on my ass, and I'm not getting anything out of this, so to hell with it." So, I figure I'm not really performing any great social function that I'm really needed for, so I don't mind if I quit at 5. Sometimes if I feel I'm doing something really important, I'll work a little bit later, but I usually figure nothing is that important that I can't pick it up again tomorrow morning. I mean, *if I were working with people I really liked and they didn't want to be let down or something maybe I'd do more.* But I don't feel that way about it.

With neither a sense of performing a worthwhile service to one's clients nor a sense of collegiality and the commitment to one's professional peers that accompanies it, there is no longer any compelling reason for this burned out legal aid attorney to maintain the involvement and concern about her work that she had when she began.

New mental health professional Douglas Furth also suggested that colleagues were an important source of encouragement for him. Like Margaret Williams, he believed that he would have been more stimulated, creative, and "turned on" in his job if he had had more opportunities to discuss his work with colleagues. He said:

> I don't feel anyone is there who is encouraging me to try new stuff and be creative and is right there with suggestions. There's no one doing that. A couple of other places I worked, there were. There's just no direction or encouragement. So, any encouragement has to come from me . . . That's all right. It's not horrible. But it's not the same as someone coming and talking to me occasionally. "What's going on? Have you done this? Have you done any family work?" There's no one there saying that to me. It all has to come from me. I have to broadcast it all myself.

In the final analysis, it is *encouragement* that colleagues provide the novice working in a public institution, and, frequently, loneliness and social isolation imposed by the work setting prevent novices from receiving that encouragement during this critical transition in their lives.

BARRIERS TO COLLEGIALITY

Despite its importance to novices, professional collegiality was often elusive in the public human service settings in which they worked. They found that professional work could be—and often was—lonely. Their descriptions of their work situations suggested several causes of this loneliness and isolation. One was conflict and hostility between individuals and groups. Another was differences in values, theoretical orientation, and seniority among professional colleagues. Yet another cause was the workload and role structure of the professional job. Finally, collegiality appeared to be frustrated by interpersonal norms or patterns of social interaction regulating behavior in both formal and informal settings. When all of these barriers existed in a work situation, as was often the case, there was little likelihood that satisfying collegial relations could develop.

The Impact of Individual and Group Conflict

When people work together, there are many possibilities for friction, jealousy, and conflict. Competition for scarce resources can turn colleagues into combatants. Differences in status and loyalty can become a source of envy and hostility. Any perceived difference in treatment can lead to resentment and bitterness. In large, bureaucratic organizations, these opportunities for conflict among individuals and groups occur frequently. When they do, collegial relations are jeopardized, and professional status does not make one immune.

High school teacher Cynthia Noble was fortunate to share the same lunch period as her principal. She was also fortunate that he chose to eat with his staff, for she was able to have more contact with him than would have otherwise been the case. However, she soon found that this felicitous situation was resented by colleagues who were not so lucky.

> I have the same lunch hour as our principal, and in my lunch hour I feel that everybody really likes him and we get along really well. We sit at the same table, and nobody's afraid of him. If somebody wants to tell him they think he's all messed up in the way he's running the school, they tell him. But evidently, there's a lot of hostile feeling towards our whole lunch hour because we have the "chosen" lunch hour; we get to eat lunch with the principal. On Fridays, we have some gourmet lunch. Evidently, a lot of the other teachers really think that's terrible that we do that and that it's only the principal's lunch hour that can do it. They could do it too, as far as that goes, but they don't, and so there's some bitterness about that.

In bureaucratic organizations, apparent influence with superiors is a valuable asset that rarely seems to be allocated evenly among all members. Thus, apparent favoritism often becomes the focus of much envy and rivalry. Although this rivalry is not necessarily incompatible with a collegial climate, it can become so in many settings.

A particularly good example of how interpersonal conflict in the work setting can interfere with the development of collegial interaction was presented by public health nurse Sarah Prentiss. She described in some detail how an undercurrent of hostility among certain members of her work group affected all of them. She and the other new nurses in the group were especially bothered by the tendency to make one of the members a scapegoat:

> We had kind of the scapegoat thing. You can see it; you can name almost everybody. We had a meeting one time, and every time this one nurse said something, people put her down. Well, we had this meeting on "failure to thrive," and she brought up maternal bonding. And that probably is one of the most important things in failure to thrive, or a lot of people think it is, and she brought it up, and boy, one of the other nurses just put that idea right down. She said, "Well, everybody knows that!" And then it was brought up again by another person in the group and everyone accepted it. And you could see the first person knew what was happening, and she complained about it afterwards. And Mary and I saw it, and we talked about it. We felt so bad because that was our chance, right then, to say, "Hey, let her talk."

Sarah believed that the collegial atmosphere in her work group suffered because of such interpersonal conflicts, which were not adequately discussed and resolved within the group.

Of all the interpersonal conflicts affecting new professionals, those related to an underlying tension between old staff and new seemed to be among the most severe. This conflict took many forms. While it rarely erupted to the surface, its subtle presence could impede the development of collegiality and social support for new public professionals.

Social cliques represented a major area in which the rift between older professionals and novices was evident, and they were a source of tension. In many cases, the older staff in an agency had already developed relatively stable and fixed social cliques. Although the new staff gradually might be absorbed by one of the existing cliques, acceptance did not come quickly or easily. Needless to say, many new professionals resented exclusion, as Cynthia Noble did:

> The older teachers have their little group, and the only time they come to the new people is when they want something from us. They never just come and say, "Why don't you come, we're doing this tonight," or, "We're going to talk about this." And they toss out little announcements that say, "Education Association Meeting tonight," but they're like the announcements I put up for a math department meeting when only the math department is invited. They never seem very open. It turns out that the education meetings are always in the teachers lounge, and, the way things are situated, if I stay after school, I have to walk through the teachers' lounge to get out of school. I've walked through them a million times, and when I walk

through everyone just gets real quiet. They've never said, "Why don't you stop and sit in, this is an Education Association meeting." So even though I'm part of them, I'm kind of upset with them. I think they're a little cliquey group, and they don't really care about the new teachers. I see no effort to get the new teachers involved, and I wouldn't mind being involved. But I'm a little bit on the shy side where I'm not going to approach them and say, "What can I do?"

On the other hand, while the new professional may be viewed as an intruder into already established social groups, lack of close, collegial relations between older and new professionals may simply be a function of differences in interests, needs, and concerns. The needs and interests of a professional change over time. What is critically important to a neophyte may be of little interest to the practitioner with several years of experience. These differences in concern as a function of experience may contribute to the difficulties many new professionals experience in trying to develop collegial ties with "veterans."

This was certainly true for new high school teachers. Cynthia Noble's description of her first meeting with her department summed up the experience of others in her situation:

I felt very out of place. There were only three people at the math meeting, and the other two guys had been teaching math for seven or eight years and were really interested in a lot of things that I haven't even gotten into yet, like how overall courses work within their district and what they could do to change courses. I'm only involved now with four courses and I know a little bit about the other courses in our district, but not very much. There were a lot of things like that they wanted to talk about, and I was really out in the blue. I wanted to talk about procedures they use to grade tests quickly, efficiently, and fairly, and things like that. To them, that was such old hat. These are my immediate problems, but it just didn't work because I was so new and they were so much older.

It is always difficult being the "new kid in school," the one who is not yet part of the group and who seeks information and behavioral cues others take for granted. What seemed especially difficult for the new professionals was the apparent lack of concern or interest from their older peers.

Perhaps older teachers minimize contact with newer ones because, paradoxically, they know newer teachers may be having problems and so they do not want to interfere. Sarason and his colleagues, in describing their experiences as psychologists consulting in the public schools, noted that they were often asked not to go into a teacher's classroom because the teacher was new and might be having problems (Sarason, Levine, Goldenberg, Cherlin, & Bennet, 1966). Thus, new teachers seem to be avoided at the very time they would probably welcome collegial contact from which they might gain the knowledge and insight necessary for solving those problems.

A less benign interpretation is offered by Ryan (1970) who contends that older teachers view the new teacher both as a personal threat and a threat to the social order of the school. As a result, they tolerate less deviant behavior in a new teacher than they would in an older colleague; warm, positive interaction between older and newer teachers is limited. Further, there may be resentment of certain privileges or options available to newer staff members that until recently had not been available to anyone. Douglas Furth found that the older workers in his mental health agency resented it when new workers took advantage of the "flex time" scheduling of work hours.

Although these factors undoubtedly impede the development of collegiality between old and new professionals, the most important factor may be differences in values and philosophy. Changes in philosophy and technique have occurred in many professions during the last 20 years. As a result, new practitioners are likely to differ considerably in their professional orientation, and these differences can be the source of conflict and mistrust between old and new members of a profession.

Staff differences in treatment philosophy or theoretical orientation were especially important in mental health settings. In Douglas Furth's agency, the staff seemed to be split into two groups: the older staff members favored psychoanalytic theory and treatment, and the newer staff members supported transactional analysis (T.A.) or a more eclectic approach. According to Douglas, those associated with one group had little interest in or even tolerance for those who supported the other. There was always a certain level of conflict and hostility between the two factions. When Douglas had been working at the agency for three months, he said:

> The split is getting more clear.
> [Interviewer: "The split between the older people and the newer people?"]
> Yeah . . . The older ones are not into T.A. However, a number of the new people are T.A., and some are more like me: you couldn't classify them as anything, particularly. . . . They're eclectic, and the older ones are analytic. And that does create problems which we have brought up. There was even talk about having a separate T.A. clinical seminar, an analytic clinical seminar, and then neither of these clinical seminars. And then some people really didn't want that because they said they wanted to learn from the others. Well, there's the attitude, apparently among the older staff, that—"Well, what's there to learn from the newer people? What do they know?" And then there's an attitude among some of the new staff: "Well, who wants to learn this analytic shit?" That's underneath it. No one says that, but I hear it from a number of the newer people.

For a novice like Douglas, who did not feel strongly identified with either treatment approach but believed he could benefit from both, this division within the agency was especially detrimental. He came to feel marginal with both groups, and his isolation within the agency thus increased.

Another difference in attitudes between older and newer staff members occurred as a function of experience in the "real world." Veterans were likely to see novices as too "idealistic and naive;" novices were likely to see their older colleagues as "callous and cynical." In the case of Cynthia Noble, the older teachers' attitude toward their work and students led her and other new teachers to avoid contact with them. She said that she avoided many older teachers in part because she did not want to be influenced by their negative outlooks. During our third interview, Cynthia declared:

> There's something about the other teachers and their attitude toward students that we [two other new teachers in her school] kind of don't like.
>
> [Interviewer: "What's that?"]
>
> Oh sitting around in the cafeteria at lunch and saying, "So-and-so's in my class the fourth time; he's such a zero," and everybody goes, "Yeah, yeah, yeah, yeah." You know, the first week at school, a lot of that filtered into me, and I found that I was looking at these kids with bad attitudes. So I try and stay away from that. It's getting to the point where like two or three days a week I don't eat in the teachers' cafeteria. I just didn't want to hear about it anymore. I didn't want to hear, "So-and-so is so dumb that he did this today in my class." And they'll come up with a story about what some kid did, and it's probably a true story, and it's funny. But that really prejudices me against the kids, especially when I don't know them because then all I've heard about these kids are the bad things.

Cynthia described how the older faculty members responded with little concern for the students when one of the newer teachers raised a problem during a faculty meeting:

> A couple of young teachers were sticking up for students in a particular incident in the last teachers' meeting. This one teacher spoke up and said, "I'm really upset about the condition of the girl's lavatory in my hall. There's no wastebasket; there's no paper towels; there's no hand towels; there's no blow dryer; there's nothing there for them to really clean up after they use the toilets." And then one of the other teachers says, "Oh, there's all that stuff in my hall, and they don't use it anyway." So then one of the other teachers says, "The moral of the story is, 'Don't hold hands with girls from _____ High School!'" So then someone says, "Well, don't hold hands with the guys, either. Have you ever seen the guys' johns?" And then they start putting down the kids for their bathroom habits, which was funny, but for the length of time that we dwelled on it—and I thought the first teacher had a legitimate gripe, and everyone made a big joke out of it.

Although Cynthia and the other teachers would have liked more contact and acceptance by older colleagues, these differences in attitude and perception discouraged them from bridging the gap. If they were lucky, they might have the opportunity to develop a more collegial relationship with one or two other peers who were as new as they and shared the same values and concerns. But when these colleagues were as inexperienced as they, there was a limit to what they could learn from each other, and they lacked the wider sense of collegiality with older colleagues that they had expected would occur in their work settings.

Like high school teachers, poverty lawyers differed in their values, aspirations, and perceptions. In fact, they differed much more from one another than the new professionals initially realized. They assumed that older colleagues—and certainly colleagues who were new like themselves—would share their values and outlooks. But they soon found that this was not the case. Some also found that it was difficult for them to work closely with someone who viewed the work so differently. Because of these differences in outlook, many professionals tended to avoid others in their field and developed a pattern of working on their own. As the following quote suggests, Margaret Williams had some definite opinions about the world and found it difficult to be "collegial" with co-workers whose views were radically different. The interviewer asked her what her colleagues were like, and she answered:

> Pooh! Well, the people in this office are so different, I cannot believe it.
>
> [Interviewer: "One from another?"]
>
> One from another and all from me! I can't believe the diversity. We have one man who started after I did. He was out doing private practice for criminal assignments and stuff. The real reason he's here is to get trial experience to go into private practice, and it seems his main motto is, "Protect yourself." I think he does fairly good work, he wants to win cases, but he doesn't really care what happens to the client. He wants to win cases not because it'll do good things for the client but because the more cases he wins, the better off he'll be when he wants to go into private practice.
>
> [Interviewer: "And you don't like that very much?"]
>
> Well, it's not my attitude. I mean, I don't like to lose cases either, but it isn't because I'm worried about what's going to happen when I go off into whatever kind of thing I'm going to go off into eventually.
>
> [Interviewer: "What other kinds of people are there?"]
>
> Well, there's another female attorney who's—she and I don't get along at all because of something not to do with work. She doesn't talk to me at all, as a matter of fact. She's in a lot of feminist stuff, which I'm not as involved in in the same way. She's been doing a lot of radical politics for a long time.

Similar descriptions of unexpected differences in professional orientation and personal values occurred in all the groups of new professionals. Such differences were a particularly strong contributor to the distrust, conflict, and hostility that led to the isolation experienced by many new public professionals. Even though they paid a heavy psychological price for their isolation, many novices preferred it to contact with colleagues whose values and approaches to practice were anathema to them.

Differences in values could be especially sharp and troublesome when the new professionals were required to work with those from other professional disciplines. Increasingly, the interdependence of community problems and resources brings professionals from different agencies and traditions together in collaborative efforts. When this occurs, the participants frequently find that their goals and orientations differ sharply. These differences can be a source of much stress. For instance, school social worker Nick Fisher was expected to spend part of his time in "consultation" with teachers and principals, the goal being to change school practices that contributed to emotional problems in children. But he found it difficult to bring about much change in the system through these consultations. He complained that the teachers and administrators were "condescending" and did not take his efforts seriously. As he put it, "I'd spend a lot of time talking to someone, and they'd see it as a coffee break where I'd see it as consultation. And it wouldn't change them. It was really frustrating." He went on to say that he was doing less and less "consultation" as a result of the frustration and was instead focusing on work with individual students. But he was still bothered by the small impact such individual remediation made. He said, "It's still band aid work. You're only working an hour a week, and it lets the mass of the system continue to tear them apart the rest of the week. It's not good, but I don't know exactly what else to do. . . ."

During another interview, Nick gave this example. He was asked by the teachers at one school to give them a "plan" for working with a difficult and troubled student who was to remain in their classrooms. He developed the plan and spent much time going over it with the teachers. He later found out they never followed it, and there was absolutely nothing he could do about it. He was powerless to influence the educational process as it affected his clients. And he increasingly came to see the teachers as adversaries rather than colleagues. Thus, the combination of competence, individual hostility, social cliques, and differences in needs as well as in attitudes all led to considerable interpersonal conflict in the new professionals' work settings; this conflict was a major barrier to the development of collegiality and social support.

Role Structure as a Barrier

There were, of course, some settings in which conflict among professional colleagues was not as great. Even in these situations, however, the structure of roles could create insurmountable barriers to collegial interaction. Factors built into organizational roles, such as heavy workloads or competing obligations that took professionals away from their work group, could prevent newer and older colleagues from establishing the social interaction sought by the novices.

The detrimental effects of heavy workloads on the development of collegiality were illustrated by poverty lawyer Margaret Williams. Like most law school graduates, Margaret had many gaps in her knowledge when she began her job, and she had hoped that more experienced colleagues would be available to "show her the ropes." Unfortunately, she quickly found that to receive this kind of help, she had to ask for it herself; it was not provided as a matter of course. In fact, she sometimes had to make valiant efforts to collar a busy colleague for assistance. Because she and the other lawyers working in the office did not have enough time for their own clients, they had even less time for one another. As a result, the social climate in the office was cold, impersonal, and harried. As she put it, "I get thrown out of people's offices all the time because they're busy." The message she received from her colleagues was, "We don't have time to help, too bad." She said that she wished her agency followed the practice used in many large firms in the private sector in which "every new person is assigned to somebody who's more experienced so that they've got some direction immediately." Unfortunately, in a neighborhood legal aid office, such a practice seems to be an unaffordable luxury.

The stresses and strains built into the role structure of legal aid offices contributed to another factor impeding collegiality: rapid staff turnover. When asked what the atmosphere of her office was like, during an early interview, Margaret answered:

> I stay away as much as I can! Everybody does his or her own thing. Nobody seems to have a whole hell of a lot of experience and I haven't learned very much from very many of the people here. And it kind of bothers me. I've been here probably longer than most. There have been two people in this whole office that I think have been here over a year. The Legal Services program is kind of known for high turnover. They don't pay very much. It's supposedly very low prestige, and also the caseload. Most of it isn't very interesting. And so, after about a year or so, people just get out. They just can't handle it anymore, and I'm going to [get out] if I can.

Compared with poverty lawyers, the public health nurses we interviewed had more manageable caseloads. However, they spent most of the day alone, away from colleagues, driving from one patient's home to another, and working alone with patients in their homes. Like public health nurses, the high school teachers worked in a role structure that impeded supportive collegial interaction. Most of their workday was spent in a classroom with 30 students, isolated from other classrooms and their professional colleagues. Also, even when teachers are able to escape from the classroom for brief periods, the American high school provides many distracting and competing activities that make them less available to each other. In most schools, extracurricular activities such as athletics make heavy demands on the time and energy of faculty members. In fact, two of the new teachers we interviewed explicitly stated that their willingness to sponsor after-school clubs or teams seemed to be as important as their classroom performance in determining whether they would be invited back to teach the following year. Although their view may have been somewhat distorted, the behavior of older colleagues to whom they turned for help suggested that extracurricular activities were indeed important and could be an obstacle to collegial interaction among teachers. Math teacher Cynthia Noble's experiences were not unique in this respect:

> Actually, in my department, I feel really neglected because the other two guys in the department are coaches, and they're more interested in football right now. I don't know, they're always out on the football field it seems like. If I track them down, they'll talk to me, but they're never around after school when I need them. . . . I just feel guilty even to ask them for ten minutes of their time. But I mean, I see them after school in the hall, and I say, "Can I talk to you?" And they say, "Well, I've got to go out to the football field." I don't have planning period or lunch with them, so it's really hard. Occasionally, I'll just interrupt their classes to go talk to them.

In all of the professional groups we studied, the structure of organizational roles sometimes impeded collegial interaction. Even when other factors in the setting were favorable, heavy workloads, rapid turnover, or expectations for extracurricular commitments could interfere with the development of social support for the novice professional working in a public institution.

The Influence of Interpersonal Norms

One final barrier to collegial interaction in public institutions was the influence of interpersonal norms. Even when new and older professionals could overcome the barriers of mistrust, conflict, and role structure, a genuine exchange of stimulating ideas and social support seemed to be impeded by certain patterns of social interaction in their work settings. Certain topics seemed to be taboo, and to raise them in discussion too often was to risk being regarded as a "deviant." Even in situations in which supportive collegiality was most expected, such as in staff meetings, there were intrenched patterns of communication that prevented it from occurring.

"Joking around" was a common example of how norms of social interaction among professionals could impede the kind of collegiality sought by the novice. In many settings, discussing something serious in the presence of more than one colleague seemed to be strictly forbidden. Discussing a *work-related* topic in a serious way was especially "in poor taste." The usual style around the office coffee pot or in the faculty lounge at lunch was a bantering, sarcastic style of communication that jumped quickly from one topic to another. Although this kind of light interaction probably provided a welcomed escape for emotionally drained veterans, the novices often found that it interfered with serious discussion of work experiences.

The agency of mental health professional Douglas Furth was a good example of this more general phenomenon:

> Staff there, often when they need time to talk about what's happening with them, they get into this joking thing. And that's not enough for me, and my hunch is it's not enough for them, either. I really want to get right at it when something's coming up with me because I know how good I can feel. Often, I need only a little bit of time to get there. But I have to have a lot of people there to do it because some of them are busy or gone or something.

The staff room at lunch in Douglas' agency was the place where "joking around" as a mode of communication among colleagues reached its ultimate level. Douglas quickly gave up any ideas he might have had that lunch would be a time for serious discussion of work-related concerns.

> Oh boy, in the big room when everybody eats together, forget it. No one talks. There are a few favorite subjects—jokes about sex, that's standard, and everyone digs on that for a few minutes. But you know, after that it gets to be a drag: somebody's dog, and what somebody brought for lunch, and two or three other subjects. So you know, for ten minutes I enjoy it. Ten, fifteen minutes, I like seeing everyone and just chattering away.

The new professionals might not have become so frustrated with "joking around" in some settings at work if there had been any place where more serious, constructive, work-related interaction occurred regularly. Unfortunately, even their formal staff meetings were characterized by patterns of interaction that stifled creative problem solving or mutual support around work-related issues. The staff meeting usually was the only formal setting in which the professionals came together for serious discussion of their work, and more often than not those meetings were used simply as a rather inefficient vehicle for one-way communication of the most basic administrative matters. They frequently seemed to have degenerated into meaningless rituals that people completed as quickly as possible.

The weekly faculty meetings at Cynthia Noble's school were typical:

> Teachers' meetings aren't mandatory, so you don't get everyone there. They're after school, and they last maybe 10 or 15 minutes. They just do business; there's not a lot of extra stuff that gets thrown in. It's just, "Here's this item, this item, and this item. Think about them and we'll send a ballot around on it." There hasn't been too much to discuss at teachers' meetings. And then, as usual, the coaches are never there. Usually the kids keep me trapped in my room, and, by the time I get there, they are all over. The first time I managed to get to one the principal was walking out saying, "Teachers' meeting over. There's nothing to talk about." They're in the teachers' lounge and there's room for about 13 people to sit, so everyone's just about sitting on top of each other. Nobody could sit there for an hour or anything; it's too uncomfortable because there's not room. So they're real quick.

Unfortunately, many new teachers expect that these meetings will be forums for discussion of their teaching experiences, issues, and problems—settings in which collegial interaction is nourished and sustained. Like Cynthia Noble, they are soon disabused of this notion.

The experiences of new public health nurse Sarah Prentiss were similar to Cynthia Noble's; however, in Sarah's case there was some hope of change. Staff meetings were held weekly at the county health department where Sarah worked, and she had hoped that they would offer an opportunity for meaningful communication and exchange of ideas with her colleagues. But, as in the high school setting, the meetings were initially disappointing on this score:

> Maybe I'm more social than some of the others because, you know, you're out in your car, you're by yourself, really, and our meetings, I think, should be sharing of ideas. You know, some of those nurses have been there for years, and several of them have their master's degrees, and they really do have a lot to offer. And they really weren't sharing it. I don't like to sit in a meeting and have someone tell me what we're doing to do for the week and then get up and leave. We'd have meetings that lasted five minutes, and it's ridiculous.

Like the teachers' meetings at Cynthia Noble's high school, the staff meetings at Sarah's agency were short, perfunctory, and disappointing for a novice seeking knowledge, growth, and intellectual stimulation. Fortunately, Sarah was able to bring up and discuss these concerns about her group with her supervisor and other staff members, and the ensuing discussion cleared the air considerably. One reason Sarah was able to do this was that she had the moral support of two other new nurses, who were also members of this group and shared her frustration and disappointment. Together, they were able to confront some of the conflicts and tensions that impeded collegiality.

Staff meetings in Douglas Furth's mental health clinic were also disappointing. He described them in this way:

We were talking about case presentations, which had been pretty much a drag. A lot of people won't admit it, but I think really that's how some people I know feel. There's no one there giving direction to what's an important concept to look at. People say whatever they want. It's like a hodgepodge. One person will say something, and someone will respond, and it won't be directly to what the first person said. And then, the presenter is lost in the process. There's no one saying, "Is this important? Do you want to stay with this?" It's sort of a joke. The mode is you present, and really what happens is someone tells you what to do. Everyone is telling you what to do. And even though we had this big rap that people wouldn't do that, unless the person asked for it, they're doing it anyway. We didn't change anything. There's no one to say, "Wait a minute." No one has that role, and people are real hesitant now to say that kind of thing because the split is getting more clear. . . . So, I haven't felt it yet, like the real excitement of sharing in a staff meeting. And no one else has ever reported feeling that way either.

Undoubtedly the failure of these staff members to really listen to each other is a common characteristic of the human condition. One frequently finds articles in the popular magazines lamenting the loss of the "art of listening." But the new public professionals in most cases expected that their colleagues would be different. Professional collegiality is expected to transcend the normal barriers to meaningful human communication, and sometimes this happens. But, frequently this communication does not occur even when the participants all come from the same profession. Collegiality does not develop as expected, and the disappointment for many new professionals is considerable.

CONCLUSION: THE REALITY
OF PROFESSIONAL ISOLATION

It must be stressed that the elusiveness of collegiality, like the strains that have been discussed in previous chapters, is not universal. There were five new professionals in our study (out of 28 subjects) who did find close, warm, supportive collegiality in their work settings. They were a minority, but their experience does show that professional collegiality can and does occur in public human service institutions. In Chapter 9, we shall examine the factors that seem to contribute to greater collegiality in public professional work settings. Unfortunately, these conditions are rare.

For a few new professionals, supervisors can provide the same kinds of social support as colleagues. When this occurs, isolation from peers may be less disconcerting. However, for most of the new professionals interviewed, supervisors were inaccessible physically and psychologically. There are always the evaluation and organizational control aspects of the supervisory relationship, which complicate the giving and taking of social support. In law and teaching, there is no expectation that supervisors will serve this function. In mental health and public health, there is more of a tradition for it, but close, open, and supportive relations between supervisors and novices were still rare in our sample. Ultimately, the new professionals must rely on their peers.

Despite the importance of collegiality to many new professionals, it would be a mistake to assume that all of them miss collegiality equally. As mental health professional Douglas Furth observed, all workers probably suffer when collegiality is absent from their work experiences, whether they admit it or are even aware of it; however, some new professionals clearly miss collegial relations less than others. In fact, some actually seek the isolation characteristic of the new public professional work experience. For instance, mental health professional Nick Fisher said that he was glad that he worked in a public school system in which he was more isolated from professional colleagues than he would be if he were working in a counseling agency. The reason was that he did not want to be exposed to the negative values and attitudes he associated with professionalism, the kinds of attitudes toward clients, for example, that Cynthia Noble found in older teachers and tried to avoid.

But the new professionals who increased their own isolation paid a price, as they themselves acknowledged. Being a new professional is a psychologically stressful, emotionally demanding experience even when one can turn to colleagues for advice and support. When sympathetic colleagues are not available for any of the reasons we have noted, the struggle to become a professional is even harder; loneliness and isolation become an added burden to carry. Also, it is through serious discussion of one's work that stimulation and fulfillment, otherwise missing, can be actualized.

The value of social interaction was unexpectedly demonstrated by the response of many of our subjects to participating in the study. Several noted that the interviews helped them gain new perspectives on their work and alleviated some of the tension and unhappiness they felt. Participation in our study provided a vehicle through which they could receive support and engage in serious discussion in a way that was not possible at work. Of course, we were outsiders and not as familiar with the technical aspects of their work as their professional colleagues would have been. However, we were available for discussion of any aspect of their work that was important to them. We gave them an opportunity to think things through in a way they rarely could do with others. We were nonjudgmental in a way their colleagues usually were not. Through their participation in our study, these new professionals were able to pierce the isolation that must be even greater for those without such an opportunity.

The idea that social interaction and support help combat psychological stress is, of course, not a new one. In one of the earliest studies of psychological stress, Grinker and Spiegel (1945) noted that soldiers in combat who were members of units in which cohesion was higher were less susceptible to excessive stress and neurotic breakdown. Group cohesion helped reduce the tension and anxiety associated with combat. More recently, Maslach (1976) suggested that human service professionals would be less susceptible to burnout if they were involved in a "support group," a regular opportunity to discuss their feelings about their work experiences with others going through the same experiences. Discovering that their problems were not unique and being able to vent their feelings of frustration, anger, and anxiety would be important aspects of such an experience.

However, it is not interaction in itself that is crucial; its focus and content can be detrimental as well as helpful. For example, there is always the danger that group sessions will degenerate into unpleasant and personally destructive "group therapy." The interchanges could increase alienation, stress, and frustration rather than diminish them. One of the earliest studies of professional burnout found that burnout is highly contagious: when a high percentage of the staff in a setting is burned out, new staff members are likely to become burned out as well (Schwartz & Will, 1961). In fact, the more they interact with colleagues, the more quickly and completely will they burn out.

Similarly, in a study of graduate students preparing to take qualifying exams, Mechanic (1962) found that, when all the students were under stress, interaction with one another merely seemed to potentiate anxiety. In our own research, we found examples in which contact with colleagues increased the strain for the new professionals involved, as when colleagues engaged in behavior or supported values that the novice thought were wrong.

More importantly, however, these proposals that professionals form support groups in their work settings are organizationally naive. Our analysis of the lack of collegiality in public human service institutions has suggested that supportive interaction among professional colleagues is blocked by several systemic barriers such as heavy workloads, isolating role structures, interpersonal mistrust and conflict related to differences in professional orientation and philosophy, and strong norms of communication and social interaction that are antithetical to collegial support. It is likely that any attempt to create "social support groups" in such settings will be undermined by the same systemic barriers that currently inhibit the development of supportive interaction among peers.

Thus, it is not interaction with colleagues by itself that is missing in the work experiences of most new public professionals, but rather a particular kind of interaction *and the social conditions necessary to support it.* The new professionals thought that collegial interaction would be one of the benefits of professional work. They looked to their colleagues, especially the more senior ones, for technical advice, emotional support, confirmation of their abilities, and intellectual stimulation. They rarely found these things, either because their opportunities for interaction were limited or becasue interaction rarely had these qualities. As a result, a sense of professional isolation and loneliness developed early in this stage of their careers, and the concommitant stress was considerable.

As they gave up the ideal of collegiality and adjusted to a work culture in which it rarely occurred, they became the "veterans" who would be as unavailable for the next generation of novices as the earlier veterans had been for them. In this way, the elusiveness of collegiality becomes an enduring aspect of the new professional's experience in public human service institutions.

PART II

COPING AND CHANGE

6

THE FATE OF IDEALISM

In the previous section of this book, we saw that the initial period of a professional career in a public institution is often filled with tension, pressure, and frustration. To be sure, there are many satisfactions: it is also a time of novelty, challenge, and excitement. Furthermore, as the time passes, the crisis of competence is usually resolved at least in part, and it is gratifying to realize that one has weathered the storm largely through one's own efforts. However, during the first six months or so (it may be much longer for some, rarely shorter), the stress is usually great.

As new professionals are trying to cope with this stress, they are also changing in many ways. In virtually every case we studied, there were changes in attitudes, beliefs, and perceptions during the first year of fulltime professional functioning. The actual changes varied with the subject, as did the amount of change. Some individuals underwent major transformations in values and belief. Others changed in more limited and modest ways. But the outlooks of all the new professionals we interviewed did change. The initial period of professional endeavor in a public institution is a time of change as well as of stress and turmoil.

Although the nature of the change in outlook varied with the individual, there were certain general tendencies in the group we studied. Specifically, change during this initial stage of the professional career seemed to occur in five areas. First, in most cases, the professional modified the work goals that he or she had initially set out to accomplish. Frequently, this modification took the form of accepting more modest, less ambitious goals. Second, there was a strong tendency for the new public professionals to reduce or restrict their levels of personal involvement in their jobs. Many withdrew emotionally and physically from the professional-client relationship and from the job itself. They reduced the psychological role of work in their lives and increasingly sought gratification and fulfillment elsewhere.

A third change was manifested when the new public professionals tended to shift the responsibility for failure from themselves to others. Rather than blame themselves for shortcomings and limitations in their efforts as they initially did, they began to blame their clients or "the system." A fourth area of change concerned general attitudes toward people: over time, there was a tendency for the new professionals to become less idealistic, less trusting, and more conservative in their attitudes toward clients and people in general. Finally, there was increasing concern with self-protection and self-enhancement. Gratification of personal needs in work became more important. The novices became more concerned about economic rewards. They also became more sensitive about infringements on personal autonomy. Thus, over time, many new public professionals changed in ways that directly affected their involvement in work and the services they provided.

In this chapter, we shall focus on what appeared to be the initial changes: modification of one's goals and aspirations for work, reduction in the sense of personal responsibility for the outcomes of one's work, and a decline in idealism. These changes did not occur in all of the subjects, but they tended to occur in those who experienced the greatest stress in their jobs (Wacker, 1979). They were often followed by other changes, especially a decline in one's psychological involvement in work and an increase in concern with self. These latter changes will be considered in Chapter 7. Appendix B contains a description of the method used to assess changes in attitude as well as statistical summaries of attitude change by professional group.

CHANGE IN GOALS AND ASPIRATIONS

The new public professionals usually began their careers with high goals and expectations. Teachers hoped to "reach" every student and believed that this was an appropriate goal. Mental health professionals believed that one should project sympathy toward all of one's clients and that one should help each client change in discernible ways; temporary palliation was regarded as insufficient. But one of the first things to change in the face of stress and strain was the loftiness of the novices' goals. Teachers came to believe that reaching every student was unrealistic, and they began to focus their efforts on making a more modest impact on a more restricted subgroup of students. Similarly, those in the other professional groups coped with the strains of the first year by lowering their goals or adopting new ones that were easier to achieve. In fact, 15 of the 20 subjects for whom we had data changed their internal goals and standards during this period (see Appendix B).

Adopting More Modest Goals

There were many ways in which the new public professionals coped with stress in their work by adopting more modest goals. *Concentrating on just a few clients* was a common strategy for dealing with an excessively large caseload. At least eight subjects used this method. Lawyers were especially likely to use this coping mechanism. The mental health professionals who worked in schools and were responsible for a high number of cases also tended to use this strategy. For instance, Nick Fisher, a new school social worker, admitted, "What I found myself doing was getting involved in two cases and sort of ignoring everything else that I promised to be doing." A new psychologist, Mark Canner, began a discussion group for eight carefully selected students and concentrated his efforts on that. The two hours each week he met with this group was the only time he felt he was utilizing his skills and really making a positive impact.

The teachers initially hoped to reach every student in every one of their classes, and they too, in at least two cases, relinquished this goal soon after beginning their tenure as teachers. Cynthia Noble said that she was finding some time to work with a few students individually, but she was only working with those who were the easiest with whom to work; "They're the kids that have shown an interest and need the help and also are the easiest ones to work with. The really hard ones, I put off until at least next semester."

Unfortunately, there was sometimes a lingering sense of guilt about concentrating on just a few clients and abandoning the goal of reaching them all. As Nick Fisher put it, "I'm deeply involved with maybe three students at the high school, and the other social worker is maybe involved with six. So what does that do to the other 300 kids [who had problems and needed help]?" He went on to say that the teachers and other school personnel "get to the point where they don't depend on me an awful lot and that's frustrating, because you don't have that much effect. All you can do is give platitudes, accentuate the positive sort of stuff. That gets kind of bad." Thus, concentrating on just a few clients did reduce some of the work pressure for several new public professionals, but sometimes at a cost. For many, it was not easy to give up the goal with which they began their professional careers.

In other instances, the new professionals coped by *cutting corners*, doing things they had told themselves they would never do, simply because the workload was too heavy. Cynthia Noble confessed that, although she believed it was important to work out homework problems before she assigned them to the students and initially she had done so, she no longer was doing this by the second month of her first term. Chemistry teacher Calvin Miller admitted that he found himself doing things that he did not like when they were done to him when he was a student:

I had some real dingbats for teachers, and I said, "I'd never do that," or, "I wouldn't want to be like that. . . ." I find myself even now, when I'm facing the reality of the situation, catching myself at times doing some things that they would have done and saying, "Wow, here I am doing exactly what I said I would never do," and yet having to do it. Some of the things are having kids do things for the sake of doing them—the busy work idea. It's hard to justify everything that you're doing.

Another common strategy used by new public professionals was to consciously *focus on the positive*, to savor "little victories" whenever they occurred, no matter how small or insignificant. Nick Fisher said, "You have to sort of lower your expectations, and also keep track, I think, of the positive things that you do." A related shift in attitude and perception was *to accept signs of success that were initially discounted.* This occurred for new mental health professional Sherman Reynolds during his first months of work. Initially, he was skeptical about the validity of testimonials from his clients. It was nice when they were thankful and appreciative, but it did not necessarily mean that he had really helped them. But as the emotional strain of working hard and getting little concrete evidence of efficacy increased, he began to change his opinion about the validity and importance of client reactions. He said, "I guess sometimes clients would be really thankful, talk about how I'd helped them. Even initially I had clients who were really profusely thankful. Sometimes it leads to some doubt about whether they're just trying to please you . . . but I'm beginning to accept their subjective view of things now as much as my own objective view."

Becoming more specialized was another way in which some new professionals adopted less ambitious goals as time passed. Many began with the goal that a practicing professional should be a "creative generalist," flexible and versatile enough in skill and approach to be able to deal with any problem that a client might have. They abhorred the tendency to select or mold the client to fit what the professional could do, ignoring the rest of the client's situation. But many of our subjects gradually came to see this initial ideal as naive and unrealistic. The crisis of competence put a premium on doing something well, and they realized that the more they specialized, the more likely they would be to gain distinction and a sense of accomplishment. In other words, they came to believe that if they did not specialize more in their work, they would never feel competent and would never be regarded as competent by clients and peers. At least eight of our subjects decided to become more specialized during this initial stage of their careers, and only two chose to become less specialized. (These two chose this course for job security; they thought that they would be more attractive to future employers if they broadened their base of experience and expertise.)

A particularly good example of the tendency to value specialization more as time passed was poverty lawyer Margaret Williams. When she began her first job, Margaret did not intend to specialize, but over time she found that having expertise in one area added immensely to her sense of competence, and so she became the "landlord-tenant law" specialist in her office. In her last interview, she said:

> I get calls from people saying, "I understand you know a lot about landlord-tenant laws, and so-and-so told me to call you. I'm having a problem with my landlord." I'm the only person in our office that does landlord-tenant now.
>
> [Interviewer: "Is that by choice, or did it just kind of happen that way?"]
>
> Yes, it was by choice. I work in landlord-tenant court two days a week ... I get people calling me up all the time. I'd say half the poor people's problems are troubles with their landlords, so nobody else in the office would know what to tell them.
>
> [Interviewer: "And that's a real change because when you started off, you said you didn't know anything and you didn't know what you'd say to your first client, and now you're an expert."]
>
> Well, I'm not the big expert in town, but I would say I'm certainly the expert in my office. You know, it's nice to know you know something about something, and I do. So that's good.

In the case of new public health nurse Gloria Bennet, her desire to become a specialist came as a radical change in her long-term career goals. In the initial interviews, she had said that she especially liked her work as a general public health nurse because of the variety of things in which she was able to be involved. She believed that this was one advantage of public health nursing over hospital nursing. But at the beginning of our last interview, she announced her intention to quit and return to school in order to become a specialist in a relatively narrow area of nursing. Her strong desire for greater competence and respect, as well as an intrinsic interest in the area in which she planned to concentrate, had led her to change her views about the importance of variety versus specialization in professional work. Once again, specialization came to be seen as more favorable because it seemed to be linked to valued career rewards.

One other example of a shift toward more modest, attainable goals was the *abandonment of social change goals and a concentration on individual remediation and change.* For instance, school social worker Nick Fisher initially complained that the *system* was the major cause of emotional difficulties in children and that the best thing he could do in his role would be political organizing and community organization with parents. During his first year, he did fight the system on one or two occasions, but, in general, he withdrew into his own personal work sphere, concentrating on close, intimate counseling with three adolescents. By focusing on work with individual cients, he made his work more rewarding and less frustrating. His autonomy was high. Community organization and social change were simply too difficult and, in the short run, too unrewarding.

New mental health professional Douglas Furth represented another example of this phenomenon. During his first months on the job, he attempted to revitalize his community mental health agency and to increase collegiality and intellectual stimulation in the staff. His initial efforts not only met with limited success, but his colleagues began to regard him as "weak" and as a "trouble-maker." He feared that his efforts would increase his social isolation rather than decrease it, so he gradually gave up his efforts to change the social climate of his agency. He learned that the best strategy was to "lay low" and work quietly behind the scenes to protect and maintain his personal privileges and autonomy.

Adopting New Goals

In some cases, the new professionals adopted new goals that were pursued simultaneously with the old and increased the likelihood that the professional would achieve some fulfillment simply because more goals meant more chances for success. There were several examples of this phenomenon. For instance, poverty lawyer Jean Chalmers spent some of her time preparing and delivering public addresses before various assemblies. The purpose of this public speaking was to raise awareness of prison conditions and the plight of the poor. She especially valued opportunities to speak before groups of law students because she believed she was helping to get more lawyers into the poverty law field. Although this public speaking aspect of her work was not something she had initially planned on doing and was sometimes an annoying distraction, it provided another goal and alternative source of meaning and fulfillment in her job.

For some of the new poverty lawyers, client contact was simply a means to only one end: legal victory. But a few invested this aspect of their work with added meaning and fulfillment by recognizing other goals that could be accomplished by it. For instance, Jean Chalmers said that she spent more time with clients than did many of her colleagues because she thought that it was a way of using law as a means of political education and organization. She was seeking to increase the clients' skills, to educate them about how the system worked and what they could do to change it. Also, her legal work could become the focus of collective effort:

> I provide a certain skill to the people I represent, and they use it. They use it any way they want. . . . I like to use legal cases to educate people. . . . What I like to do is keep lawsuits going, large ones, so that people can work collectively. They trust each other, and, by trusting each other and working together, at least we can make a coalition and try to change things and at least try to reduce the paranoia, let them know there are others in the same situation, and that they can, as a group, deal with problems and not be fearful of the Parole Board.

Providing personal counseling and social services to some clients was another extralegal way in which the new poverty lawyers could increase fulfillment in their work. Margaret Williams confessed that she enjoyed playing counselor and social worker with some clients even though she was "not supposed to waste her time" on it. She said that some of these clients got very attached to her when she did this, which was good for her "ego." It is easy to see how this could happen considering this excerpt from an interview with poverty lawyer Jean Chalmers:

> This man would call me, and there was nothing that I could really do at that point, legally, but it was very important to talk to him and he became a very good friend of mine. It was just to keep his spirits up. After awhile, all we could talk about was this huge party we would have when he got out [of prison] —it helped him just to know that there were people out there who cared and that if he had phone calls that had to be made, we would make them for him. And when he finally got out, we did have a huge party. I kept saying we were going to have to dance, and he kept saying, "I haven't danced in years," and I said, "You'll find a woman there," and we had a great party for him. He was concerned that he wouldn't have the proper clothes, and we took him shopping. But it was that type of thing: just so he would know that there was someone out there, because talk about a sense of alienation! When these guys get out of prison, they're taken to the nearest bus station and that's it.

When the new poverty lawyers can expand their role to include this kind of "social work," the results can be extremely gratifying for them as well as for the clients. Unfortunately, as we have seen in previous chapters, there are many aspects of their work situations, such as crushing caseloads and restrictive organizational rules, that make such an expansion of role and function difficult. As Margaret Williams admitted, playing social worker and counselor was something she had to do surreptitiously; it was forbidden by agency policy. And whenever she took an extra few minutes to help a client on a more personal level, there were dozens more she was neglecting.

Other professionals also seemed to adopt new goals during this initial phase of their careers in response to unexpected role pressures. For instance, the school curriculum was often broad and flexible enough to allow new teachers to shift their teaching objectives in response to classroom experience. An example occurred in the case of Carol Potter, a new teacher who came to realize that, contrary to her initial expectations, her students found it difficult to study a language intensively day after day without a break. Therefore, she began to teach French culture to them on some days instead of language. They responded favorably to this shift, and the teaching of culture became a new teaching objective in her classroom. So when students had difficulty learning as much language the history and culture." The new goal provided an alternative source of fulfillment for both teacher and students.

One final example of the adoption of a new goal was the acquisition of skill and competence. Initially, skill and competence were seen by the novices as means to an end; the only goal of any real importance was positive change in a client's condition. But during this initial phase of their careers, many came to define their own learning and professional development as a major goal in itself, apart from any immediate positive effect this may have had on clients. For instance, new poverty lawyer Reginald Smith derived great satisfaction from being able to improve his skill in negotiation and bargaining. He told of his elation when he discovered on his own that, if he listened to what the other party had to say, they would tend to listen and accept what he had to say. Listening respectfully seemed to increase his chances of persuading another person to give ground. For Reginald and other new professionals, discovering these skills and perfecting them became an added dimension of their work, an alternative source of satisfaction when they failed to help a client or felt less than competent in other areas of practice. In effect, they redefined the psychic rewards that were most meaningful to them in their jobs; adopting new goals in their work helped to sustain commitment and enthusiasm.

Whether they lowered their goals or added ones that were more possible to fulfill, modifying their initial goals and aspirations was a major way in which the new public professionals coped with the stresses and demands of their work. Like the new priests studied by Hall and Schneider (1973), their initial idealism gave way to a more cautious realism about what they and other professionals could do to relieve personal suffering and promote personal growth. Also, it frequently seemed clear that this change in outlook contributed to the coping process. Perhaps public health nurse Sarah Prentiss expressed it best when she said, "I think the idealism thing—I don't know. I think that enthusiasm and idealism is good as long as it doesn't hurt you, but it was hurting me. It was; it was really bugging me because I was really expecting things to be like I wanted them to be and they weren't. But I realized that, and I'm glad I did."

The new professionals were often reluctant to give up the ideals and goals they were taught to value during earlier socialization, but when these ambitious aspirations became too dissonant with their experiences, when the gap between real and ideal continued to loom wide, most of the new professionals adopted more modest goals or developed new ones that could provide alternative sources of fulfillment and satisfaction. By lowering their sights, they increased the likelihood of personal success. Whether such changes in attitude were beneficial for clients and society remains to be seen.

FEELING LESS PERSONALLY RESPONSIBLE
FOR THE OUTCOMES OF WORK

Related to the change in goals and aspirations in new public professionals was the tendency to feel less personally responsible for the results of their work.

Initially, they were more likely to feel that what happened in their work was primarily the result of their own efforts. If a student did not learn, the teacher was using the wrong approach. If a depressed and neurotic client continued to engage in the same self-defeating behavior, the therapist lacked the necessary sensitivity and skill. If the innocent victim went to jail, the fault was probably the attorney's; a better, more thorough preparation of the case and a more effective cross-examination of the key witness for the prosecution would have secured the client's freedom and ensured that justice was done. Over time, many of the new professionals modified this belief. Rather than blaming their own ability, motivation, or training, they would increasingly blame the clients for failures. "Blaming the victim" (Ryan, 1971) became increasingly prevalent. In other instances, the new professionals might "blame the system" rather than the client. In either case, there was a tendency for the professionals to become less critical of themselves and to feel less personally responsible for the outcomes of their work.

Of course, there were some who tended to define their responsibility in more limited terms from the very beginning. But among those who initially accepted the responsibility for what happened in the helping relationship, the pattern clearly was to do this less as time passed: 15 of the 19 subjects who could be rated on this dimension changed in this way (see Appendix B). And, as in the case of changing goals and aspirations, this modification in the sense of personal responsibility seemed to serve a psychological function. By minimizing their own roles in the outcomes of their work, they reduced some of the pressure they were experiencing and protected their precarious self-esteem. The frequent occasions of "falling short" (Chapter 2) became less devastating when the novice attributed the cause to some factor outside of his or her own control.

In some instances, the new professionals seemed to reduce their sense of personal responsibility by adopting a kind of fatalism about the outcomes of their work. They did not necessarily blame others for falling short; they simply came to believe that there were certain limits to what they could do, and there was no way of moving beyond those limits. High school teacher Cynthia Noble articulated this view when she described her frustration with an unmotivated student in one of her classes. The interviewer asked, "Does that make you feel like you're doing something wrong, or do you think it's the kid's problem?" Cynthia answered:

> A lot of it is their attitudes, and it's really hard for me to change their attitudes. The student came right out and told me that the counselor told her that she wasn't going to need this course. So if she wasn't going to need it, why should she be in there, and she wanted to drop it. I can give her a million reasons why she should take the course, but as long as she feels that the counselor told her that she doesn't need it and she's not going to need it, then I'm not going to change her attitude. So, it's resolved.

In this example, the new teacher blamed both the student and the counselor to a certain extent for creating the situation, but the primary belief expressed in this statement seemed to be that whatever the causes, there would be situations in which a teacher simply cannot change a student's attitude. To try would be futile. In Cynthia's case, this attitude was different from the more optimistic one with which she began her teaching career.

In other instances, the new professionals denied their personal responsibility by adopting rules or principles that "got them off the hook." For instance, high school teachers Alice Harris and Merton Douglas both said that they believed they had no responsibility for helping students who did not show at least some effort to help themselves. In Alice's case, the comment was made in reference to grading papers. "If kids don't take time to study, why should I spend time writing comments on their papers?" In Merton's case, the response was more general and severe; he said he ignored students who would not try even a little. Apparently, he believed that he was not responsible for any student who did not try.

Mental health professional Nick Fisher adopted a more elaborate rule that limited his personal responsibility and couched it in terms that made it seem "clinically" respectable—even necessary. He said:

> Teaching and social work are a lot the same. Teaching is an impossible job. You can't really do what you're supposed to do, and so everyone goes home thinking that they really fucked up the year. But I think I was a little bit aware of that at first, with feelings of being incompetent. I think the T.A. (transactional analysis) thing really helped me because what it really said was, "It's not your responsibility that the client succeed; all you really are is a facilitator rather than a rescuer. Once you get into the rescuer role you're bound to fuck up the clients because you're playing games. . . ." That just really laid it on me that I don't have to rescue these people. If they really want to change, I can do a lot to help them find the ways to do it. I can present facts and present things to potentiate their choice of changing. But if that's not their choice, I can't do anything. That really seems to me to give the client a lot more dignity, too.

Although Nick Fisher's thinking about the professional's responsibility seems to be more psychologically sophisticated than the new teachers', in both cases there was a tendency to limit that responsibility and, in so doing, reduce the stress and pressure experienced by the professional. Whether such a limiting of professional responsibility also benefits the client, as Nick suggested, probably depends on the situation.

In addition to drawing a line when professional responsibility is concerned, some new professionals went one step further and actually blamed clients when difficulties occurred. A good example of this attitude was poverty lawyer Perry Curtis. Most of the legal aid clients with whom he worked were compliant and grateful, but there were those who became dissatisfied and even hostile. Over time, he came to label these the "troublemakers." And, despite the fact that clients usually had to wait seven months or more after contacting the office before they could even see a lawyer and despite the fact that the caseload for a lawyer in Perry's office was in the hundreds and likely limited the quality of service provided to the typical client, he did not blame either himself or his agency when a client became disgruntled. Instead, he regarded the cause as something wrong in the client's head. The troublemakers, in his view, were that way because they were "psychotic" or "nuts." Or, when he was feeling more charitable, he might attribute the clients' dissatisfaction to their economic deprivation or to society's generally negative attitudes toward lawyers, which influenced some people to be more critical than they might otherwise be.

Another example of the growing tendency to "blame the client" came from an interview with new public health nurse Sarah Prentiss. During the initial interviews, Sarah felt responsible when a client was resistant, apathetic, or hostile. She felt that she had done something to "turn off" the client. But when we returned several months later for the follow-up interview and reminded her of this attitude, she responded, "I don't do that anymore . . . because it's not me. I really don't think that it's me because I think that I've had too many positive experiences and I don't come on too strong." She went on to describe a recent example. When she had gone out to a home and introduced herself, the mother said in a tone mixed with hostility and fear, "I don't know how you got our name. We don't need you. We don't need anybody." Sarah said that she did not pursue this case further because the woman's reaction was probably caused by her "low mentality" and there was just "no way I could get anywhere with them." Sarah did concede that the mother's refusal might have been due to a sense of pride, but then added, "I don't know if it would even be pride in *her* case." Although there may have been factors contributing to the client's initial hesitation and resistance, including something Sarah had done or said, Sarah chose to attribute the cause primarily to the woman's alleged mental deficiency. The most significant aspect of this situation, however, was that just a few months before Sarah would have critically examined her own possible contribution to the outcome more than she did on this occasion. Over time, she increasingly came to blame the client when an intervention failed.

The same tendency was noted in the development of high school teacher Carol Potter. In her final interview, she said that she had come to believe that whether a student does well is to a great extent a matter of his or her personality and interests. Although it was still hard for her to accept the fact that some students were not doing as well as others, she now felt less guilty and depressed about the situation because she had shifted the responsibility from her shoulders to theirs.

"Blaming the system" was another way in which the new public professionals increasingly limited their sense of responsibility. For instance, school psychologist Mark Canner stated that he was largely ineffective because the constraints that the system imposed on his role prevented him from engaging in effective practice. If the system just did not get in the way, he would be effective. Although there seemed to be much validity to this belief, it also seemed clear that as time passed Mark became increasingly less likely to critically question his own performance. The "system" became a convenient scapegoat on which all failure and inadequacy could be blamed.

Another example of "system blaming" was high school teacher Merton Douglas' attitude about his general business class. Of all his classes, this one was the most troublesome and least satisfying. Initially, he tried to improve the climate and performance of the class, but gradually he seemed to give up. As he did so, he adopted the rationalization that "General Business is a dumping ground," a convenient place for the counselors to place students with scheduling problems or insufficient motivation or ability to study anything else. It was not Merton's fault that the class was so poor; it was not even the students' fault. They all were simply victims of a system they could not control. Such a belief made the frustration and disappointment somewhat more bearable for this new teacher and gave him the "right" to "cut his losses" and reduce the amount of emotional energy invested in this unrewarding effort.

Chemistry teacher Calvin Miller, by his final interview, was also blaming the system for the persistent lack of motivation in his students. For him, the problem seemed to be all of the extracurricular activities that competed for student interest and effort:

> It's hard to get them interested in your class when they've got all these other things going on. How can you be interested in school when you've got swimming coming up and gymnastics. So you sort of learn, that's okay ... that helps me realize, "Okay, they're not always going to be enthusiastic or interested." You know, on certain days this is going to be work.
> [Interviewer: "And if they're not enthusiastic it's not necessarily because you're doing something worse?"]
> Right, not because of me, or the subject matter, or whatever.

It is, of course, impossible to say whether Calvin's new attitude is more realistic than it was when he tended to blame himself for all failures. But this new attitude did have the effect of reducing the extent to which Calvin, as the teacher, felt responsible for what happened in the classroom.

There were many other examples of blaming the system. Some of the new professionals began to attribute lack of client responsiveness to the barriers generated by the professional-client relationship. And, of course, one could always blame the largest "system" of all: social and economic forces that permeate all of society. When poverty lawyer Perry Curtis was not blaming the client, he advanced this interpretation to account for the anger and hostility directed toward him by some clients. "I think it's just the economy. They're angry at everyone. The government's cutting back on welfare benefits—at least there are talks about it. It's election year and everyone that's up for election is bad-mouthing welfare because that's the thing to do this year. So it makes the clients angry."

To be sure, not every new professional we interviewed blamed clients or the system for problems encountered in their work. There were a few who continued to believe that they could reach every client and that, with continued effort, they could find more effective methods that would enable them to achieve this goal. They resisted the temptation to minimize their own responsibility by blaming either clients or the system. They did realize that their clients in public human service settings were among the most deprived members of our society, that there were factors in the clients, in their families, and in their communities that made them unresponsive and difficult to work with. But they did not use these external factors as a rationale for feeling less responsible themselves. Unfortunately, the new public professionals who did not tend to minimize their own role during the time we studied them represented a relatively small minority (4 of 19 for whom there was data). They tended to be the ones who found themselves in unusually supportive work situations in which workloads and role demands were manageable. For most of our subjects, the pressures of the job made it difficult to continue feeling personally responsible for what happened in their work. They did not need the added burden of guilt. And so, when they fell short, they increasingly found it less stressful to blame others rather than search for causes in their own performance.

THE DECLINE IN IDEALISM

Previous research and theory on professional socialization has emphasized the decline in optimism and the rise in cynicism during the early stages of professionalization. For instance, an early study of medical students by Eron (1958) found that, during their four years of medical school, the students became significantly less idealistic and significantly more cynical, as measured by paper-and-pencil attitude scales. The more in-depth, naturalistic research by Becker and his colleagues (Becker et al., 1961) tended to confirm this finding. Similarly, a study of new lawyers by Carlin (1962) found that they, too, tended to become less idealistic and less concerned with ethical issues during the initial part of their careers. On the other hand, Eron found that law students did not become more cynical during the course of their studies. In fact, there was a slight trend in the opposite direction. Thus, attitudes such as cynicism, idealism, and humanitarianism have been of great interest to students of professional development.

In our own research, therefore, we were interested in studying the extent to which new professionals in the public sector became more cynical, pessimistic, and conservative. Two attitudes seemed relevant: trust and sympathy for clients and conservatism. Conservatism refers to a tendency to approve of less liberal social policies and practices, such as a teacher's belief that "law and order" in the classroom is necessary to maintain a good learning climate or a lwayer's belief that criminals have to be prosecuted to the full extent of the law "to be taught a lesson." We found that 10 of the 19 new professionals for whom we had data became less trusting and 8 became more conservative during the time we interviewed them (see Appendix B). As in the case of the other attitude changes, the subjects who changed most in these areas also seemed to be among those who experienced the most "reality shock" during the first months of their work. For them, role conflict and overload tended to be higher, and there was less collegiality and more difficulty with clients, fewer opportunities to experience a sense of competence, and less variety, meaning, and intellectual stimulation in the job.

In order for this evolution from idealism to cynicism to occur, the loss of trust in clients seemed to be critical. As described in Chapter 3, the discovery that clients often lie and attempt to manipulate their "helpers" was an unexpected, disturbing one for the new public professional. For many, this discovery not only changed their attitudes toward those particular clients; the effect seemed to generalize and influence their attitudes about all clients. And for some, their attitudes about people in general were influenced as well.

For instance, new high school teacher Eugenia Barton had a difficult first term. Near the end of it, she said, "High school kids will do you in . . . I wouldn't count on my high school kids to help me at all." She was only sorry that she had been too idealistic initially, so "gullible and stupid . . . too easy." She mentioned the old maxim of teaching, "Don't smile until Christmas," and said that she had not believed it when she began her career as a teacher. But by November of her first year, she had become a believer. She said that she had been naive to believe that if one treats kids with respect, they will reciprocate. She vowed that in the future she would not be as "flexible" or "trusting"; she would have "written rules" and would allow no deviations. Her trust and belief in students— and the young in general—had been shattered. She bitterly complained, "Kids have no sense of responsibility for school equipment, no sense of ownership or feeling that this is their school." Although her classes were better the next term, there remained in Eugenia a residue of bitterness and distrust toward her students. The extent to which this change in attitude affected her interactions with her students and *their* attitudes and behavior can only be guessed.

A similar change occurred in the attitudes of high school teacher Carol Potter. Soon after she began teaching, she decided she would not remain in the field. Although she came to enjoy it more as time passed, she was still planning to leave teaching when last interviewed. A major reason was that she simply did not like what she observed in the students. She complained that there were "an awful lot of discipline problems," that students were disrespectful and impudent.

She came to believe that students had "no respect for each other or for anybody else." New high school teacher Cynthia Noble, though intending to remain in teaching, made almost the identical observation, saying that students seemed to have "changed a lot in five years;" there was "no sense of responsibility," and the lack of respect and consideration they displayed was "frightening."

Disillusionment and cynicism infected several of the new poverty lawyers as well. Reginald Smith confessed during one interview that "this job has made me less trustful of people." And Margaret Williams, a poverty lawyer who was very bitter about being "chumped" by her clients said, "Now, I don't expect the clients to be telling the truth. You know, there's a chance they are and there's a chance they're not. You know, they're protecting themselves and they hope you buy their story." Thus, in many new public professionals, unrealistic expectations about their clients led to a "backlash" reaction in which positive, trusting attitudes toward clients and people in general changed to negative, cynical attitudes. Like the lover in the saying, "Hell knows no fury like a lover scorned," these idealistic and trusting novices reacted strongly to their initial confrontation with the less appealing aspects of their clients' behavior.

However, by no means did all of the new professionals change in their attitudes toward people. Some retained their trust and positive regard for clients. For instance, poverty lawyer Jean Chalmers claimed that her clients rarely lied to her, that they usually had no reason to do so because of the kind of law that she was doing, and, that when they did lie (or "exaggerate" as she chose to put it), it was because of what prison conditions had done to them. Her sympathies clearly remained with the clients. Her trust and positive regard for them had not been shaken by her work experiences during the initial stage of her professional career.

Also, even those new professionals who became more bitter and cynical about people often continued to waver between their old and new beliefs. For instance, poverty lawyer Margaret Williams became so angry and bitter about the people she represented that she thought of going to work for the prosecuting attorney as a way of getting back at them. But, at certain points in our interviews, she would assume a different stance and become more sympathetic and understanding. In the next breath, she might become angry and unsympathetic again. The following excerpt illustrates this phenomenon. She had just described how she had recently been mugged outside her office and how angry and bitter the experience had made her:

> I know a guy who was in the state penitentiary for armed robbery. He's now a major league basketball player. He got out of crime. He's in good shape now and he's not getting involved in it any more because he struck it rich. He said that if he hadn't made it big in sports, he'd probably still be doing the same kind of stuff because he says it's one of the only ways to stay alive in the ghetto because there

aren't any jobs and you cannot live on what you get from welfare. You just can't.

[Interviewer: "But, at the same time, you say personal robbery you still find. . . ."]

I still can't stand it, and something's got to be done about that. I mean, there must be a way for people to live without putting guns in other people's heads. I feel really sad when I know it's the end of the line for some people, but I still don't think—I wonder what you do? You say, "Well Jesus, they ought to be able to get a job." You know, there are jobs out there. Just because they don't want to do a day's labor. . . .

Here we see a new professional struggling to find and retain the idealism and sympathy for the underdog that she had had when she began her professional career just a few months before. The old attitudes were there; they had not been totally lost. But increasingly she regarded her clients—and poor people in general—as ungrateful, selfish, manipulative criminals for whom "law and order" was the only conceivable response. She might never completely lose her sympathy and understanding, but her attitudes had clearly shifted away from the strong, absolute, uncompromising idealism and faith she had had when she began.

Although there were probably many different causes of the changes in attitudes observed in our subjects, the interviews suggest that in most cases the shifts were direct responses to the pressure, frustrations, and demands experienced on the job. Although these aspects of the work experience could unquestionably be found in other jobs, they are more likely to occur in the work situations of public professionals. There are few jobs in which the gap between what is normally expected and what is usually found seems to be so great, and the "reality shock" that results has many effects on the individual. We have considered three of those apparent effects here: changes in goals and aspirations, reduction in the sense of responsibility for what occurs in one's work, and decline in liberalism. In the next chapter, we shall consider some other changes in attitude and behavior that seem to occur in response to the demands of professional work in a public setting.

7

THE FATE OF COMMITMENT

The public professionals interviewed for this study began their careers with lofty goals, idealism, and strong positive regard for clients. They also felt a strong commitment to work and a willingness to make self-sacrifices for others. Personal gain in the form of monetary rewards, security, or prestige was seen as relatively unimportant. They hoped that the work itself would be intrinsically rewarding and the major source of psychological gratification in their lives. In Chapter 6, we examined what happened to the optimism, idealism, and liberal outlook of the novice public professional. In this chapter, we shall examine the fate of self-sacrifice and psychological involvement in work.

FROM PERSONAL INVOLVEMENT TO ALIENATION

Over time, most of the new public professionals in our study withdrew from work. Initially, the withdrawal took the form of greater emotional detachment in the professional-client relationship. They forced themselves to be more "objective" and "professional." They forced themselves to identify less with clients and to empathize less with clients' worries and concerns. In addition, many of them also began spending less time at work, and they did not take their work home, physically or emotionally, as much as they had initially. And, most strikingly, they began to look to non-work activities for psychological fulfillment. The role of work in their lives shrank. As they withdrew from their jobs, they found that the frustrations, disappointments, and grievances experienced at work seemed less important. Thus, "work alienation" made work more bearable, even more satisfying. Like other changes in attitude and behavior discussed, it seemed to serve an adaptive function.

Emotional Detachment
from the Helping Role

In our discussion of the intimacy dilemma faced by many new professionals (Chapter 3), we saw that a major source of uncertainty and stress in professional-client relationships concerned the issue of personal involvement with clients. On the one hand, there seemed reason to believe that greater emotional involvement with clients would facilitate the development of client attitudes and motivation necessary for the helping process. On the other hand, there was the fear that this emotional involvement could jeopardize the professional's credibility and ultimate effectiveness. Our assessment of change in attitude over time suggested that, more often than not, new professionals resolved the conflict by reducing emotional involvement: this phenomenon was observed in 11 of 19 individuals for whom there were data (see Appendix B).

To a certain extent, this reduction of emotional involvement was probably desirable. When new professionals identified too much with their clients, as many initially did, objectivity and effectiveness were hampered. Some of the novices seemed aware of this problem and reduced their emotional involvement in a way that was adaptive.

There were several examples of this emotional detachment in the interest of *role effectiveness*. For instance, new teacher Cynthia Noble said that although she found that students responded well when she gave them individual attention, warmth, and acceptance, she was afraid that this closeness could be disruptive.

> I don't know, a lot of kids need a friend, and I'd like to be able to be their friend, but I don't want to get too chummy with them because then you get other kids being jealous—"So and so is teacher's pet"— and then you can run into all kinds of troubles. . . . Most of the kids that I have given attention to, it's been giving them academic attention. I try not to just sit around with a bunch of kids and just chit-chat unless it's based on something academic because then those kids learn too much about me. And then you start getting into all sorts of private—well, not really relationships—but something comes up and they know everything, more than the other kids in the class. So I try not to let any of the kids know any more about me than anybody else.

Although Cynthia felt that both she and some of her students lost something because of her decision to maintain a certain amount of distance in the teacher-student relationship, she ultimately came to believe that her overall effectiveness in the role would be compromised if she did not do so.

A similar rationale for emotional detachment was provided by poverty lawyer Reginald Smith. In his case, role effectiveness seemed to require that he maintain emotional detachment and objectivity when dealing with court judges and referees whom he found despicable. Anger was the emotion that had to be controlled in this instance:

> There's one referee over at the juvenile court, who shall remain name-less, who's just well known to be a hanging judge. He would find guilt on almost anything. He probably believes these kids come in here guilty. And it kind of bothers me because a lot of times I go into court having to represent a client with a pretty strong case, which I think, had it been a jury trial, there would have been enough evidence to establish a reasonable doubt. When kids come up and say, "I felt guilty the minute I walked into the courtroom," well, what can I say to that? It's true. With this particular referee it's true. Any kind of crime that's black-white or with a white victim, he's going to find guilty. No matter what, he's going to find guilt. . . . But of late I've been able to have more success I think with this particular referee than have other people in the office. I've been able to get him to do some things that are out of character for him to do. And I think it's largely because I've approached him on a cool kind of professional basis, even when, in my opinion, he doesn't really have a clear under-standing of—you know, I feel I've got to live with him. As long as I work with people in the court and I'm going to have to be coming into his courtroom, I might as well not let the situation between him and me get to the point where he's going to take out his anger on my clients.

In this case, the new professional was concerned that the client would ultimately suffer unless he could maintain emotional distance. A sudden outburst of emo-tion directed toward the prejudiced referee could draw harsh consequences for the client, who would be the scapegoat for the referee's wrath. Thus, Reginald Smith learned to hold his anger in. He was becoming a "professional."

Emotional detachment however, did not always occur in the interest of better performance of one's role. The novices we interviewed also became in-creasingly detached from their clients as a means of *self-protection.* Strong empathy with the client could be a source of much pain for a professional work-ing in a public institution. As we saw in Chapter 2, new professionals often fell short in their efforts to help, and failure was difficult for them to accept. Emo-tional detachment offered a means of reducing the pain of failing. Poverty law-yer Perry Curtis worked in a neighborhood legal aid office in which he specialized in domestic relations matters, an area of legal practice in which some of the most emotionally sensitive and painful issues must be handled, such as divorce cases in which custody of the children is contested. He expressed the function of emotional detachment in a revealing way when he said, "The heavy caseload has an advantage in that it makes it very difficult to get emotionally involved in any single case because, frankly, you really just don't have the time to spend on the case."

There were many examples of the use of emotional detachment by new professionals as a way of coping with emotional overload or doubt about their capacity to help. Initially, emotional detachment might occur with a single case or situation that was particularly stressful. For instance, mental health professional Douglas Furth described how he frequently "turned off" to one particularly frustrating client to whom he was assigned:

> The fact is, there are only two clients I have now that I don't like working with. One's a woman who—it's called a multiproblem family. If you name the area, they're hurting, and it just feels overwhelming. And the woman will talk [make sounds of someone babbling] at me, and I don't want to hear her after a minute. You know, we're not getting anywhere. Okay, maybe she is. She could be ventilating a lot. It could be useful. You know, she just could be discharging a lot of stress, and that could be useful. I don't always want to be used that way. I mean, there's certain people I'd rather do that with than others. This is a woman whom I don't like to do that with. So, I'll listen for a minute or two, and then I'll say, "Okay," and I'll just cut her right off, and I'll say, "Look, I think this is the best way that I can work with you now." And I'll say, "Let's pick one area and let's work on it," and then I'll cut it short. I won't even see her for an hour. I won't do it. It's too difficult for me with that particular woman.

In working with this particularly needy and frustrating client, Douglas used emotional detachment in more than one way. Instead of listening sympathetically and allowing her to ventilate, as he did with other clients, he assumed a more directive, task-oriented style. He "cut her right off," apparently without much regard for how she might *feel* about his doing that. He referred to her and her situation with a label ("multiproblem family"). He caricatured her speech by using a sound that suggested she said very little of importance. He quickly focused in on an area, a small part of her life situation isolated from the rest. (This in fact may be a useful technique for dealing with personal problems, but in this case, it was another way in which Douglas established some emotional distance between himself and the client.) Finally, he ended the sessions before the hour was completed, a most direct way of limiting his involvement with a difficult, unrewarding client.

Over time, emotional detachment toward clients might become more pervasive. It no longer occurred in response to a particular client or situation; it became a general attitude toward work. A particularly good example was poverty lawyer Margaret Williams:

I don't feel as sorry for the clients as I used to. I mean I used to feel
with them. I used to do more social work type stuff. At this point, I
just say, "I'm a lawyer and I don't do that kind of stuff. You can cut
your own red tape," which they can.

[Interviewer: "You don't give as much sympathy as you used
to?"]

No. I used to all of a sudden get very upset and spend half the
morning making phone calls and finding out what happened. I mean,
at this point, I'm ready to tell them to call action line or something.
. . . I used to get all hyped up about somebody's name change or a
guardianship or whatever, and I don't care anymore.

Perhaps Margaret's initial concern and worry about her clients was excessive. It
may be difficult to justify spending half the morning just to find that a person's
Social Security check had been lost in the mail and that another would be sent
out. On the other hand, Margaret seemed to have believed that her attitudes had
shifted to the opposite extreme. After less than a year of practice as a poverty
lawyer, she no longer empathized with clients when they felt distressed. In fact,
she now expected their reactions were exaggerated, that things were not so bad.
She saw the unhappy, worried, and distressed client as a nuisance who had to be
"cooled out" as soon as possible so that Margaret could get on with her work. In
a short period of time, she had apparently come to see the expression of concern, sympathy, and compassion for the client as "social work," something that
was outside her jurisdiction. She did not always feel this way, but she believed
that she was coming to feel this way much of the time. Lying by clients and an
excess of routine work in her job had contributed to an ever-increasing emotional detachment in this young poverty lawyer. At this point in her career,
Margaret hoped to be able to leave legal aid and enter reform law in which she
would have little client contact.

Thus, over time, many new public professionals became more emotionally
detached in their work with clients. But there were exceptions. For example,
there was new public health nurse Gloria Bennet. In discussing the emotional
stress associated with terminating work with a patient, she noted that she had
avoided the tendency to engage in excessive emotional detachment as a way of
not being hurt:

I don't tend to keep my distance more from patients now than in
the past. Sometimes it's hard, because when it comes time for you to
close them, you know that you have to leave and there's nothing else
you can do for them. Then they get really upset. "Can't you just
come back this time or that time?" So like a lot of the time, I'll
close them, but if I'm in the area, I'll stop by and say, "Hi," or
something. That's something that makes the job satisfying.

Both her sensitivity and the structure of her job enabled this public health nurse to handle an emotionally difficult situation without resorting to the emotional detachment employed by so many other new professionals working in public human service settings. Unfortunately, Gloria Bennet seemed to be an unusual person in an unusual job situation. Also, even she had periods when she wanted to separate herself from the patients and avoid emotional involvement. "Sometimes I don't feel like listening to people. I don't feel like helping them by being a sounding board. I just want to go in and earn my money and leave. That's natural, but I guess you have to realize that you're going to have times like that." Perhaps Gloria Bennet's awareness and acceptance of the fact that there would be times when she felt less sympathetic and emotionally sensitive helped her to minimize these occasions in her work. However, the pattern was different for many of the other novices we studied. For them, emotional detachment increased during the initial phase of their careers.

Psychological Withdrawal from the Job

Most new public professionals began their careers with the expectation that their work would be their central life interest, the major source of personal expression and fulfillment in their lives. They had sacrificed and worked hard to become professionals in large part because they did not want their work to be "just a job." They did not want to create an impermeable barrier between their work and non-work lives. Unfortunately, during the initial stage of their careers, many of them began to change their views about the role of work in their lives. This change seems unfortunate because, in most cases, the decision to relegate work to a less significant role occurs when work is found to be less meaningful and fulfilling than they had hoped it would be. Psychological withdrawal from work makes this lack of fulfillment somewhat easier with which to live; like the other changes in attitude we have examined, it usually seems to be a means of coping with a stressful work situation.

Most of the new professionals in our study began their careers by throwing themselves into their work. Their lives as students were finally over. They were ready to enter the "real world" and make an impact on it. The excitement and anticipation, the desire to do well, and the sense of responsibility to their clients, agencies, and themselves propelled them into their jobs. They were ready—in fact, eager—to give up all other interests and to make work the primary interest of their lives. The way they allocated their time reflected this sense of commitment; high school teacher Victoria Goble was not atypical in stating that she allocated "90 percent of the time for school and 10 percent for sleeping." When not in the classroom, she was preparing for the next day; when not actually preparing, she was thinking about what had happened at school, going over each class period in her mind, playing out different ways of dealing with the problems she had confronted. It was demanding and tiring, but also exciting.

The first weeks of work were similar for other new public professionals. For instance, high school teacher Cynthia Noble was determined to spend all of her time on her work if necessary. Work was the first priority for her. In fact, when asked to define the "ideal teacher," she described someone who "is fair, works hard, and is really interested in the work." Working hard and being interested in the work reflect high psychological involvement in one's work, and most new professionals valued this outlook and initially came close to realizing it. Soon, however, the new professionals' attitudes toward work began to change. They began to limit the amount of time they spent on work and to keep it from infringing on their personal lives. This was a more limited involvement in work than they had initially planned.

The impulse to limit one's physical and psychological involvement in work had positive as well as negative motivations. In some instances, it seemed related to a newly emerging "philosophy of life." The new professional came to believe that it was "wrong" or "unhealthy" to invest so much of one's self in work, that doing so interfered with other important aspects of one's life. Teacher Calvin Miller was initially highly invested in his work, spending most of his time in work-related activities. After six months in the classroom, however, he was hoping to change this pattern—not only because he felt tired and worn down, but also because he felt that there were, or should be, outside interests in his life.

> I'm really involved in my work and so it sort of has carried over into my personal life. And at times it has bothered me that I'm doing so much at work.
> [Interviewer: "Why? You're getting a little tired of it?"]
> I'm getting a little tired of it, and I'm sure that I'll have other things to do. Part of the thing was coming down here and not really knowing that many people, moving down here to a new area, and really wanting to do well in this job. So I was really willing to put a lot into it. As I meet more people and have more interests outside of school, then I'm going to be spending less time there.

There was a similar pattern in the situation of poverty lawyer Reginald Smith. During our final interview, it became clear that he was no longer psychologically involved in his work. In fact, it was impossible for the interviewer to keep him on the subject of his job because he was more interested in talking about his search for personal identity outside of work. He continually returned to long, reflective discussion of his feelings about himself, his relations with his mother and close friends, and his attempt to determine what kind of person he really wanted to be. He said that this personal exploration had, in part, been precipitated by his job: acquiring professional status had forced him to deal with a question with which he had not dealt before, the question of identity. All of the years he was in school, working hard to become a lawyer, he had never had time to ask himself that question, much less explore it in any depth. Now that he had become established in a job, he felt that he could withdraw into himself and invest his emotional energies into an area of existence that had been neglected. Also, it seemed clear that he believed that his quest for identity could not be carried out within the confines of his job as it was structured. Job and personal life were seen as separate areas; greater investment in one meant less investment in the other. When asked what his priorities were, he said:

> Well, I think that my priority now has shifted out—I'm pretty comfortable in terms of my work situation. I've settled upon a role for me, professionally. . . . So my priority right now is to find out some things about me, to try to find out who I am and what I want to be. . . . When you're in school, you never have to deal with, "Who am I?" You know it's there, but there are so many other things you have to deal with just to get through school, you never deal with that. . . . I never had time to think about it. I had to think about school and didn't have to deal with me, to be more introspective about me. . . . The job can kind of take a back burner . . . because I'm more important than the job. . . .

Reginald hoped to eventually go into labor law, but he was content to stay in his present job "for the time being," to use it as a moratorium during which he could maintain minimal involvement in work while pursuing the quest for personal growth and identity outside of work. Also, he was savoring the lack of pressure in his current situation. "I'm not rushing. I'm trying to make myself slow down. I'm finding that I'm more relaxed and not quite as tense. I'm able to relax and I feel comfortable."

Like Calvin and Reginald, some new professionals were comfortable about their disengagement from work, seeing it as a positive development, often long overdue. Other professionals, however, were not comfortable about their growing disengagement. Social worker Nick Fisher, for example, illustrated the complexity of the new professional's relationship to work and the conflict and ambivalence that may be present. Before returning to graduate school for his degree in social work, Nick had been a classroom teacher. At one point in our interviews, he described how those years of teaching, as well as important events in his personal life, led him to believe that an intense psychological involvement in one's work represents an unhealthy desire to escape:

> When I was teaching, I threw an awful lot into my job, and I realized that an awful lot of what I was putting into my job was sort of compensating for the inadequacies that I felt in my personal life. . . . I think that toward the end of my teaching I felt like I was handling teaching real well; I really convinced myself that I was very good at

that. It just became a given and no longer something I had to prove. So because of that I came to concentrate more on getting fulfillment in other parts of my life. . . . During that three or four year period when I began to focus less on my job and fill those gaps I began to see that there was more involved in my life. . . . My school work was more like an escape. Now I find I feel myself very involved in the process of becoming me, and it makes it hard to turn that off and get into the job. . . . You know, theoretically you should have a job where you could be growing all the time at the same time as working. But you can't always do that. And so I find myself having less energy for my work than I should, maybe, or feel comfortable with.

On the one hand, Nick presented his disengagement from work in a positive light: once he no longer had to prove to himself that he was a competent teacher, he could turn his attention elsewhere, and his involvement in the job slackened. He rationalized his decline in involvement by assuming that both he and his students would be better off if he were less involved, if work were less of an "ego trip" for him. Intense involvement in his work could be an attempt to escape from the responsibility of working on other issues in his life, such as a marriage that eventually ended in divorce. On the other hand, he was vaguely uncomfortable with the limited involvement in work that was now reoccurring in his new career as a mental health professional. He realized that "theoretically" one's work could, and perhaps should, be an arena for personal growth and fulfillment. But he also had learned that his work as a professional in a large public bureaucracy could not always fulfill those needs. Thus, his psychological withdrawal was in part an escape from a job that had lost meaning as well as a positive attempt to maintain a more balanced, less work-oriented existence.

For some new professionals, the amount of time spent on work changed little during this period, but the psychological meaning of that involvement did. Like poverty lawyer Perry Curtis, they continued to work hard out of a sense of obligation to their clients, not because the work was a stimulating or fulfilling part of their lives. When asked how central a part of his life work was, Perry replied:

I think I'm somewhat toward doing the bare minimum in the sense that I hate work. I just hate the routine of it. My ideal would be to pick and choose the cases I want and just work on these. The work ethic has never been strong in my—I spend a lot of time on the cases I have, and I get caught up in them. I say to myself, "Boy, I'm going to take Wednesday afternoon off." I haven't done it yet. I get tied up. One of the main reasons is that I feel I have an obligation to my clients, which is very important to me. But I enjoy my free time. I enjoy doing other things. I enjoy vacations very much. Even if I don't do anything but vegetate for three weeks, I enjoy the vacation. . . . Work is not the most important part of my life.

Although attorney Perry Curtis spent much time on his work, he did so primarily out of a sense of obligation. He did not *enjoy* work the way he enjoyed his hobbies or his vacations. One also sensed that work occupied a rather small place in his life in terms of its psychological meaning.

For poverty lawyer Shana Phillips, the change in work involvement during the first year was a more radical one. Shana threw herself into her work when she graduated from law school and passed the bar. In fact, she had been absorbed in her work all during law school and continued to be so when she assumed her first position as a lawyer in a poverty agency. She typically worked six and a half days each week, but the amount of time she devoted to work was only part of her commitment. There was nothing else in her life that received so much of her effort, her attention, and her caring. She worked in a high-pressured, competitive agency in which the norm seemed to be that work *would* be one's life; everything else should be subjugated to it. It was to be the major source of self-esteem, fulfillment, and meaning. If there were ever a conflict between one's work and a personal relationship or hobby, everything should be sacrificed for the work. This seemed to be the norm followed by Shana's colleagues, and she easily came to adopt it for herself. She believed that most of her personal needs could and should be fulfilled by her job.

But the job was demanding and frustrating. Shana increasingly felt that she was putting more into it than she was getting out of it. She felt like a rat running on a treadmill. Rather than fulfilling her personal needs, the job was making her feel needier. She began using drugs and alcohol heavily. "For a while, I was nuts. I was seeing five men and I was hustling everyone. I was even hustling the gay women I know, and I'm not gay. But just everything became sexual." Finally, she reached the breaking point. She took some vacation time and went away to spend some time on a commune with friends. When she returned, her philosophy of life had radically changed. Her priorities had shifted. One of the changes that she made in her life at this point was to sharply decrease her psychological commitment to work. She withdrew and invested much of her time and energy into other activities. In discussing the role that work now occupied in her life, she said:

> It's not a big fulfilling thing for me. It's what I like to do, and it's what I do. It's just a part of my life. It's not anything that keeps me so much in touch with my feelings, my opinions, my values. I mean, it does, but maybe in a very subtle way.
> Interviewer: "Did you conceive of law as being something different from that originally? Was it always like that for you?"]
> Oh yeah, I was going to be a big radical lawyer. I was going to be the white female version of [named a famous radical attorney]. It was a big ego thing.
> [Interviewer: "And now it's just one interest of many?"]
> Yeah, it's a source of satisfaction, but—I've learned a lot since I left school about just broadening my horizons and having other interests. Law is not everything.

Shortly after this major change in priorities, Shana changed jobs, taking a position with more autonomy and less pressure (including less client contact). She strictly limited herself to a 40 hour work week, and spent much of her time and energy outside of work in a new hobby—yoga. Her aspiration was to devote even less of herself to work than she already was:

> I have a fantasy. I have a whole new fantasy life. My fantasy life consists of someone giving me $50,000. I go to California. There's a guy there who runs a school. I would do yoga half a day for four days and then I would practice law maybe four half-days. I would take any kind of law I wanted, and I would represent who I wanted . . . I'd just like to do that for about two or three years.

Now the most fulfilling and important activity in her life was her hobby. "Yoga has become a real big part of my life . . . In terms of confidence, personally and professionally, yoga really gives you that. And it's something that you carry over. . . . It's a whole lifestyle and a whole way of perceiving. . . . I really dig it because it's a part of me. And it serves as a way to channel my anger and sense of competition." Not only did her new hobby provide an alternative source of gratification, it also helped to "channel" and discharge some of the frustration and anger that built up as she worked.

Unfortunately, as Shana withdrew from work, it became more and more difficult for her to maintain her motivation. To her chagrin, she found herself cutting corners at work and taking advantage of the flexible and autonomous conditions in her new job. "There's a supervising attorney at my new agency who is just a big teddy bear. Sometimes when you're in a situation like that, you tend to abuse the other person's flexibility. Occasionally I see myself slipping into that. I even start having motivational problems where I just don't want to do anything. After awhile, I get bored."

Although many of the novices were clearly dissatisfied with their work and remained so during the period we knew them, decreasing psychological involvement was not necessarily accompanied by decreasing satisfaction with the job. In fact, poverty lawyer Shana Phillips and several other subjects in the study actually seemed to become more content with their work as their psychological involvement diminished. For Shana, work was most unpleasant when she was still invested in it and looked to it as the primary source of fulfillment in her life. The gap between what she wanted from the job and what it offered was greatest at that point. As she withdrew, her expectations and desires for her job decreased. Thus, the job was less disappointing. Frustrations, role conflicts, ambiguity, lack of variety and excessive routine, conflict with clients and co-workers—all of the typical sources of stress and dissatisfaction experienced by new professionals in public institutions—were less upsetting because the job was less important. In other words, increasing alienation from work seemed to be a coping mechanism for many young professionals, a way of protecting themselves from the stress and discouragement they would confront each day if work continued to play a dominant psychological role in their lives.

However, there were exceptions to this picture of withdrawal from work. A few of the subjects in our study maintained and perhaps even increased their psychological involvement in work during the initial phase of their careers. For instance, Diane Peterson's work situation was one of the best in our study, and she responded by maintaining a very high level of involvement in the job. When not involved in some activity directly related to work as an alcoholism therapist, she would usually read books or journals in the field or attend professional conferences and workshops. After years as a frustrated and depressed homemaker and mother, she found her work exciting, meaningful, and fulfilling. She was enthusiastic about the work she was doing from the very beginning and maintained this enthusiasm during the months we followed her. In fact, her work life became so absorbing that she allowed her children to go live with their father, whom Diane had divorced a few years earlier. "I even gave up all my kids for the fact that they didn't fit into my priorities right now." At another point, she summed up her feelings about work in these terms:

> One has to start realizing, "Am I going to make this an 8 to 5 or 9 to 5 job, or am I prepared to give an awful lot more of myself?" I'm really seeing now that my hobby is my job. It involves reading more and just being involved more. Maybe it'll be joining a women's group or two, infiltrating and finding out what they're doing with alcoholism. This is a whole life. It's not just a job.

One can seriously question, as Diane did, whether this kind of total involvement in one's work is "good." Perhaps some readers will be appalled that this mother "sent her children away" because she believed her work was more rewarding and she wanted to devote herself totally to it. Perhaps this was not only a selfish action but one that will have deleterious consequences for both mother and children in the years to come. Such questions are difficult to answer, not only because so much important information about the situation—past, present, and future—is missing, but also because what ultimately is at stake is a question of value. What constitutes the "good" life? How should life be led? In the ideal world, how much psychological involvement in one's work is optimal?

In considering such questions, two important points should be emphasized. First, these questions become central ones for most new public professionals early in their careers. Second, the general trend for them is to become less involved in work and more involved in non-work areas of life as time passes (13 out of 23 did so). Although this shift in thought and action is not always a response to a disappointing work situation, it frequently is. "Work alienation" became common in the novice professionals we studied, and it usually seemed to be a way of coping with an unpleasant job.

If we had not studied these young professionals in the context of their work, we might have assumed that the change in their attitudes was unrelated to those work experiences. But this would have been an incomplete and inaccurate interpretation. Numerous observers of current American culture have written about what seems to be a basic change in young people's attitudes toward life. Increasingly, these cultural prophets have argued that the young (and many of their elders) are turning away from the world of work, looking elsewhere for psychological fulfillment and growth. Roszak (1969) saw this trend as part of what he called the "counterculture." Reich (1970) referred to it as the "greening of America."

Although these observations may have some validity, our research on the personal experiences of young public professionals suggests that such changes in attitude are not occurring in a vacuum, nor do they necessarily develop in middle or late adolescence. It would be incomplete to suggest that poverty lawyer Shana Phillips' withdrawal from work was caused by her vacation from work, which included contact with the "counterculture" during her stay at a commune. Clearly, this experience contributed to those changes in attitude and behavior, but, when she went to that commune, she was already running away from a work situation that had prepared her for that "conversion." She redefined the role of work in her life primarily because she could not maintain that intense, total involvement in her job. And she could not do so in part because of the nature of the job, the kinds of disappointments and pressures she experienced every day, with little psychological (or financial) compensation. The few new public professionals employed in work settings in which the psychic rewards outweighed the costs, such as alcoholism therapist Diane Peterson, did not withdraw from work. And it is unlikely that a visit to a commune by Diane Peterson would have convinced her that she could do so. Only a change in the job, in the balance of psychic rewards and costs, could have done this. Thus, most of the new professionals did withdraw from work and sought fulfillment elsewhere, and most of them developed this attitude only after finding that professional work in public institutions was not as rewarding as they had been led to believe.

INCREASING CONCERN WITH THE SELF

One would expect that professionals, especially those who choose to work in the public sector for salaries usually less than those paid in the private sector, would be unusually altruistic. Although there are exceptions, this assumption is probably valid—for new professionals. However, over a very short time this altruism often fades. One of the changes that seemed to occur in many of our subjects was that their own welfare and personal gain became more important to them.

The most concrete manifestation of this increasing self-interest was the change in attitudes about salary. While most of the subjects did not noticeably change their attitudes toward their pay, at least seven did so, and the apparent reason for the change was revealing. Generally, dissatisfaction with the salary occurred most often when the new professional had been frustrated in her attempt to secure other kinds of rewards from work. A salary that seemed adequate for a fulfilling, interesting, personally meaningful job came to be seen as quite inadequate for a job filled with worry, frustration, and daily assaults on one's personal dignity.

The poverty lawyers were a good example of how attitudes toward salary were linked to degree of fulfillment. The two frustrated idealist—Shanna Phillips and Margaret Williams—began with little concern for how much they were being paid. As Margaret put it in an early interview:

> The problem with legal services is that it doesn't pay very much, it's not very high prestige. . . . They don't pay you any more than 15 grand a year, I don't think. Anybody's got a family to support can't do it. I don't want to sound like an elitist, but who needs it? I can live fine on what I'm making, and I have no complaints. I'm not going to leave because I want more money. As far as I can tell, I like doing this kind of work. . . .

At another point in this early interview, Margaret said that she was making so much more money than she had when she was a student that she felt absolutely rich. She was especially impressed because she even had enough to buy a used car. But at our final interview, six months later, her attitude had changed considerably. She now complained not only about the way she "was being treated," but also about "the way I'm being paid." She said that she had been asked to write a brief for an in-service training workshop on her own time, and her response was, "For the amount they're paying me, hell if I'm going to do it on my own time." In describing her current salary, she said, "I did get a raise, but it was an automatic raise. It wasn't because of my great work. Now I'm making $13,500. Great!" The sarcasm in this statement was clear. The change in her attitude toward her salary was a reflection of her bitterness about the way she had been treated by clients, colleagues, and administrators.

The reaction of poverty lawyer Shana Phillips was similar. She articulated especially well the relationship between frustration in her job and increased concern with extrinsic rewards:

> I have about reached the point where I've had enough. I think you could generalize about a lot of people that get out of law school. In the first year or two, they are very idealistic and they want to help folks. The next year or two, they want to help folks *and* make money. The next year or two, they just want to make money. And I can see that process happening to myself.
> [Interviewer: "Well, what causes that? What is it that does that? Is it that public service law is not paid very well at all?"]

Well, it doesn't pay that well, but I think that it's more than that. It's just the reality of practicing law. . . . I mean, in a way, it's a brutalizing process, the criminal justice system is, for the clients and for everybody who works within it. It happens to the probation officers; it happens to the judges. It just happens—because I *have* been interested in making more money. That's definitely been happening the last few months. And what I say to myself is, "Why am I working 55 hours a week for all this aggravation?" And I see myself wearing out. And I say, "Well, I can see doing it for $25,000, but I can't see doing it for $15,000."

[Interviewer: "I see, so it's not just money, it's the work as opposed to the compensation for it."]

Right. When you're getting hassled by everybody from the judge to your client and working as heavily as you're working and burning out, you say, "Why am I doing this? It can't be for the money because the money isn't there. And maybe if there was more money there, it would be more worth my while. I could see putting up with what I'm putting up with." I see it as kind of analogous to even a factory worker. I mean, their jobs are so monotonous and so dehumanizing, and everybody complains that, "Gee, these factory workers want all this money and they want this and that." To put up with that aggravation, I can understand it.

Nine months later, Shana's attitudes toward financial compensation had continued to shift; monetary rewards had become even more important for her. She was even willing to take on cases about which she had moral qualms if the pay was good. She was beginning to do private work on the side to make more money, something she had never thought she would be interested in doing:

Well, I'm getting more traditional in the sense that I want to make money, and I want to be able to do things that I want to do. I don't always take the cases that I could, simply because the person might not have money. It depends. Sometimes I do outside cases. I just kind of sneak them in there. Like now I'm writing an appeal for a friend. But it's an armed robbery and a rape, and I would never do a rape before in my life. I would always just turn them down. I would just refuse to take the. . . . One guy personally, I just did not like him, but when he retained me, I took it. And he was just a punk, but I guess you can't like all your clients.

Even more striking than the growing concern about financial compensation was the new public professionals' increasing desire for autonomy. New professionals in every group came to value autonomy more during the first year of their career. The only field in which the majority did not change in this way was high school teaching. Even in this field, three of the seven subjects were more concerned about their autonomy at the final interview than they had been when they began teaching. In general, 14 of 21 subjects became more concerned about personal autonomy during this period.

In early interviews, the novices in our study usually concentrated on frustrations and satisfactions directly related to role performance, such as client characteristics and behavior, achieving a sense of competence, and so on. The new professionals at this initial stage were more likely to be concerned about the lack of social support in their work settings than about the lack of autonomy. For instance, new high school teacher Cynthia Noble was probably typical when she said that she would actually welcome being told what to do when she first started. She would gladly have traded some of her autonomy for more guidance and emotional support from co-workers and supervisors.

However, it was not many months before the content of the interviews noticeably changed. The novices spoke less about their individual job demands and responsibilities and more about organizational politics, conflict over control and resources, and the ultimate implications of these issues for their own autonomy. They increasingly came to value autonomy and became more aware of how policies and actions throughout their organization could impinge on that autonomy.

A particularly good example of this shift in concern was mental health professional Douglas Furth. Initially, he was primarily concerned about securing acceptance and support from his colleagues. However, his efforts in these directions were largely unsuccessful, and he gradually gave up. As his hope for collegiality and emotional support receded, his desire for autonomy increased. For instance, one of the things he was most concerned about during our final interview was his work schedule. The agency's flexible schedule policy allowed him to arrange his time so that he only had to go into the office four days a week. But some of the older staff had been grumbling about the "privileges" of the newer ones, and there was a possibility that the flexible schedule policy would be eliminated. Fortunately for Douglas, this change in agency policy did not come about, for it would have severely limited his freedom. Initially, Douglas had fought for greater staff unity. After six months, he was fighting to protect his personal autonomy. To a certain extent, this change was a response to political events in the agency. But it also seemed to reflect a shift in Douglas' personal values.

Poverty lawyer Margaret Williams was another subject who became increasingly aware of organizational politics and personal autonomy. During our initial interviews, her primary complaints concerned excessive routine in the work, lying and other disagreeable behavior of clients, and lack of guidance and support from colleagues. She said nothing about organizational conflicts or the issue of autonomy. During her final interview, however, these were the major concerns. She discussed the ongoing conflicts between the paralegals and the professionals and between the agency and the governing board. She also spent much time criticizing the administration's efforts to increase the "accountability" of the legal staff. She increasingly resented what she called the "big brother attitude" that seemed to pervade the thinking of the "people downtown." Much of her job frustration and disillusionment had become focused on the administration, and the protection of her professional autonomy had become one issue over which Margaret and other new public professionals could dig in their heels, fight, and perhaps even win for a change. As their larger ideals and hopes evaporated and dissolved in the day-to-day reality of practice, they were replaced by more limited and narrow concerns of self-interest, autonomy, and "turf." Having "lost" so much, the new professionals tenaciously protected the privileges they had.

ATTITUDE CHANGE
AS A MEANS OF COPING

The last two chapters have described a number of changes in attitude that occurred in many new public professionals during the initial phase of their careers. The major element that these changes seemed to share was their psychological function: virtually every change helped the novice cope with the stress and strain experienced on the job.

For instance, lowering one's goals and aspirations alleviates the crisis of competence; more modest goals are more easily attainable. The incidence of success increases and the incidence of failure decreases. Also, because more modest goals can be attained through one's own efforts, one is less likely to feel frustrated, helpless, and inadequate. The sense of mastery increases. Minimizing personal responsibility also alleviates the crisis of competence, for if one assumes that the cause of falling short is a defect in the client or a barrier in the system over which one has no control, the sense of personal inadequacy is reduced. The burden of guilt is eased, and some of the sting associated with failure is removed.

Psychological withdrawal from work also contributes to the coping process. As long as the neophytes were highly invested in their jobs, frustrations and difficulties were especially painful. But as they withdrew psychologically and the role of work in their lives was reduced, as other, non-work pursuits became the primary arenas for need fulfillment, the stresses of work became less threatening. The crisis of competence was reduced because one's self-esteem was no longer so dependent on one's job performance. The lack of interesting, stimulating, intrinsically rewarding activity in work becomes less disturbing as alternative sources in one's "life space" are identified and tapped.

This view of the adaptive function of attitudes and attitude change is not an original one. In fact, Katz (1971) developed it in a classic essay on attitude theory. In that essay, he argues that attitudes contribute to the maintenance of psychological equilibrium. They help provide meaning and order to the world, enhance and protect self-esteem, alleviate fear and anxiety, and thereby preserve one's peace of mind. Even when attitudes and beliefs become a source of stress and anxiety (as in the case of a paranoid's delusions), they may well represent attempts to avoid an even more distressing or harmful situation. (For instance, the paranoid's delusions make him vigilant and, in his mind at least, less likely to be caught by surprise and harmed by clever enemies.) Thus, conceptualizing the attitude changes that occur in new public professionals as attempts to cope with stressful work situations is consistent with general psychological theory.

Current writing on "burnout" has emphasized this adaptation perspective. For instance, Maslach (1976) has proposed that professionals who experience stress in their relations with clients employ "detachment mechanisms." These include the use of derogatory labels for clients, impersonal and superficial communication with them, "going by the book" or following a set formula in work with clients, thinking of clients in terms of clinical labels and diagnostic categories, and sarcastic humor. These detachment mechanisms protect the professional from guilt, frustration, and anger. They are psychological defense mechanisms.

If this stress-coping-adaptation view of the change process were valid, one would expect a positive relationship between the amount of stress and strain experienced in the job and the amount of attitude change observed in the new professional. A study of our interviews, by Wacker (1979), found just such a relationship. In this study, Wacker asked one group of raters to estimate the amount of psychological stress experienced by each of the new public professionals. She then asked a second group of raters to make independent assessments of attitude change on seven different dimensions (see Appendix B).Thus, for each subject, she had a "stress" score and several "attitude change" scores. She computed the correlation between these scores for each of the four professional groups. In general, she found strong positive correlations between stress and negative attitude change. In other words, the greater the stress and strain experienced in their first jobs, the more likely were the new professionals to change their attitudes, and the changes were usually negative. Of course, these results do not establish a causal relationship, but they are consistent with the notion that the negative attitude changes that occur in many professionals early in their careers serve a defensive function: they are responses to, and attempts to cope with, excessively high levels of stress.

However, this explanation of why new professionals change as they do is different from the usual one found in the literature on professional socialization. The more typical view emphasizes the role of social influence. For instance, McPherson (1972) described how the nonverbal behavior of veteran school teachers communicated their disapproval of certain practices by neophyte teachers. These cues ultimately led to a change in the neophytes' behavior and attitudes. The novices were susceptible to influence by older colleagues because they identified with them and used them as models. Also, their older colleagues controlled important rewards and punishments. For instance, to be rejected and ostracized by one's co-workers would be extremely painful for most new teachers; therefore, they comply with demands and change their practices.

The social influence explanation for professional attitude change is not incompatible with the coping and adaptation explanation offered here. In fact, both processes probably occur. The new professionals we interviewed were influenced by colleagues, supervisors, and even clients. However, a careful study of their experiences from their own subjective viewpoints suggested that the desire to alleviate the anxiety, frustration, and guilt associated with their old attitudes was a more potent force for change than the influential efforts of others. In other words, the primary motive for adopting more modest goals or withdrawing from work or becoming emotionally detached from one's clients was not to conform and win the favor or approval of others; the main motive was to reduce high levels of stress and tension. Social influence and comparison may have facilitated these changes, as when a supervisor or older colleague said sympathetically to a new professional, "Well, you know, no one is able to reach *every* client. Sometimes clients just aren't motivated to change, so don't worry about it." However, the primary impetus for change came from the psychological disequilibrium associated with the "reality shock" of work, and the changes that were made seemed to be ways of restoring equilibrium. The new attitudes and behaviors were primarily adopted not because they were favored by others but because they reduced psychological distress.

CONCLUSION: PROFESSIONAL ATTITUDES AND THE PUBLIC WELFARE

During the last two decades, unionization and collective bargaining by groups of public professionals have become more prevalent (Oppenheimer, 1975). Many citizens seem to have been upset by this trend; an excessive concern for salary and financial reward seems to be "inappropriate" for professionals in public service. Many have asked, "What has happened to altruism and selfless dedication in teachers, lawyers, physicians, and nurses? Why have they become so greedy and callous?" Such questions assume historical changes in professional dedication that may or may not be real. But our study of change in new public professionals supports the notion that many do in fact become more self-centered and concerned about extrinsic rewards during the early part of their careers. Also, our in-depth interviews suggest that, to a large extent, this change occurs because of the relative imbalance between what the professionals put into their jobs and what they get out of them in terms of psychic rewards. Many new public professionals begin their careers with relatively little concern about money. The intrinsic rewards of their work—such as the gratitude of clients they have helped, a sense of accomplishment, and intellectual growth and stimulation—are what they are most concerned about. However, most fail to find these rewards, at least to the extent they had expected. Consequently, they turn to other forms of compensation that are more concrete and, through collective action, sometimes more attainable. Those who seek to know why public professionals unionize and increasingly emphasize wage demands in collective bargaining should look at the nature of the work professionals are asked to do.

Perhaps it is no coincidence that the changes in attitude observed in the new public professionals mirror the changes that have occurred more generally in our society during the last decade. Many observers (such as, Lasch, 1979; Goldenberg, 1978) have noted a growing "narcissism" during the last few years. Concern with the plight of the needy and with social change, characteristic of the 1960s, seems to have given way to an obsessive preoccupation with one's own welfare and individual "growth." There are many theories and explanations for this shift in attitude, and there is probably some validity to many of them. However, this study suggests a possible cause not mentioned previously: the disillusionment experienced by the growing numbers of new professionals who work in the public sector.

Many of the new professionals of the 1970s were the idealistic and committed students of the 1960s whose activism helped make the plight of the poor and the need for social change dominant themes in this country. Their idealism and concern for others led them to choose professional careers and then to choose public agencies in which to practice their professions. Unfortunately, their confrontation with the world of work proved to be more demanding and less fulfilling than they had expected. The structure of their jobs and agencies made it difficult to practice in the way they had hoped. Success occurred less often than they had ever imagined. Colleagues were less stimulating and supportive. The work was more routine and uninteresting. Clients were often not very pleasant. As a result, the new professionals began to lose their compassion, their sense of commitment. They began to withdraw from a vocation that was no longer as meaningful and compelling as it had once seemed. Ultimately, many began to concentrate on their own personal success and welfare. If they could not do so much to help others, at least there were concrete ways in which they could help themselves. This scenario is probably too simplified to fit the diversity of experiences and change found in young, public professionals. However, it does seem to accurately describe the general pattern that many of them followed, and, as such, it seems to offer at least a partial explanation for what happened to the selfless commitment of the young. Not only did their work as professionals in public institutions fail to serve as an adequate vehicle for actualizing their ideals; it also represented a major emotional crisis and a drain on their coping resources that made it increasingly difficult to maintain a concern for others and the larger society. When people are under great stress, when their self-esteem is threatened, and when their goals and desires are frustrated, concern with the self increases while concern for others declines.

Thus, the changes in attitude and outlook that occurred in the new public professionals we studied and that have been described in the last two chapters not only mirror many of the changes in national consciousness that have been occurring during the last decade. They are, in fact, a major cause of those changes. To the extent that professionals collectively help define the historical climate of a society at any given point in time, the plight of the new public professional influences us all.

PART III

SOURCES OF VARIATION
IN EXPERIENCE

8

FOUR CONTRASTING EXPERIENCES

In the previous sections, we examined the patterns and trends of the entire sample of new public professionals. In general, the new public professionals experienced much stress and strain. A number of factors contributed to this stress, the crisis of competence being one of the most important. The professionals' attempts to cope with this stress led to changes in their attitudes and behavior, particularly psychological withdrawal from work and loss of initial idealism.

However, not all of the subjects followed this pattern; there was a noteworthy minority who experienced more manageable levels of stress and/or did not burn out. In this chapter, we begin our examination of the sources of variation in new professional experience. Four case studies are presented. Two represent typical examples of the stress, strain, and change described previously; two depict exceptions. Two are high school teachers, and two are lawyers. By comparing and contrasting these four individual experiences, much can be learned about the factors that may influence the degree of stress and burnout experienced by new public professionals. Chapters 9 and 10 shall discuss more generally the variations in organizational setting and in individuals that seem to affect burnout.

THE LOSS OF COMPASSION:
MARGARET WILLIAMS, POVERTY LAWYER

Margaret Williams represents one of the most vivid examples of the loss of idealism in new poverty lawyers. Intensely idealistic and socially concerned when she entered legal practice, she experienced high levels of stress, conflict, and disillusionment in her first job as a lawyer. Within a short period of time, her attitudes toward work and life shifted in ways that she herself would have defined as negative when she first began her career. Thus, her case offers potentially valuable insights about the complex relationship between expectation, need, stress, and change in the new public professional.

At the time she was first interviewed, Margaret was 24 years old. Her parents were highly educated and involved in managerial or professional work. She had attended a prestigious law school from which she had graduated eight months before. She had gone to work for a neighborhood legal services office in a large city shortly after graduation and was still employed there. Much of her work involved landlord-tenant law. However, she was called upon to represent impoverished clients in a wide variety of both minor and major civil proceedings. She was not married, but was living with a male lawyer.

Margaret had been an undergraduate during the late 1960s and had become active in radical political causes. Her politics were still radical when she finished her legal training, and she sought a poverty law position in order to actualize her social values through her work. Unlike many young lawyers who seek poverty law jobs as a temporary placement for developing trial skills, Margaret expected to pursue a lifelong career as an advocate for the poor and dispossessed. Poverty law was not a self-serving means to an end for Margaret; it was the fulfillment of a career goal she had formed many years before as a young political activist.

In some respects, poverty law was what Margaret had hoped it would be. When she was a law student, she was concerned about taking a job in which she would be compelled to do things she felt were morally wrong. A strong career need was to find work in which it would be possible to maintain her moral integrity. Her current job fulfilled that need. At one point, she said, "I'm really glad that I'm doing this because I don't have any moral qualms about the work I'm doing." She described another lawyer she had met who was representing a landlord in an eviction case. He was trying to get a family evicted, and she asked him, "How do you sleep at night doing this kind of shit?" She felt sorry for him because there was nothing else he could do. At least none of the cases she had to take represented a moral dilemma. For an idealist like Margaret, who could not separate work, life, and human values, preserving moral integrity was important.

However, in other respects, poverty law work in a neighborhood legal services agency proved to be a bitter disappointment for Margaret. She claimed that, when she first took this job, she was misinformed about what it would involve. She said she was told that she would have the opportunity to handle reform law, which she preferred for at least two reasons. First, in reform work the facts are known, and one attempts to establish new interpretations of the law. Not only is this type of work more intellectually stimulating and challenging, but it is also the type of work she had been trained to do in law school. In law school, one researches the law and knows the facts. However, in legal practice, the law is always clearcut; it is the facts that are in dispute. For Margaret, this type of work was less intellectually stimulating, less creative, and more limiting.

Also, she felt the potential impact of her work was relatively slight. At one point, she described her work as a "big band-aid," and said she was frustrated that it did not lead to "real" change. At another point, she said that she had become dissatisfied with the routine, "diddly shit" nature of the cases. Her work seemed to lack real meaning because it did not challenge legal and social institutions. Instead, the basic legal and social practices remained unquestioned while she spent days on the phone finding out why a client's Social Security check had been delayed.

On the other hand, the issue of meaning in work was a complex one for Margaret. At times, she believed that her work really did "make a difference," especially as a way of helping needy individuals. She said that she took few sick days because her clients really depended on her. At times, she really got satisfaction from helping people solve their personal problems. Thus, there seemed to be a basic, unresolved conflict for Margaret between the need to make things a little better for individuals and the need for more basic social and political change. She seemed to accept both goals as legitimate, yet in her present work she often felt unfulfilled because she was limited to helping individuals.

Margaret's discontent with her work also seemed to be related to another unfulfilled need that was more difficult for her to recognize and accept: the need for recognition, prestige, and fame. She confided at one point that she would be happier if she could do work that really "made a splash." She talked admiringly—and enviously—of a friend who had acquired much publicity and had become a "legend" through his legal work. She went into great detail describing one of his press conferences. When asked about her future aspirations, she responded that she would like to work in an agency in which the lawyers have very little direct contact with clients and work on big "test cases." Clearly, Margaret was attracted to the limelight.

Her idealism and moral commitment to serving others made it difficult for Margaret to recognize her more egoistic, less altruistic strivings. In fact, she strongly criticized ambitious colleagues who seemed to have a bias in favor of the "big" cases. She contrasted herself with co-workers who seemed to have little concern about what happened to their clients and who tried to win cases simply for the sake of winning and the positive consequences it would have for their careers. When she did so, she did not seem to realize that she, herself, had personal needs that had little to do with the welfare of others. Although Margaret tended to set herself apart from others, there was probably a strong but often obscure conflict between altruism and egoism in her as well.

One other aspiration Margaret talked about was the development of professional competence. When she took the job, she had expected that she would learn much from her co-workers. This did not happen for three reasons. First,

Margaret found it difficult to relate to them initially because they did not share her own political and social beliefs: most were more conservative, one more radical. Second, because of the high turnover in neighborhood legal aid, most of her co-workers were as inexperienced as she. Finally, because the workload at her agency was extremely heavy, the lawyers felt too pressured and busy to spend much time exchanging ideas about cases. Thus, because her co-workers did not provide the opportunities for learning that Margaret had sought from her first job, she came to dislike them as well as her job. She also complained about her supervisor, partly because of his inability to provide leadership and a sense of direction in the office, but also because she felt he did not know enough about legal practice to facilitate her professional development.

Thus, Margaret helped to fulfill several personal needs through her career, including recognition, fame, moral integrity, intellectual stimulation, social impact, and increased competence. Some of these needs were fulfilled, but most were not, at least not as fully as she had hoped.

Margaret's growing disappointment with work seemed to contribute to a rapid change in her attitudes toward clients. Initially, she said she responded to all clients and problems with concern. However, she admitted that eight months after she began the job, she no longer responded to them in a uniformly positive way. She felt that she had become callous and uninterested in the more routine cases, and these made up the bulk of her workload. There were many factors contributing to this shift in attitude: the heavy workload that made it difficult to respond warmly and compassionately to each client and contributed to her resentment of clients who pestered her about "bullshit cases" (she referred to these clients as "cranks"), her realization that many of her clients lied to her, and the experience of being robbed twice by clients. Although she said that she still felt real sympathy and concern for those few needy, honest clients with especially compelling cases, by the final interview she viewed the typical client as ungrateful, interfering, nagging, dishonest, and threatening.

The change in Margaret's attitudes toward clients perhaps contributed to noticeable changes in other important social attitudes as well. She began to resent the agency's board of directors and some of the local community people it represented. She noted that she had become less sympathetic toward criminals. Rather than making excuses for them as she had in the past, she found herself becoming angry toward them. However, there was still much conflict and ambivalence concerning these attitude changes. During one interview she made a strong "law and order" statement, saying "I'm getting really intolerant of a lot of things ... Like in a college town, you can say, 'Oh, street crime is just a product of racism and poverty and we must understand, blah, blah, blah.' Well, when a gun's stuck in your head, you stop understanding. And I have had that." Yet, only a few minutes later, during the same interview, she talked sympathetically about a former armed robber she had met who pointed out to her that, when there are no jobs at all in the ghetto and one is dependent on welfare, crime is really the only "career" that makes sense. But the longer Margaret remained in this job, the more her attitudes shifted in a conservative direction. By the final interview, which took place more than a year after she began working as a poverty lawyer, she described her attitudes as "cynical" and "paranoid," and she was seriously thinking of changing sides and going to work for the prosecutor's office.

One other set of attitudes that showed change were those related to work itself. Initially, she was concerned about her professional competence (and the perceived lack of it) and was unhappy because she did not receive enough emotional and technical support from her co-workers and supervisors. Gradually, as she became more comfortable with her own performance, her dissatisfactions centered around issues of autonomy, control, and office politics. Also, while in an earlier interview she expressed little concern about her salary and said she was making more than enough, in the last interview she said she was dissatisfied with her "meager" salary, did not like the way raises were handled, and resented an in-service training program because it required additional time without additional compensation. Finally, while she complained about the lack of variety in her work during the early interviews, she increasingly chose to narrow it further by becoming the office specialist in one area of law, greatly enhancing her professional prestige and self-esteem.

Thus, in little more than a year, Margaret's attitudes toward society, clients, and work had undergone dramatic transformations. Clearly, one factor in this process was the structure of her job, including the heavy workload, poor support services, excessive routine, poor supervision, and so on. Also, by working in a rough, deteriorated section of the inner city and coming into daily contact with the "wretched of the earth," she had been subjected to traumatic, brutalizing experiences (such as being robbed at gun point by three large men), which had a profound impact on her. In addition, she seemed to enter law expecting to bring about dramatic and rapid social changes while achieving personal recognition and fame. Few jobs could have fulfilled these expectations, and the unresolved conflicts she experienced made it even more difficult for her to accommodate to her work situation.

Another source of difficulty seemed to be the lack of effective coping aids. Unlike many of the other poverty lawyers, Margaret did not identify with a general, abstract conception of the legal system and her role as a lawyer in it. She approached her work in an immediate, spontaneous, and personal way. She was the "great white knight" venturing forth to do battle with evil on behalf of good. When she found that the poor clients with whom she strongly identified were not as pure and good as she had thought and that they did not think of her as being at all different from the other "outsiders" whom they had learned over the years to fear and despise, Margaret had nothing on which to fall back. She also coped poorly because of her failure to develop any psychologically rewarding endeavors outside of work. If she had been able to shift some of her psychological investment into more rewarding activity outside of the job, she might have been able to accept more of the work-related strain. But throughout the initial part of her career, work was her whole life. Thus the frustration and disappointments of poverty law created a deep wound that gradually led to profound changes in Margaret's attitudes toward work, life, and society.

COMMITMENT AND FULFILLMENT IN THE LAW:
JEAN CHALMERS, REFORM LAWYER

Unlike most poverty lawyers interviewed, Jean Chalmers was able to remain socially committed, compassionate, and fulfilled in her work. Her resistance to the disillusionment and burnout experienced by most others seemed in part to be related to what she brought to the job: her personality, her preparation in law school, her abilities, and the framework through which she viewed her work. However, equally important (perhaps even *more* important) was the structure of her job and the nature of the setting in which she worked. By comparing her with Margaret Williams, one gains an unusually clear picture of some of the factors influencing early career development in public professionals.

Jean was a single, 28-year-old lawyer who had been working about eight months when first interviewed. Her parents were high school graduates. Her mother was a homemaker, and her father managed a small business concern. After graduating from a prestigious state university, she worked in VISTA. It was here that her interest in law as a career really began to crystallize. She went to study law at a less prestigious, university-affiliated, urban law school. During law school, she worked as a law clerk in an agency that handled appeals for indigent clients. Her law school also had an "urban law clinic," which gave students early experience in handling real cases and working with low-income clients. After graduation, she found a job in an agency specializing in reform cases and class action suits on behalf of various disadvantaged groups.

In her preparation, Jean was different from some of the other public lawyers interviewed in at least two ways: she had more actual experience in legal aid settings during law school, contributing to more realistic expectations regarding what could be done, and she was a bright student attending an institution in which the students generally were of a "lower caliber" (her words). As a result, she may have felt more self-confident and secure during those school years and received more positive regard from faculty than others interviewed, who were equally gifted but attended more competitive law schools where their talents were less recognized. In other words, Jean seemed to be a "big fish in a small pond." Given the especially strong need for recognition and success characteristic of the new lawyers we interviewed, this "small pond" situation in law school may have helped Jean develop a strong professional self.

Whatever the origins, Jean came to her first job with fewer illusions and more practical ability than the other poverty lawyers. She said that from the start she did not believe that she would "save people" through her work. In fact, she saw herself as frequently defending "the system" and playing by "their rules." She saw the need for compromise and working at a slow pace.

While this framework through which she viewed her work might seem more compromising and less idealistic than the views espoused by some of the other public lawyers interviewed, in fact it supported for Jean a continuing commitment to reform work. In some respects, she seemed to have minimized the extent to which she rejected the status quo and challenged it in her work. However, while she had no illusions about either her role or what the "system" would permit, she engaged in cases that helped bring about reforms consistent with her ideology (for instance, helping women prisoners become more self-sufficient by providing them with law libraries). She had not become disillusioned, and she had not abandoned her commitment to social change, in part because she viewed her work from a carefully thought out larger perspective, one which took account of the legal system as it actually was and clearly articulated how one lawyer's day-to-day work could contribute to larger social goals.

In addition to this well-articulated perspective, Jean brought to the job unusual skill in the interpersonal aspects so crucial to the effective practice of law. For instance, she described how she could usually obtain vital, highly sensitive information from informants by approaching them in a friendly, nonthreatening way and patiently listening to them talk. This interviewing skill facilitated performance of the interpersonal aspects of the work, a major weakness and source of frustration for many other young lawyers interviewed. Thus, one factor aiding Jean's adjustment to work was the skills and the "larger perspective" developed before she came to her job.

As suggested, Jean entered law primarily in order to secure greater social justice and improve the quality of life for the disadvantaged. In this respect, she and Margaret were alike. However, unlike Margaret and the other poverty lawyers, she had been able to maintain her concern and commitment for at least 18 months on the job. She continued to express concern with the legal rights and human welfare of those confined in our prison system. She described her clients positively, at times even affectionately and admiringly. She seemed to have remained compassionate and sensitive toward them.

For instance, she indicated that she was always available by phone to prison inmates whose cases she was handling because she knew it was important for them to have someone to talk to. Although the office secretary became perturbed when the clients called collect and frequently there was nothing that Jean could do about their personal problems when they did call, she continued to recognize the psychological value of those contacts for the clients.

She could even view clients who lied with charity and tolerance. Unlike several other lawyers interviewed, Jean tended to minimize this problem and rationalized it in terms of what the prison setting does to prisoners. She also criticized her own profession, suggesting that many lawyers are incompetent, dishonest, or both. She felt that it was not surprising for disadvantaged clients, whose previous experiences had shaken their faith in the legal profession, to believe they needed to lie and manipulate.

Jean's patience and concern for clients was in part supported by the adoption of goals that went beyond just winning cases. She stated that she spent more time with clients than did the other lawyers in her office because she wanted to use law as a way of "organizing" and "educating" the disadvantaged. She viewed client contact as a way of increasing the client's personal and political effectiveness. These additional goals gave client contact more meaning and provided optional sources of accomplishment.

Jean's resistance to disillusionment did not mean that she was totally without cynicism. In discussing the social programs for the poor created during the 1960s, she said, "If you had burned the money, you would have gotten the same thing." She also had no illusions about the motives of those who want to help the poor. According to Jean, government and church groups were willing to support some legal aid for the poor because it was nonthreatening: the poor were given no real power. Defending a poor person in an auto negligence case was hardly radical.

On the other hand, Jean was less hostile toward the establishment than she and other young lawyers tended to be before beginning their careers. For instance, she stated that she trusted prison officials more and did not believe that they carried out reprisals against prisoners involved in reform cases, even though some of her clients claimed they did. Thus, there did seem to have been some shift in her attitudes, toward greater cynicism about reform and more tolerance for and trust in "the establishment" (or at least some of those working for it). And, like other young, progressive lawyers, she was concerned about "selling out" her principles. She described one friend as an "ex-radical" who sold out after working one year with the "other side." Jean said that she did not think she would be immune from the pressure to change in such a situation, so she would never take that sort of job.

Jean probably did not even realize all the ways in which she was helped to resist "selling out" in her first job. Always being on the side of the disadvantaged in adversarial situations probably helped her retain her ideals, but other young lawyers in similar positions lost their sense of commitment relatively quickly. Equally important in helping her preserve her commitment was her workload. Jean worked in a special branch of legal aid that handled only reform work. Clients did not walk in the door with relatively trivial, routine problems. In fact, in most cases the lawyers in her agency sought out the clients, choosing those whose cases would provide a vehicle for effecting some type of reform that the lawyers had been researching and working on in other ways. Even their physical location, 20 stories above the street in a large office building, helped insulate them from the daily client pressures that became so overwhelming for those working in neighborhood storefronts. Thus, while Jean Chalmers worked just as much as the other poverty lawyers (perhaps more), the pace was slower, more under her own control, and less pressured than in most legal aid offices.

Jean's job was less frustrating in still other ways. Reform law provided considerably more variety, challenge, and intellectual stimulation than criminal law or neighborhood legal aid. As Jean said, there was something new all the time, and one had the chance to sit down and think about the challenging new problems. Reform law also allowed her to utilize and consolidate the skills learned in school, for she had to research law as well as facts.

Jean's job also rated high in meaning and significance. When she won a case, the entire legal system changed in a small but discernible way; potentially, thousands of individuals could be affected. Unlike the legal aid lawyer working to help a single individual, Jean worked to change the whole system. The job also seemed more meaningful because she was one of the few lawyers in the state doing reform law. And she had further specialized within her agency and field, making her own contribution truly unique. She spoke with some pride about her many invitations to give speeches about a field in which she had quickly become one of the leading "experts."

Thus, Jean's job allowed her to do work whose impact and uniqueness made it particularly meaningful in terms of her own social values. In fact, this opportunity to perform a role so consonant with her social values was a critical factor in her ability to retain those values. She was one of the few lawyers interviewed who had been able to do something about her "politics" through her work. It was not surprising that after almost two years, she stated that she was extremely satisfied with her job, had no plans to do anything else in the future, and remained content with her relatively low salary despite the long hours and her awareness that others with less experience were earning much more in different jobs.

In addition to the work itself, Jean's job was made more satisfying by those with whom she worked. There was a positive social climate among the ten people in her office. Co-workers were described as very friendly and "like a family," frequently getting together outside of work. Also, because there was less workload pressure than in the typical neighborhood legal aid office, everyone constantly checked everyone else's work, in a spirit of cooperative support rather than criticism or evaluation. Not only did this practice contribute to a collaborative atmosphere, it also enabled a new worker like Jean to learn from models. In a more isolated work setting, there would be much less opportunity for this modeling to occur, and there would be greater anxiety for a longer period of time as the novice learned through trial and error.

Another positive aspect of the office was that the other lawyers, like Jean, seemed to be highly dedicated to their work and less interested in using it as a "stepping stone." (While Jean attributed their dedication to their "values" and "compassion," the positive, rewarding aspects of the work in reform law probably had much to do with her co-workers' sustained commitment.) In concrete terms, this longer time commitment to the work meant that her colleagues had more experience and expertise than the typical group of lawyers working in neighborhood legal aid. Thus, they were able to contribute to the professional development of a new lawyer such as Jean.

The agency's director did much to sustain this positive social climate. Jean believed the atmosphere was so warm and relaxed because the director was that way himself. She described him as someone who did not like being an administrator or giving orders to people. However, he was available to provide advice and direction when Jean had a work-related problem. (For instance, he even gave her reassurance and advice on how to cope with one co-worker in the office who tended to be hypercritical and unfriendly.) Jean had much respect for the director, a highly competent lawyer who had remained in public service for many years despite the low salary and hard work.

For a woman attorney, the sexual composition of the office also seemed to contribute to its supportiveness. Of five lawyers, three were women. Jean believed that because of this favorable male/female ratio, there was none of the hostility or condescension toward women that one might find in male-dominated, professional settings.

Despite the many positive aspects of her job and the strengths she brought to it, Jean did find it stressful at times. Like other new professionals, Jean was initially insecure about her own competence, and the "crisis of competence" was a major source of stress during this stage of her career. She soon realized that she had learned only the "basics" in law school and that the "real learning" began when she started her first job. According to Jean, her major frustration was that she could not "learn fast enough." The burden of responsibility in reform work, the feeling that her mistakes could "hurt" many individuals, made the issue of competence especially pressing.

So acutely aware of her inadequacies, Jean became especially sensitive about others' evaluations of her. During one interview, she remarked that lawyers tend to evaluate each other largely on the basis of perceived competence, not on the basis of how "nice" a person is. This emphasis by her peers on competence increased the tension and pressure, the need to "prove oneself," that she was already feeling. These concerns made her more vulnerable to the opinions of co-workers, and the only colleague of whom she spoke negatively was one who was especially critical of her mistakes.

Fortunately, the major change that occurred between the initial and follow-up interviews was in her sense of competence. After 18 months on the job, she reported feeling less anxious about her performance. However, she also admitted that a lingering sense of inadequacy continued to haunt her.

In addition to Jean's concerns about competence, there was what she called the "balancing problem," the conflict between keeping up with cases, keeping up with clients, and keeping up with the "public relations" aspect of reform law. Concretely, this problem was one of conflict between three distinct roles: research, counseling, and public speaking. While these three roles probably provided a level of variety that made the work more interesting, they all demanded time and effort and required constant "balancing." Nevertheless, it was clear that the intrinsic rewards of the work far outweighed the disadvantages.

To summarize, Jean Chalmers was one of the few idealistic and "socially committed" new lawyers who had been able to sustain this attitude for any length of time. While a carefully thought out, well-articulated perspective for viewing her work clearly helped her in making a relatively successful adjustment, the support of the work setting was also critical. Her situation provided a particularly clear picture of how one's first job influences both personal fulfillment and social commitment in a professional career.

LEARNING THE HARD WAY:
CALVIN MILLER, HIGH SCHOOL TEACHER

Calvin Miller, a 23-year-old unmarried chemistry teacher, seemed to have experienced more discontinuity and stress than most of the other new professionals in the study. He moved alone to a new town just a week before starting to teach in an unfamiliar school. He had no established circle of friends. He found himself completely on his own with no outlines or materials left from the previous teacher and no one but his students to give him feedback. He was disappointed with his students, and he increasingly blamed their lack of motivation and ability. Initially, he put much pressure on himself to do well, and felt he was under pressure from external sources to prove himself worthy. Soon after beginning his job, he entertained thoughts of quitting and only seemed genuinely excited by his summer plans to begin work on his Ph.D.

Calvin's decision to teach came during college after realizing that he typically took on helping roles throughout school and within his family. He remembered no outstanding teachers who might have been role models; in fact, he most remembered that he had had "some real dingbats." He rather courageously chose an inner-city school in which to do his student-teaching because it was the "hardest" and because he knew there was an excellent chemistry critic-teacher. Although he described his student-teaching as a "good experience," he seemed unsure of himself in the teaching role when he began his first job. Apparently, he felt that student-teaching had prepared him as much as possible and so was not dissatisfied with it. However, he was not at all prepared to deal with the responsibilities and demands of teaching.

In fact, lack of preparation and a sense of uncertainty were continuing themes in Calvin's experience as a new teacher. Much of this was compounded by circumstances in the work setting. Calvin did not learn that he had secured his job until late August. He was required to use a book he had not seen before, reading through it quickly over the weekend before school began. He did not know what had been done before because the former teacher had taken almost everything with her. No one told him how to deal with the many unfamiliar bureaucratic procedures of opening day; these proved to be more difficult than he had expected. Calvin also did not know what the lab facilities were like and had not seen the lab book. Finally, throughout his first year of teaching he continued to be uncertain about how to present material: what to include and what to leave out, what to emphasize, how fast to move, and so on.

This personal uncertainty and lack of formal orientation were exacerbated by Calvin's isolation from other teachers; he needed and wanted much more assistance and support from co-workers than he received. Not only did he need information about teaching procedures and school procedures, but he also wanted the support and reassurance that come from discussion of mutual experiences. Calvin said explicitly that it helped him to hear about the problems older teachers were having. "It makes me realize it's the situation," he said in one interview. He was eager to hear that he was not the only one having those problems, but there was little opportunity to talk with other teachers. There were, in fact, at least three obstacles to collegial discussion of teaching problems in Calvin's school. First, there seemed to be an unspoken norm against it. For instance, when he checked with another chemistry teacher to make sure they were covering the same material at the same pace (they were to switch classes at midyear), the other teacher expounded to him on the concept of "teacher's domains." This older teacher seemed to believe that to offer suggestions, give advice, or even ask a new colleague about his teaching was an unpardonable interference, an intrusion into another's domain, a violation of one's "turf." Thus, although Calvin would have welcomed advice or discussion, his attempts to obtain it seemed to violate some implicit prohibition.

A second obstacle to collegial discussion of the teaching experience was the structure of the job. The only time Calvin saw other teachers was at lunch. Most of the day, he was "alone" in his classroom, cut off from social interaction with all other adults. In fact, even three months after the term began, many teachers still did not know him; some supposed he must be a student.

Finally, most of Calvin's colleagues did not talk to him about work because they had lost all interest in it. Calvin felt that, with one exception, all the other science teachers had everything "down pat" and were not interested in teaching anymore. They were more interested in "sports or hobbies or extramarital affairs" than in the educational process.

In addition to limited and unsatisfactory contact with his colleagues, Calvin had little contact with the principal. He thought the principal was "wishy-washy," reserved, and unapproachable, keeping his distance between himself and the faculty. Thus, in general, Calvin lacked supportive, helpful interaction with older, more experienced colleagues. Isolated from both principal and co-workers, he felt very much on his own and alone during his first year of teaching.

Another source of strain for Calvin was the demanding workload. Calvin seemed to be overwhelmed by the amount of work he had, especially in the beginning. He always brought much work home with him. Also, he felt it important to become involved in extracurricular activities in order to show students that he was interested in them and to get to know them outside the classroom. He chaperoned dances, attended football games, and sponsored a team sport.

Calvin found certain aspects of the work to be particularly difficult. For him, the need to constantly make decisions in the classroom was especially demanding. He said, "You have to decide everything . . . even deciding for these kids what they should learn, what they should know . . . what they should do today." The burden of responsibility was heavy, much heavier than he had realized it would be. At one point, he summed it up by saying, "If you can't make decisions, don't teach."

Student behavior also made the work more onerous. Most frustrating for Calvin was the students' lack of interest in school. Actually, his students were more motivated than the ones he had taught in the inner-city: 60 percent were college bound and would try even if the material were difficult. But maintaining their attention, interest, and motivation was a constant battle, one that Calvin felt he lost more often than not. His students increasingly complained that class was boring; as their boredom increased they became more difficult to deal with. He believed that all of the other activities in their lives, such as extracurricular events, made it difficult for them to be interested in class. By the last interview, he complained, "The most frustrating thing to me in the job right now is that at times the students aren't as interested or as turned on by it as I am." He was seriously considering leaving teaching and going into fulltime research for this reason. He believed the ideal teaching situation was college, where it was the student's responsibility to learn, and his fault alone if he flunked, where there were no hassles from students, and it was possible to just lecture.

Despite his student-teaching experience in a "tough school," Calvin had many concerns about discipline. One student in particular was "pushing him," which meant, apparently, almost complete defiance. This student threw things, did not leave the room when Calvin told him to do so, made the other students laugh, and had once started a fire in the room. This problem was especially stressful because Calvin believed he had contributed to it by his own lack of skill. He thought he had "let things get out of hand." He was especially afraid he would get a reputation for "lacking control." He was uncertain and confused about how firm to be. On the one hand, he thought that teachers "really have to be careful" not to hit or even touch students. But if they did not find other ways to be firm, the classroom became chaotic. He admitted that he was just "feeling his way" in learning how to handle students. He said, "It's really hard for me to get down on people," and he considered this a major weakness. His critic-teacher's primary criticism, he said, was that Calvin did not "get mad enough." But Calvin complained that was just not his nature.

Calvin finally decided that he had not been firm in decisions, and by the follow-up interview he said that he had learned to be "tough" and to anticipate problems. The new approach did seem to "work," for students no longer tested him or pushed him.

Calvin was also uncertain about how friendly and informal to be with students. While he initially felt that he was having no problems relating to most students at their level outside the classroom and then having them respect him as a teacher back in the classroom, he soon admitted that it was "hard for me some-times to draw the line and get my kids to really 'snap to.'" By the follow-up interview, six months after he began teaching, he was still finding that maintain-ing the distinction between being a friend and being a teacher was difficult. He hadn't seemed to be able to cope effectively with the "big deal" some students made out of finding out his first name. On the other hand, he believed that treat-ing a student more as a person made the student more willing to work. The ques-tion of personal relationships with students proved to be a continuing source of concern.

Parents were yet another source of concern. Calvin said that he was com-pletely unprepared for the interference from parents. In the inner-city, no one ever complained about "anything." But in the predominantly middle class com-munity where Calvin took his first teaching job, he felt he had to "watch what I do." Many parents were professionals; they had the time and energy to take an active interest in their children's educations; they were comfortable in the school setting, and they were not intimidated by school teachers. The problem was made worse by the fact that Calvin was not sure that his principal would always back him up. Thus, Calvin felt vulnerable in his contacts with parents. Their constant scrutiny of his performance from a distance was another source of pres-sure and tension he had not expected.

Calvin's concern about students and parents occurred in the context of a great desire to do well in his first job. Like the other new teachers, Calvin was worried about the bad job market. He had sent out 50 applications and obtained three interviews. The other two positions were less desirable in their future pros-pects and teaching conditions, so he felt "very, very lucky to get this job." If he did not do well, he could be fired, and dozens of other unemployed teachers would be eager to take his place. Also, because there had been so much competi-tion for this job, he believed that he had to "justify" the school's selection of him. Furthermore, he was "following in the footsteps" of an outstanding teacher who reputedly had been committed, concerned about students, and able to get "every kid to work to their potential."

Calvin also seemed to suffer because of his own high, internal standards. He said he always pushed himself to "to do his best" and was hard on himself when he fell short. Thus, as in the case of most other new professionals, there were strong external and internal sources of pressure to do well in his first job.

Unfortunately, Calvin was rarely able to discern how well he was actually doing in his work. He said, "It's fairly easy to get negative feedback, but hard to get positive feedback, because when the kids are doing alright, then they're quiet." Although Calvin did receive formal evaluation and feedback on his performance three times during his first year, he found it disappointing as a measure of his progress or an aid to further growth and improvement. While he reported that the principal was pleased and gave him a few minor pointers on questioning technique that were helpful, Calvin was scornful of the areas included on the evaluation form and felt that it was of little help. On his evaluation, the principal said that he thought Calvin had improved and that he would recommend that he come back the following year. The evaluation seemed to be based on only one brief observation in one of Calvin's classes, and he had wanted much more specific feedback and advice. Calvin had asked the central office administrator in charge of the science curriculum to observe him, evidently wanting someone with expertise in his field, but he had not come yet, and Calvin sounded fairly cynical about him: "He's probably just pushing papers." Thus, in addition to the lack of informal contact with co-workers, Calvin did not receive knowledgeable or generally useful supervision from the principal. Calvin knew he needed help and made some effort to obtain it. But those who should have been the primary sources of assistance simply did not respond adequately to Calvin's initiatives.

The combination of all these factors contributed to a growing sense of alienation in Calvin. By the follow-up interview in February, he admitted, "There are days when I'm bored." The excitement of the new semester was already wearing off. He was worried that he might become more bored with work and "drop out" like so many of his colleagues. Their lack of interest, as well as the students' and principal's, made it difficult for Calvin to maintain his own interest and enthusiasm. The lack of student interest was particularly destructive because, without it, the work became tedious and dull—a "job" rather than a "calling." And as *he* lost interest, the students became even less interested and more difficult. Thus, the boredom and understimulation of teaching became part of a vicious circle from which it was difficult for Calvin to escape.

Over time, Calvin's idealism also waned. His goals and perceptions concerning students changed. He gradually abandoned what seemed to him to be the perfectionist ideal of "reaching" every student. He came to believe that student performance depended more on the student's "given ability" and less on the teacher. He also came to believe that, no matter what a teacher did, some students would not like the class and would not want to work. Initially, he had attempted to reach *all* of his students, but, by the follow-up interview, he minimized his sense of personal responsibility for student interest, ability, and performance.

As Calvin's goals became more modest, maintaining discipline and control in the classroom was increasingly seen as a sufficient end in itself. For instance, when the new class assignments were made at midyear, he found that he was "stuck" with the defiant student who had given him so much grief during the first term. However, Calvin set out to be "tough" with him and the class from the start, and the defiant, disruptive behavior stopped. The student now spent the hour in the back of the room with his head down, and Calvin could not make him do anything in class. But Calvin seemed satisfied with the situation: the student was still not participating or learning, but at least some semblance of peace and order had returned to the classroom. The elusive and difficult goal of "reaching every student" was quietly abandoned by Calvin in the struggle to maintain order and save his "reputation."

Calvin's commitment to teaching as a career also weakened during the first year. He began to reduce his intense involvement in his work, for he did not want his life to continue to center around school. And he said that he might quit teaching eventually, especially if the students "kept getting worse." He seemed more excited about the athletic team he was coaching after school than about his teaching and was looking forward to taking courses during the summer in oceanography and environmental chemistry. By the last interview, Calvin had decided to begin work on his Ph.D., a degree that would presumably be his ticket out of the public school classroom forever.

Thus, like so many new public professionals we studied, Calvin Miller experienced a difficult, frustrating, stressful first year of practice. It was a time of great effort and little reward, of bitter disillusionment and loneliness, of inescapable conflict and self-doubt. In response to this stress and strain, Calvin survived by changing what seemed to him to be the only thing he could change: his goals, his aspirations, and his commitment to students and teaching.

UNIQUE TEACHER IN A UNIQUE SETTING: ALICE HARRIS, HIGH SCHOOL TEACHER

Alice Harris was a 22-year-old art history teacher. Of all the new teachers we interviewed, hers was the most stimulating and rewarding work situation. She escaped many of the difficulties, frustrations, and pressures experienced by the typical new teacher, and her energy, enthusiasm, and self-confidence exceeded that of the others. In examining Alice's style and her work setting, one finds many factors that might have contributed to her positive experience.

First, Alice's commitment to teaching occurred earlier than most of the other teachers'. She decided during her senior year of high school, as a result of her experience with two "great teachers," that she wanted to teach, preferably an interdisciplinary course such as intellectual history. She saw teaching as a "profession," not just something to fall back on. (This contrasted with other new teachers who did not have positive "role models" or for whom teaching was really a second choice.) In college, Alice's commitment to a particular way of teaching history was reinforced. She thought there was no other way to learn history than to look at the whole culture, and she hoped to teach in a program based on this approach. Fortunately, when it came time to do her student-teaching, there was a nearby high school that had such an integrated program, so she was given a placement in which she felt "this is where I belong in terms of my own orientation."

In addition to fulfilling Alice's hopes in terms of content, the program also provided an unusual team-teaching situation. While initially Alice did not feel a part of the team, as she developed a closeness with her critic-teacher, that teacher helped her to become involved with the others. They all did things socially, so Alice did not feel like a student-teacher, and she said that at the end of her student-teaching year, "They hated to see me leave."

Alice always had lunch with the other student-teachers in her building and found that her experience was very different from theirs. While she interacted with a whole team of teachers in related but diverse fields, the other student-teachers interacted with only their critic-teachers. And they often had problems communicating with that teacher while Alice never did. "Everything was always talked out between us. I never did anything I didn't feel I should." Her critic-teacher did not push her or expect too much too soon, as the other student-teachers often felt theirs did. Alice's teacher was sensitive to her feelings and communicated her trust that eventually Alice would be very involved. As a result, when Alice did start teaching, she felt comfortable in the role.

Although Alice said that she enjoyed every minute of student-teaching, she admitted that the pressure caused her to develop a "real bad nervous condition." It disappeared as soon as she finished her student-teaching and did not reappear. Alice was the only teacher who felt she was under more stress during student-teaching than during her first year on the job.

The credit for Alice's positive student-teaching experience seemed to lie both with her placement and her own ability, not with her teaching preparation, which she termed very poor. She felt that the content of the intellectual history courses she took had been fine, but she received little usable help from her "methods" courses in education. She concluded that she needed more exposure to *high school* teachers, not college professors, more exposure to "not bright" *kids*, and more relevant discussions of problems to be encountered in the future.

Through both luck and hard work Alice obtained her first job at the same high school where she had done her student-teaching. First and probably most important, she had performed well as a student-teacher, showing she could handle discussion classes as well as large lectures. Also, she had made friends with everyone in the humanities program and "felt really a part of it." When one of the program's teachers decided to take a year's leave, he thought Alice could take his place if she spent the whole summer preparing and making up the two credits she lacked in the particular field. Without any official assurance she would get the job, Alice went ahead and took an independent study course all summer, writing lectures so she would be prepared in the fall.

Alice was fortunate in another aspect of her job. Initially, she taught only three-fifths time (at midyear, it was raised to a four-fifths appointment). This meant that she was free every other hour throughout the day and finished early. Although she prepared lectures for large groups, she had no seminar responsibilities after her lectures. She had no "lesson plans" to prepare or papers to mark every day, and, in her own words, she had "lots of time during the day to spend preparing."

The teacher who went on leave had remained in the area, and he and Alice had become very close friends. He had given Alice many of his own materials, and Alice said, "Without his basic framework I would really be lost. It's been an enormous help." This other teacher had had no help himself during his own first year, which he described as a "disaster." Alice acknowledged that she enjoyed "resources unusual for a first-year teacher" and that her experience was a "special circumstance."

As might be expected, Alice described her adjustment to her job as easy: she knew where to get materials, she knew where supplies were stored, and she knew everybody she needed to know. "I felt right at home when I started." Not only was the teacher on leave helpful, but so were all the members of her team.

Alice was the only new teacher to describe her colleagues in enthusiastic terms. "They're really great!" she exclaimed. Some were not "the best," she admitted, but they were all devoted to the course, and none were "lazy." She felt that the nature of the humanities program demanded that the teachers be close and become good friends because they had to work together so closely and cooperatively, planning the course and sharing materials. She took notes on all of their lectures to tie her own into what the students heard in the others, and she shared her materials with the other teachers to illustrate some of their points.

Lunchroom conversations among her teammates were very different from the usual teacher small talk. Alice said that they always talked about interesting intellectual issues and ideas—new books they had read, for instance—and not just trivia. As a result, she said, it was "really a learning environment . . . really fun." Later she described them as "always joking around, laughing, just having a good old time."

Not only were they fun and stimulating, she also felt they were very supportive if anyone had a bad day. "If all else goes bad, you can always count on the team to cheer you up." Furthermore, if she had any real worries about her work, she asked her team members and felt that they gave honest feedback.

The only difficult adjustment that Alice felt she had to make during the first year was "getting used to doing the three classes and not getting tired after one class. You really lose a lot of energy if you put a lot in." Learning to pace herself and "restrain" her enthusiasm was something she was doing out of necessity because she found herself losing her voice by the third lecture of the day. She said she sometimes became so excited she yelled.

Since Alice had done her student-teaching in the humanities program, the caliber of students she now had came as no surprise, but she was unique in her positive description of them, with good reason. Her course was an elective, with an established reputation for difficulty, so only bright, capable, and fairly ambitious students chose it. They were all college-bound seniors, and Alice described them as "loving" the course. "They want to know, and they're curious. They're just terrific!"

Student reaction and feedback were important to Alice. She often asked the students what they thought about a lecture. She also tried to meet students by having them come in for help, stopping to speak to them in the halls, talking to those in the front rows, and going early to lectures to greet them as they came in.

While establishing and maintaining a proper student/teacher relationship was problematic for some new teachers, for Alice it did not seem difficult. She had clearly given the matter some thought and had concluded that if she had not had a successful student-teaching experience and established good relationships with her students then as a teacher, she would have felt insecure and wanted the students' friendship now. But she felt she did not need to "compensate" by seeking friendship instead of respect. From the beginning of her student-teaching, she "felt I was doing a good job," and her 10th graders even told her, "Oh, I love you!" Although she had seniors now and was worried about the narrow age gap, she had discovered that it was not a problem.

Perhaps as a result of her insistence on maintaining a friendly and warm but distant teacher/student relationship, Alice said she had no problems with students or discipline. Sometimes they would tease or test, but she thought that she immediately and firmly put an offender in his place and found that other students were supportive, telling the offender to "shut up." She found that she could be "nasty" to a student who got out of line and the next day he would be "fine." She acknowledged that teaching in a lecture situation precluded her emotionally identifying with her students and helped her maintain the distance she wanted. Alice also had a special relationship with her principal. He had been the teacher of her critic-teacher, and he had made jokes about Alice's being "the third generation." She was looking forward to being observed by him, in fact, because he had been on the humanities team himself and was therefore more knowledgeable than someone else would have been. Alice did not like the fact that administrators were perceived by teachers as separate from them and as enemies. Unlike other new professionals, Alice perceived the limitations of administrators as residing in the *system* rather than in the individuals or their personalities, and she felt that, were she in such a position, she would not be strong enough to combat the "bureaucratic imperatives" that plagued administrators. As in other instances, Alice was unique in expressing awareness of such issues.

Although Alice was unusually satisfied and positive, there were aspects of her work situation that she could not tolerate. What aroused Alice's greatest vehemence, if not real anger, were the "awful" teachers' meetings, which she termed a complete waste of time. Interminable arguments went on about nothing, and one could not skip them because "someone would tell on you." She complained that some of the teachers she worked with were "catty." Bad teachers and older, uncommitted teachers also aroused Alice's ire. She disliked the teachers she saw in the teachers' lounge who never worked and showed filmstrips every day. Their major interest usually was coaching. She coped with her dislike by avoiding those teachers.

Although dedicated to her work, Alice tried to limit her involvement. She had been advised to leave schoolwork at school, and she considered that advice "constructive," believing that she had to "draw the limits, not spend your whole life at school." She felt that getting too wrapped up in school to the detriment of the rest of one's life was an "impulse of the new teacher," to which, if she were single, she would probably succumb. But her home commitment prevented it. Having a family was ultimately her first priority, and anything else was going to have to fit into that priority.

Overall, Alice expressed the highest level of satisfaction with her job of any of the new teachers. "If I can teach in a program like this, I'll never want to go anywhere else or teach any higher level," she said. "I don't feel a lack of anything." Although she thought there might be more work involved in the humanities program, it was more intellectually satisfying to her. She thought the economic ceiling might be a "big thing" for some of the older teachers, but it was no concern for her. She said sadly that she would truly miss some of her students when they graduated in June, a sentiment not expressed by any other teacher we interviewed.

CONCLUSION

In this chapter, we have examined in detail the experiences of four new professionals. Alice and Jean had unusually positive experiences, while Calvin and Margaret encountered much stress, frustration, and disappointment. In comparing and contrasting these four individuals and their work situations, several potentially important factors immediately stand out. First, the two "successful" novices seemed to bring more realistic attitudes to their jobs. Second, they appeared to have received better preparation; they had had certain training experiences that were more relevant and helpful. Third, their workloads were more manageable. Fourth, Alice and Jean received more support from co-workers and supervisors; they worked in a more collegial setting. Also, both the nature of the work and of their colleagues provided more intellectual stimulation than Margaret and Calvin found. Jean and Alice also worked in special programs that had unusually clear, consistent, and distinctive goals and philosophies. Finally, the two more satisfied and committed novices seemed to have found work situations that allowed them to practice as they had hoped to when they entered their professions.

In the next three chapters, we shall use these case histories as well as other materials to identify important characteristics of individuals and settings that generally seemed to influence the amount of stress and negative change that occurred. We shall be concerned with the factors that contribute to differences in the experiences of new public professionals.

9

THE WORK SETTING'S IMPACT ON BURNOUT

Although all of the new public professionals interviewed found their work situations to be difficult and, at times, frustrating, there were important differences in those situations. In fact, there was considerable variation within each professional group as well as between them. As we came to know the new professionals better and followed their trials and tribulations over time, we began to notice how certain aspects of their work settings affected their experience. Factors such as the workload, the quality of supervision, the amount of intellectual stimulation and variety, and the clarity and complexity of organizational goals seemed to vary considerably from setting to setting, and these factors strongly influenced the levels of stress, frustration, and burnout that occurred in the new professionals.

Among the many factors that influenced the early career development of new professionals, eight seemed especially important. These factors varied in the work settings of new public professionals. When they were favorable, career development was facilitated. When they were unfavorable, stress and burnout were more likely.

THE ORIENTATION PROCESS

The work setting first influenced the new public professionals through the orientation process. The public agencies we studied varied considerably in how they introduced new staff members to their work. At one extreme, there were the settings that had no formal orientation process and immediately confronted the new professional with all of the demands imposed on the most experienced workers. For instance, mental health professional Douglas Furth found a full caseload of 20 clients literally "sitting in his box" the first day of work, with a terse note written by the secretary that he could begin contacting his clients and scheduling appointments. Calvin Miller, whose history was presented in the previous chapter, learned of the textbook he would be using less than a week before school began, and he had only one day to "poke around" the lab before assuming a full load of five classes in chemistry. The transition from student to professional for these and many other individuals was sudden and abrupt, and they received little support from co-workers or supervisors in making it.

On the other hand, there was new mental health professional Diane Peterson who was eased into her new career slowly, with careful planning by her first employers. She began working in her agency on a part-time basis while finishing her last semester of school. She was assured that she would be provided with the time and the means to acquire the knowledge required for her job. During the first two months, she saw no clients; her time was totally absorbed by visits to other programs, observation of more experienced staff members at work, seminars, and reading. Gradually, as she felt more knowledgeable and competent, her responsibilities increased. Not surprisingly, she was one of the most satisfied and enthusiastic individuals seen in the follow-up interviews, experiencing little of the negative attitude change observed in other new professionals.

Another case in point was high school teacher Alice Harris, one of the subjects described in the previous chapter. She had done her student-teaching in the same school where she took her first teaching job. During student-teaching, her critic-teacher eased her into the classroom, allowing her to accept increasing responsibility and challenge at a pace that was comfortable for her. Fortuitously, she began teaching on three-fifths time basis in September. This was increased to a four-fifths time appointment at midyear. Thus, like Diane Peterson, she was eased into the role of professional gradually. In Diane's case, this "orientation process" was deliberately planned; in Alice's case, it occurred more by accident. But in both cases the results were similar: less stress, more satisfaction, and more enthusiasm for work.

There were also consistent differences between the various fields in the way orientation was handled. High school teachers typically received little orientation other than a one-day session devoted largely to instructions concerning administrative procedures. Mental health professionals, with the exception of Diane Peterson, were also provided with little formal orientation. However, only two of the seven interviewed began with a full caseload the first day. The others had some opportunity to become acclimated to their new roles as their caseloads gradually increased. The new lawyers received no formal orientation. Their introductions were similar to the mental health professionals'.

The initial period of adjustment was generally easiest for the public health nurses we interviewed. The nurses typically spent half of their time during the first two months attending lectures and demonstrations designed to familiarize them with the health department, community resources, and other aspects of their jobs. Also, they were assigned to a "field advisor" as well as a regular supervisor. The field advisor was a more experienced public health nurse, and the novices initially spent much of their time accompanying their field advisors on regular rounds. In this way, they learned the informal as well as formal aspects of their new roles. Gradually, the new nurses worked more on their own, first in the presence of the field advisor who gave continual feedback on performance, later alone. This careful orientation process was one reason that Gloria Bennet could say, "Nursing's a good profession because I've never been cut down in it. I don't mean that I've never made a mistake or I'm Supernurse, but somehow you're not just thrown up there. You have a good support system, good backing, and your confidence level is allowed to build. And it's important." Of course, even those who went through a carefully planned orientation process experienced self-doubt concerning their professional competence at times; however, their plights were not as difficult as those of professionals whose orientations were more limited.

The importance of the orientation process for new professionals is supported by an analysis that is summarized in Table 9.1. For this and the subsequent analyses presented in this chapter, two groups of subjects from the study were examined. The first was composed of the six novices who were most successful in resisting the negative changes in attitude associated with burnout. In fact, in the study by Wacker (1979) described in Appendix B, these six subjects actually developed more positive attitudes over time. The second group was composed of the eight professionals who were least successful in resisting burnout. In general, these unsuccessful novices developed the most negative attitudes toward their clients and work during the study.*

After creating these two special groups of public professionals with "positive" and "negative" attitudes, we rated the quality of the orientation received by each. If the subject had participated in a formal orientation program and had been introduced to the work in gradual increments, the orientation was rated as good. The orientation was also rated as good for three subjects who had previously worked in the same setting as students. (An example is Alice Harris who was a student-teacher at the same school where she spent her first year of teaching.) When the professional had not worked in the setting before and had immediately assumed a full workload with minimal direction or support, the orientation was rated poor.

---

*The mean change score for the six subjects who developed the most positive attitudes was +.26. The mean change score for the eight professionals who developed the most negative attitudes was -.42. The range for the sample was +.53 to -.94.

TABLE 9.1: **Quality of Orientation Process Associated with Positive and Negative Attitudes in New Public Professionals**

	Positive Attitudes	Negative Attitudes
Good Orientation	6	1
Poor Orientation	0	7

Source: Compiled by the author.

The lack of randomness in the initial sample makes the use of tests of statistical significance untenable; however, the frequencies presented in Table 9.1 are striking. All six of the successful new professionals had received good orientations to their jobs while only one of the eight novices who experienced negative attitude change had had a similar experience. Although these results certainly do not prove that good orientation generally is associated with positive career development in new public professionals, such a premise would be a credible working hypothesis.

THE WORKLOAD

Previous writing on professional burnout has cited the workload as a major contributing factor. In general, it has been found that the heavier the workload, the greater the tendency to burn out (for example, Berkeley Planning Associates, 1977; Maslach, 1976). Maslach (1976), however, suggested that longer hours by themselves did not lead to increased burnout; it is greater amounts of direct client contact that create the interpersonal strain she sees as central in the development of burnout. In fact, in a study of job satisfaction and burnout in community mental health center staffs, there was evidence suggesting that even increased client contact does not lead to more burnout when that contact is with clients who have less severe problems and are more cooperative and when there are opportunities for frequent "time-outs" from client contact (Cherniss & Egnatios, 1978a). In yet another study, Maslach and Pines (1977) found that when staff members in day care centers were assigned responsibility for supervising a specific subset of the children in the center, there was less burnout than when all staff members were jointly responsible for all children on the premises. Thus, the quality of the workload as well as the amount of work affects staff burnout in human service agencies.

The workloads of the new professionals interviewed for this study varied considerably along many dimensions. For instance, poverty lawyer Margaret Williams had an active caseload of more than 60, while reform lawyer Jean Chalmers never worked directly with more than four or five clients at a time. Not surprisingly, Jean remained more compassionate and available to her clients than did Margaret. Another poverty lawyer, Perry Curtis, thought he had more than 600 open cases. It was understandable that he became impatient with any client who might take a few extra minutes or that he said he sometimes had to "scream" and throw stacks of papers across the office in order to release the frustration. It should also be noted that while Perry and Margaret had to work with every client who came through the door, Jean and her colleagues in the reform law setting went out and carefully selected their clients, choosing only those whose cases would provide the most leverage for law reform.

The workloads of the two high school teachers described in Chapter 8 also differed in ways that probably affected their enthusiasm and commitment. As a part-time teacher, Alice Harris initially taught three classes a day instead of the usual five. Also, she taught in a special program that attracted only the brightest and most motivated, college-bound students. Calvin Miller, as well as the other new teachers, taught a more heterogenous group of students, including many who had little interest in school. Finally, unlike Calvin, Alice was not responsible for supervising a boisterous group of youths running around a laboratory full of dangerous chemicals and equipment. Thus, burnout seemed to be affected not only by the absolute quantity of clients but also by the conditions under which services were provided.

In general, there was considerable variation in the number of clients for whom professionals of the different fields were responsible. High school teachers typically taught between 120 and 150 students during a day. Poverty lawyers had caseloads as high as 600. On the other hand, three public health nurses and three mental health professionals rarely had caseloads of more than twenty-five and usually saw no more than five clients a day. For these new professionals, there was an opportunity to invest more time and effort in each individual client, and thus they were more likely to experience a sense of accomplishment in their work.

Evaluation of the workloads handled by the most successful and unsuccessful novices supports the link between heavy workloads and professional burnout. For the purpose of this analysis, a "light" workload was one in which the professional worked with, and was responsible for, fewer than 25 clients each week. The only exception was new high school teacher Alice Harris who officially worked less than fulltime during her first year of teaching and thus had more time for preparation and recuperation than the typical new teacher. Table 9.2

TABLE 9.2: Workload Demands Associated with Positive and Negative Attitudes in New Public Professionals

	Positive Attitudes	Negative Attitudes
Light Workload	5	0
Heavy Workload	1	8

Source: Compiled by the author.

shows that the novices who maintained their idealism, commitment, and compassion generally enjoyed "light" workloads: five of the six subjects in this group had light loads. On the other hand, all of the eight professionals who experienced negative attitude changes were confronted with heavy loads. For the new public professionals involved in this study, the workload was thus another factor associated with career adaptation.

INTELLECTUAL STIMULATION, CHALLENGE, AND VARIETY

In Chapter 4, we saw that, in general, new professionals in public settings were frustrated and disappointed because their work was less interesting and stimulating than they had anticipated. Although the work of all new professionals eventually came to be more routine than expected, there was considerable variation, and a few novices found work situations that were challenging and stimulating most of the time. Again, the lawyers Jean Chalmers and Margaret Williams are good examples. In reform law, the work seemed to be more varied and challenging. One was forced to work in new areas of the law, creating and developing approaches to legal problems. There was usually much intellectual stimulation in this work. However, in legal aid, most of the cases were routine matters, similar in virtually every important respect to dozens of other cases handled by the lawyer. Even if an unusual case came along, there was no time to do the thinking and research on it as there would be in the reform law setting; it was simply processed like any other case. Thus, although Margaret Williams probably used her legal knowledge and judgment more often than she knew, she eventually came to feel that most of the work she did was so routine that it could be handled by a clerk with only a high school education.

The jobs of the two high school teachers described in Chapter 8 also differed in the amount of variety and intellectual stimulation involved. Calvin Miller taught basic chemistry to students who quickly lost interest and became bored. The lack of intellectual stimulation in this kind of work was one of his major complaints about the job, and, by the end of his first year, he was thinking seriously of returning to graduate school for a Ph.D. in chemistry and a career in research. On the other hand, Alice Harris taught material on a more advanced level to a group of highly motivated students whose interest and ability constantly challenged and stimulated her. Art history is not inherently more stimulating than chemistry, but the teaching *situations* of these two new teachers did seem to differ considerably in this respect, and that difference seemed to influence their fulfillment and commitment to their work.

Table 9.3 also suggests that differences in intellectual stimulation were associated with differences in early career development. Five of the six most committed new professionals worked in jobs in which intellectual stimulation was high. Besides Jean Chalmers and Alice Harris, there was mental health professional Diane Peterson who, as a staff member in a new, experimental alcoholism program, had many opportunities for learning, teaching, and research. Professional development for herself and other mental health professionals with whom she consulted were major aspects of the job. The other examples of greater stimulation were public health nurses Gloria Bennet and Sarah Prentiss, who said they especially liked their jobs because they were able to engage in so

TABLE 9.3: Amount of Intellectual Stimulation Associated with Positive and Negative Attitudes in New Public Professionals

	Positive Attitudes	Negative Attitudes
Much Stimulation	5	0
Little Stimulation	1	8

Source: Compiled by the author.

many different areas of nursing practice and had time to read, study, and learn. None of the unsuccessful novices experienced much intellectual stimulation in their work.

SCOPE OF CLIENT CONTACT

By definition, public professionals provide services to clients. They help them to solve problems or to accomplish difficult tasks. An important dimension by which the work may differ, however, is the scope of client contact: the range of problems addressed by a professional in working with a client and the extent to which the professional sees the client in different kinds of situations. There is evidence to suggest that the scope of client contact influences the sustenance of caring and commitment in new professionals.

Maslach (1976) suggested that one cause of burnout in professionals was that they usually have only a truncated and largely negative relationship with clients. They see clients only when the clients are having problems, and they work with the clients only in the context of those problems. They do not see the clients as whole persons in all the different aspects of their lives that make them human. Frequently, as in the case of poverty law, their contacts are brief and fleeting. In classroom teaching, there is more sustained contact over time, but a particular student is only one of thirty in the classroom at any given time, and the typical high school teacher must teach five classes each day. Therefore, students rarely assume any kind of individuality for the teacher in this setting. The relationship remains limited and impersonal in most cases. When professional-client relations cover such a narrow domain of human existence, the humanity of those relationships disappears. They become cold, mechanical, and unfulfilling. When this happens, it is difficult for the professional to sustain commitment and concern.

Although the scope of professional-client relations must always be limited to public human service agencies, there was considerable variation for our subjects. Poverty lawyers and high school teachers probably had the most limited range of client contact. Not only was their contact with individual clients of brief duration, the matters they concerned themselves with were severely limited unless they expanded their roles beyond what they were supposed to be. Specifically, the poverty lawyers concerned themselves only with the legal problems of their clients, and even here they were usually concerned with only a subset of their clients' legal problems. They avoided other types of problems the clients might be having and rarely learned about aspects of their clients' lives that were satisfying, rewarding, and pleasant. For high school teachers, there was pressure to remain focused on academic concerns and avoid any discussion of the more personal, emotional aspects of their students' existences. There was always the possibility that forays into the realm of personal life would be misunderstood by the students and they would become either too familiar with the teacher or be frightened away.

Of course, not all poverty lawyers and high school teachers chose to "play the game" in this way, and this accounts for the differences within these groups in relation to client contact. Some poverty lawyers decided that part of their role was "social work" or "personal counseling" and allowed, even encouraged, their troubled and distraught clients to talk about the whole range of their problems and occasional joys. When the poverty lawyers did this, their clients—and their jobs—took on new dimensions. New sources of fulfillment became possible (as well as new sources of stress). Similarly, there were high school teachers who, with some trepidation perhaps, attempted to learn as much about their students as possible—not just their previous grades or I.Q. scores, but their family backgrounds, their aspirations, their fears, and their satisfactions. Such involvement with students or clients had its risks, and the crushing workload of most new professionals made such involvement impossible in most cases. But when they were able to successfully expand the scope of client contact, they were more likely to find meaning and fulfillment in their work. They were also more likely to maintain the sympathy for and trust in clients that they had had when they started their work. In short, they were more likely to resist burnout.

The differences in the extent of client contact were even greater across the different professional groups. As noted, for high school teachers and poverty lawyers, contact was most limited. For mental health professionals working in highly bureaucratic systems in which much time was devoted to paperwork and administrative functions or in systems in which the clientele was not voluntary, the scope of contact was somewhat wider but still limited. For instance, the range of issues a young client might discuss with a school social worker could be limited by laws requiring school social workers to report felonies committed by youths as well as by youths' distrust of authority. Mental health professionals working in smaller agencies with a voluntary clientele had a wider range of client contact, but it was still limited in that they usually met with each client only one hour a week, the meetings occurred in an office setting, and the focus tended to remain on the problematic aspects of the clients' lives. Of all the groups we studied, the public health nurses had the widest range of client contact. They saw their clients in the clients' homes; they often had contact with the clients' families; and they became involved in social, psychological, and other aspects of the clients' lives. Their focus was rarely restricted to medical matters.

Thus, the scope of client contact experienced by the new professionals differed considerably in the four professional groups we studied; and, significantly, those differences tended to be correlated with levels of stress and severity of burnout in the groups. Those groups in which the scope of client contact was greatest tended to be the ones in which stress and burnout were least severe. Table 9.4 supports this generalization; four of the six successful novices (two public health nurses, a poverty lawyer, and a mental health professional) were

TABLE 9.4: Scope of Client Contact Associated with Positive and Negative Attitudes in New Public Professionals

	Positive Attitudes	Negative Attitudes
Extensive Contact	4	1
Limited Contact	2	7

Source: Compiled by the author.

able to become aware of many different facets of their clients' lives, while only one of the eight novices who were less successful in avoiding burnout did so.

PROFESSIONAL AUTONOMY AND BUREAUCRATIC CONTROL

As described in Chapter 4, a major issue confronted by new public professionals was the unexpected infringement on their autonomy resulting from bureaucratic rules and regulations. Much to their chagrin, they were often treated as though they were small, easily replaceable cogs in a very large wheel. Also, they were frequently expected to act in ways inconsistent with their personal or professional values because bureaucratic efficiency demanded it. The new professionals often came to believe that the real client to be cared for and protected was the institution for which they worked rather than the individuals who came to them for help.

Although all new public professionals experienced this conflict between professional autonomy and bureaucratic constraint, the conflict was greater for some than for others. Bureaucratic restrictions are a fact of life in all public human service agencies, but the degree of bureaucratization varies. For instance, in a national study of child abuse programs, variation was found in perceived autonomy in the job, degree of innovation allowed, and degree of rule formalization, and these variations were correlated with degree of burnout reported by staff. In general, the more rigid and restrictive the agency, the higher the incidence of staff burnout (Berkeley Planning Associates, 1977).

The experiences of lawyers Margaret Williams and Jean Chalmers provide a good example of the wide differences in autonomy versus bureaucratic intrusion found in our sample. Although both were lawyers working in publicly funded agencies serving indigent clients, the level of bureaucratic control over the work was much greater in Margaret's situation. In fact, in the last interview we had with her, conducted about a year after she began working there, she complained bitterly about the "flak" that she and other lawyers in her office were receiving from the local community and from bureaucrats who worked in the central office "downtown." Apparently, some of these outside critics believed that the lawyers were not working hard enough and were "getting away with murder." An inspection had been ordered and an administrator from the central office was planning to make a "surprise visit" to inspect their files and records. In Margaret's situation, it was easy to regulate the work because so much of it was routine. The office processed civil disputes so similar in nature that one could estimate how long it should take an attorney to take care of any particular case. And the procedures for taking care of a case were usually so clear-cut that it was also possible to evaluate whether the attorney had done the work appropriately. But the main concern of these "bureaucrats," according to Margaret, seemed to be with efficiency: processing a certain number of cases (and clients) within a given amount of time. And it was also clear that the staff attorneys, who had no role in writing the regulations, could be "scraped" and replaced by other eager novices if they did not conform to these rigid regulations. Not surprisingly, there was growing sentiment to unionize among Margaret's colleagues.

Jean Chalmers did not experience any of these intrusions. Reform law was more complex and ambiguous than routine legal aid work. One case could occupy the time of several lawyers for several months. The numerous court appearances, the long hours of legal research, the public appearances and press conferences that were a vital part of the change process could not be catalogued, weighted, and evaluated so easily. Because the reform lawyers were breaking new ground, their work defied bureaucratic control. As long as their agency occasionally filed big suits and won some of these, they were apparently performing adequately. Even the clients were unlikely to complain because they were individuals who had already been convicted and sentenced and had given up hope of having matters reversed. These clients were more likely to feel that Jean's agency was doing them a favor, for they were approached by the agency and told that, because their cases were "special," the agency would pick up their cause and try to help them. Thus, as a reform lawyer, Jean Chalmers was more insulated from bureaucratic control than was legal aid lawyer Margaret Williams, and this further contributed to their differences in frustration, alienation, and burnout.

Significant differences in autonomy were also found in the mental health sample. Those like Nick Fisher and Mark Canner who worked in large, complex bureaucracies such as school systems or mental hospitals were more closely regulated and restricted than those who worked in smaller, more independent agencies (for instance, Douglas Furth or Diane Peterson). In the case of a school social worker, for instance, one was accountable to both the director of pupil personnel services and the principal. Classroom teachers also made demands, and, although the teacher was not above the social worker in the organizational hierarchy, the social worker had to be careful not to alienate teachers too much if he or she were to remain effective. Added to these demands and restrictions on the social worker were the usual ones emanating from the clients—both students and their parents. Thus, it was not surprising that professionals working in this situation experienced it as being "in a battle zone with bullets whizzing over my head all the time," to quote social worker Nick Fisher.

On the other hand, new social workers working in small counseling agencies, such as Douglas Furth, had only one supervisor to whom they were accountable. That person was also a social worker—a professional who tended to share the same values about professional autonomy as did the new professional. There were no other vested interests or groups within the system, such as teachers or principals, whose expectations and values differed and who could further limit one's autonomy. Also, the requirements for accountability seemed to be more lax in the small counseling agency than in the large institution, and there were fewer constraints, such as civil service regulations. This greater degree of institutional autonomy ultimately meant greater autonomy for the individual professional. In general, new mental health professionals working in these types of settings clearly enjoyed greater autonomy and freedom from bureaucratic interference than did those working in larger, more complex public systems whose very size defied understanding and individual control.

An examination of Table 9.5 reveals that the degree of autonomy in a new

TABLE 9.5: Amount of Autonomy Associated with Positive and Negative Attitudes in New Public Professionals

	Positive Attitudes	Negative Attitudes
High Autonomy	6	1
Low Autonomy	0	7

Source: Compiled by the author.

professional's job is another work setting factor associated with burnout. Only one of the eight most "burned out" novices worked in a job in which autonomy was high, while all six of the novices most resistant to burnout experienced high levels of autonomy in their work.

CLARITY AND CONSISTENCY OF INSTITUTIONAL GOALS

The goals and values of the larger institution also affected the process of adjustment in new public professionals. In some cases, the new professionals worked in complex institutions in which several different professional groups attempted to achieve many different goals simultaneously. When this was the case, problems in communication and interpersonal conflict were more common. Conflict and poor communication imposed an especially great burden for the novice, increasing his or her sense of powerlessness, isolation, and lack of fulfillment. Also, lack of consensus over goals made the achievement of a sense of competence more problematic, for no matter how competently one pursued one goal, one could always be accused of failing in achieving others.

The clarity of goals and expectations in a work setting also influenced the new professional's experience. When guidelines were unclear and policies changed from week to week, the strains associated with a weak sense of competence were greatly exacerbated for the new professional. With more experience and confidence, professionals sometimes exploited such ambiguity, using it to secure more advantageous working conditions for themselves and better service for their clients. Initially, however, greater ambiguity and conflict in goals only increased the new professional's sense of helplessness.

The importance of institutional goal clarity and consensus for professional commitment has been noted by other researchers. For instance, Reppucci (1973) argued that a clear, strong, guiding philosophy is necessary to sustain hope, commitment, and morale in any human service organization. Bucher and Stelling (1977) found that trainees in professional settings characterized by strong, clear, uniform models of practice (for example, a psychiatric residency program based solely on psychoanalytic approaches) developed stronger professional commitment and identity than did those who went through programs whose goals and approaches to practice were more diverse and vague. Further, other findings of their study suggested that the programs with greater goal clarity and consensus better supported the development of a sense of mastery in the trainees.

One of the most extensive studies of organizational behavior also suggested that institutional goal conflict and ambiguity could strongly influence a worker's satisfaction and commitment. Kahn et al. (1964) found that higher levels of role conflict and ambiguity were associated with higher stress, lower job satisfaction, and more psychological withdrawal from one's work. Organizational goals clearly influence the degree of role conflict and ambiguity that occurs in a setting, for when an organization has several different, competing goals or goals that are ambiguous, clarity and consensus in roles within the organization are likely to be affected. In other words, ambiguity and conflict in organizational goals contribute to ambiguity and conflict in organizational roles, which ultimately leads to increased stress, tension, and psychological withdrawal. Thus, for all professionals working in human service organizations and especially for novices, the clarity and degree of internal consensus regarding institutional goals seems to be another aspect of the work setting that influences professional attitudes and behavior.

The four new professionals whose stories were told in Chapter 8 provide good illustrations of how organizational goals influence the early development of the novice. Looking first at the high school teachers, Alice Harris taught in a special, interdisciplinary humanities program with several other teachers. The program was based on a strong sense of mission concerning the "interdisciplinary approach." This sense of mission was shared by all members of the team. Within their special program, the goals were clear and there was little conflict about them. All agreed that their way of teaching was the best way. On the other hand, chemistry teacher Calvin Miller was not part of a special program. He and the other new teachers we interviewed were simply part of a high school setting characterized by the weaker, more general, and more amorphous goals of public education. There was little consensus among the teachers in Calvin's school concerning their educational goals, and the conflict was even greater if one considered the views of administrators, students, parents, and other members of the community. Calvin was not supported and guided by the clear, consistent sense of purpose that was a central part of Alice Harris' work setting.

There was a similar difference in the institutional goals of the work settings for the two lawyers we studied. In Jean Chalmers' reform law agency, the single, clearly defined goal was to use the law as a vehicle for social and institutional change. Not surprisingly, it was a goal shared by all who worked there; when a program's goals are clear and focused, those who might not share those goals tend to select themselves out; they are not likely to even take a job there. Thus, the members of programs like Jean's tend to be more homogenous in their commitment to program goals, and there is little goal conflict. But the situation is very different in programs such as Margaret Williams' legal aid agency. In her program, there were multiple goals being served by the agency: for some, social and institutional change was a major goal of that agency; for others, service to needy individuals was the agency's primary reason for being; for still others, the agency provided a stepping stone, making it possible to acquire trial experience and develop valuable contacts in the local bar before striking out on their own. For Margaret, at least in the beginning, the first goal was most important. But many of her colleagues were pursuing the other goals, and there was not the same clear, unified sense of purpose in the agency that was found in Jean Chalmers' reform law setting. For these new professionals and the others we interviewed, the degree of conflict and ambiguity concerning their work settings' goals seemed to strongly influence fulfillment, satisfaction, and commitment during the first period of their careers.

TABLE 9.6: Clarity and Consistency of Work Setting Goals Associated with Positive and Negative Attitudes in New Public Professionals

	Positive Attitudes	Negative Attitudes
Clear and Consistent Goals	5	0
Unclear and/or Inconsistent Goals	1	8

Source: Compiled by the author.

The data in Table 9.6 present a congruent picture: institutional goals were clear in five of the six most successful novices, while goal conflict and ambiguity were relatively high in the work settings of all eight of the novices who experienced negative attitude changes. These eight professionals all worked in especially large public bureaucracies, such as legal aid programs, school systems, and mental institutions, where various competing groups within the institution contributed to high levels of conflict and ambiguity in goals and role expectations. They also tended to work in jobs within those institutions in which conflict was particularly high. (For instance, program goals for new teachers tend to be less ambiguous and conflicted than are those for school social workers and psychologists who work in the same institution.) Once again, a factor that varied in the work settings of new professionals was associated with differences in early career development.

LEADERSHIP AND SUPERVISION

From the beginning of our study, we expected that supervision would be a decisive factor for new professionals working in public human service agencies. For the older, more experienced professional, supervision may be less critical, but for the novice who has not yet consolidated the learning of basic skills and for whom the crisis of competence is a paramount facet of the work experience, supervision can be a major source of support or, conversely, a major source of frustration and disappointment.

Previous research on burnout and motivation in work setting has tended to confirm the critical role of supervision and leadership. In one of the earliest field studies of stress and morale—a study of combat units conducted during World War II—Grinker and Spiegel (1945) observed that group cohesion was necessary for sustained motivation and commitment in difficult and threatening situations and that group cohesion was primarily affected by leadership. Qualities of the effective leader, according to Grinker and Spiegel, included technical competence, an insistence on superior performance, impartiality in administering rewards and punishments, and a continuing concern with the "creature comforts" of subordinates. Strong, decisive leaders who epitomized the behaviors desired for the group were also effective in maintaining high levels of group cohesion and individual persistence in combat units.

These qualities of supervision and leadership associated with high morale and commitment have emerged from other studies as well. For instance, an early paper on burnout in human services cited "loss of charisma of the leader" as a common antecedent of increased burnout in staff (Freudenberger, 1975). A study of burnout in staff of federally funded child abuse agencies found that, of all the aspects of the work setting correlated with burnout, leadership was the most significant (Berkeley Planning Associates, 1977). Specifically, it was found that supervisors or agency directors who provided both structure and support for staff were least likely to have staff burn out. A similar finding emerged from a study of early career development in priests by Hall and Schneider (1973), who found that an open and trusting relationship between supervisor (pastor) and priest was an important prerequisite for continuing high morale and commitment throughout the priest's career in the church. Technical competence of the pastor also seemed to be important. In yet another study, Pearlin (1967) found that degree of alienation in hospital nurses was associated with the physical visibility and accessibility of their superiors and the ways in which superiors typically gave orders: superiors who were considerate and rational were less likely to have alienated subordinates than those who were more authoritarian. Thus, previous research on morale, motivation, and commitment in the work setting suggests that supervision and leadership is decisive and that technical competence, support, consideration, respect, and the provision of structure are qualities of supervisors and leaders associated with higher levels of motivation and commitment in workers.

Although the quality of supervision seems to be important in most work settings, it is especially critical for new professionals working in human service organizations. As Cherniss and Egnatios (1978c) pointed out, supervision in human service agencies differs from supervision in industrial settings in that professional development is a major focus. Supervisors not only monitor and correct subordinates' work in the interests of administrative control. They also attempt to facilitate the subordinates' professional development.

For the new public professionals we interviewed, supervision thus was an important factor in their efforts to achieve a sense of competence. Supervision aided the development of competence in several ways. First, supervisors could provide technical suggestions and advice that increased the new professionals' effectiveness. Second, supervisors could aid the development of competence by providing feedback to the new professionals on their performance. Positive feedback confirmed the individual and alleviated some of the anxiety concerning competence. Negative feedback, when provided sensitively and constructively, helped the new professional identify weaknesses, correct them, and thus develop greater competence and skill. Third, when supervisors were readily available for consultation, the new professionals felt less alone; the burden of responsibility was eased and the fear of harming others through clumsiness and ineptitude decreased. Finally, the supervisor could provide a point of reference. As one new mental health professional put it, he felt more competent when he and his supervisor saw a case in the same way and arrived at the same conclusions concerning treatment.

Unfortunately, the quality of supervision varied widely for the new professionals we interviewed. High school teachers and poverty lawyers did not receive regular supervision with a focus on professional development. Their supervision was largely administrative and negative: as long as they did not "make waves" and stayed out of trouble, their supervisors left them alone, except to communicate administrative directives. Some of the mental health professionals and public health nurses were more fortunate. They met at least once each week with supervisors who were familiar with their cases and provided consultation and feedback on professional issues. For instance, Douglas Furth, the new mental health professional working in a family counseling agency, described his supervision:

> I have seen a number of individuals who were in the process of getting divorced, and I haven't worked much with that in the past. And that's what I had questions about. So my supervisor and I were talking about that, and she knew how to look at the issues. . . . One of these clients just seemed to—I wondered why she even came in because she didn't respond to anything I did. So I talked about the case with my supervisor, wondering what to do there, wondering what approach to take when someone is just not responding to anything you say. So my supervisor told me some background about some issues that this woman was probably facing now, about how she probably feels about men. And here I am, a man, and I'm encouraging her to tell her feelings; and before, when she did, she probably got blasted by her husband, and things like that. That was

one area my supervisor helped me with. It was very useful for me to have that talk because, when I saw the client again, having that talk helped me to go much further and be much better with her. I really appreciated that.

Douglas met weekly with his supervisor. During their hour-long sessions, he would present issues with which he was having difficulty and his supervisor would usually be able to provide information and advice that helped him to work more effectively. As the excerpt suggests, this consultation often helped to allay Douglas' anxiety about his effectiveness by providing a frame of reference, and it contributed much to his learning, growth, and competence. However, when new professionals did not meet regularly with their supervisors, when the supervisors' role was limited to administrative control and neglected professional development, or when the supervisor lacked the ability and competence that Douglas' supervisor seemed to have, supervision did little to alleviate the crisis of competence.

These ideas concerning the importance of good supervision for new public professionals are apparent in the four professionals whose experiences we have been examining in detail. For the two lawyers, supervision and leadership in the agency seemed to be very different. Margaret Williams complained about her "boss" and his lack of help. She had hoped to work under someone who would be more experienced and knowledgeable than she, someone from whom she could learn and develop a sense of competence. She was disappointed to find herself working with a supervisor who lacked experience and seemed to be just as ignorant about many areas of the law as she. Also, his administrative leadership was weak and ineffectual. Margaret believed that when the office was criticized by people "downtown," her boss should have been a better buffer between the staff and these outsiders who were interfering with their work. She also complained that, because of his lax leadership, the office was disorganized and there were frequent conflicts among staff members concerning their respective roles and responsibilities. Margaret averred that, if her boss had been stronger and more effective, such disputes would never arise.

Reform lawyer Jean Chalmers had a very different experience with her supervisor. Her comments made it clear that she had great respect for him. Like the effective combat leaders in Grinker and Spiegel's early study (1945), he seemed to epitomize the most admirable qualities of a reform lawyer. He had years of experience in reform law and was knowledgeable and effective. He was good enough, Jean believed, to be a successful lawyer in private, corporate, or government law, but he chose instead to accept the relatively low pay and arduous working conditions of reform law because of his strong social conscience. Despite a large family to support, he continued to work in reform law and had done so for many years when Jean joined his staff. Furthermore, he seemed to take a strong interest in the work and professional development of Jean and the other attorneys working under him. He was constantly available to answer questions and offer suggestions, yet allowed Jean as much autonomy as she wished, treating her as a competent colleague rather than an inept underling. He also seemed to be sensitive to and concerned about the interpersonal climate in the office and helped Jean deal with the misunderstandings and friction that occasionally occurred between her and a co-worker. In short, Jean benefitted from a competent, admirable, supportive supervisor who gave her autonomy when she needed it and helpful guidance when she needed that. His interest and support helped her to get over the difficult times that occurred in the work of all the new public professionals and, thus, helped her sustain the commitment and enthusiasm so often lost during the initial part of a professional's career.

The differences in the quality of supervision provided the two high school teachers were not as great. All of the new high school teachers had weak, almost nonexistent supervision. Theirs was the only professional group that uniformly failed to provide supportive, involved supervision for novices. The new teachers were surprised that they saw their principals so infrequently. When they did see their principals, they rarely received help, advice, encouragement, or even constructive criticism. The only time they saw the principal without seeking him or her out was during one of their two formal evaluations when the principal came into their classroom to observe. Even then, they rarely received much in the way of useful feedback or suggestions for improvement from the principal. In teaching, the assumption seemed to be that, once novices complete the eight weeks of required practice teaching, they are "on their own" and, if support or consultation from someone else is needed, there is "something wrong" with the new teacher.

Alice Harris and Calvin Miller were not too different from this standard pattern. However, in Alice's case, there were some fortuitous factors that made the situation better. First, she taught at the same school where she had done her practice teaching; thus, her "critic teacher," who had provided unusually sensitive and helpful supervision to her the year before, was still available and could offer continuing advice and encouragement. Second, the team-teaching situation gave Alice unusual opportunities to receive help, guidance, and sympathetic support from several older, more experienced colleagues. Third, the teacher whom she replaced remained in the community and met with Alice many times to provide material and guidance. Finally, because Alice's principal had trained her critic-teacher and had himself taught in the interdisciplinary program at one time, he had a somewhat greater familiarity with and interest in Alice's work than was usually the case. Thus, although supportive supervision was not much more available to Alice Harris than it was to the other new teachers, there were several factors in her work situation that compensated for this and helped sustain her interest and involvement in her work.

Table 9.7 indicates that for the new professionals involved in this study supportive, yet nonintrusive, supervision was associated with positive career

TABLE 9.7: Quality of Supervision Associated with Positive and Negative Attitudes in New Public Professionals

	Positive Attitudes	Negative Attitudes
Good Supervision	4	0
Poor Supervision	2	8

Source: Compiled by the author.

development. None of the eight unsuccessful novices had supportive supervision. Either their supervisors were "never around unless there's a problem" or they were critical, overbearing, and/or "incompetent." On the other hand, four of the six successful novices spoke favorably of the emotional support and technical help they received from their supervisors.

PROFESSIONAL ISOLATION AND SOCIAL ATMOSPHERE

Availability of co-workers was another factor that strongly influenced the quality of the novice professionals' experiences. In fact, weak supervision could be compensated for by co-workers who were available, interested, competent, and sympathetic. However, in many cases, co-workers were neither psychologically nor physically available. For instance, high school teachers were usually confined to their classrooms for most of the day; the structure of their work setting ensured a high level of isolation and loneliness. Similarly, public health nurses spent much of each day driving alone from one home or school to another, rarely coming in contact with colleagues.

In addition to physical factors, the isolation and loneliness of the new professional was also influenced by the social attitudes of the individual and the other staff members. As noted in Chapter 5, a major source of divisiveness among professional staff in human service agencies is differences in outlook and belief. For instance, new public health nurses were conscious of more conservative attitudes toward sexuality held by some of the older nurses with whom they worked: they found it difficult to become close, friendly, and collegial with another nurse who believed that women who contracted venereal disease were "cheap" and "irresponsible." Their different moral outlooks became a barrier to collegiality. In the mental health group, colleagues often formed into divisive cliques within an agency on the basis of their treatment philosophies: psycho-analytically-oriented staff were in one "camp" the transactional analysis people were in another, and so on. In the high school teachers, different attitudes toward students and work seemed important: several of the new teachers we interviewed were appalled by older colleagues who seemed to actively dislike students (referring to them in at least one case as "the manure heap") or who were minimally invested in their work and seemed more interested in the after-school teams they coached or their weekend camping trips. Although the novices may have remained civil toward these colleagues whose attitudes they found so objectionable, they tried to avoid them as much as possible.

A similar situation occurred in the case of poverty lawyer Margaret Williams. She disliked her colleagues and had little to do with them, in part because she thought they were more interested in furthering their own careers than in helping clients or effecting social change. For her, poverty law was part of a social movement, and she could not become very collegial with other poverty lawyers who did not share this orientation to work. On the other hand, the lawyers working in Jean Chalmers' reform law agency were similar in commitment to work, career orientation, and social ideology. They were all progressive in their political beliefs, saw law as a vehicle for effecting change consistent with those beliefs, and shared a strong commitment to their work and the plight of the clients whom they represented. This homogeneity in attitude seemed to facilitate cooperation, support, and collegiality among staff members, which was an important factor in Jean's early struggles to become a full-fledged professional. Thus, in every field we studied, there were important differences in attitude and belief among staff members that affected the degree to which colleagues helped and supported one another when their work became difficult.

There were probably other factors that affected the social atmosphere of the work settings we studied; whatever the causes, though, every work setting seemed to have a distinct social atmosphere that greatly affected the degree of isolation or support experienced by the new professional. For instance, some agencies seemed to be warm, friendly, informal places to work. Staff members tended to be relaxed, cooperative, and supportive toward one another. New staff members were made to feel welcome, and everyone took an interest in the welfare of the new person. In this social atmosphere, the new professional felt much less isolated and the strain associated with newness was greatly reduced.

At the other extreme were agencies in which the atmosphere seemed to be cold, formal, tense, and competitive. Staff members tended to keep to themselves or stayed with a small clique antagonistic to all who did not belong. Jealousy and competitiveness seemed to reach pathological extremes. New staff were ignored, resented, or ostracized. Interactions among staff members, on the few occasions they were unavoidable, tended to be cold, reserved, and formal. When informal conversation occurred, usually within a clique, gossip and biting sarcasm at others' expense tended to dominate. In this type of setting, the isolation and anxiety experienced by the new professional was at its highest. Although most settings would probably be placed somewhere between these extremes, whatever the social climate of one's work setting, it seemed to influence the process of coping and change in new professionals.

TABLE 9.8: Degree of Social Isolation Associated with Positive and Negative Attitudes in New Public Professionals

	Positive Attitudes	Negative Attitudes
Low Isolation	4	0
High Isolation	2	8

Source: Compiled by the author.

Table 9.8 presents the data concerning isolation from co-workers. Four of the six successful novices worked in settings where there was much social interaction and support among co-workers (Jean Chalmers and Alice Harris were two of these four). For the professionals who experienced negative changes, isolation was the rule without exception. Thus, like orientation, autonomy, intellectual stimulation, and the other work setting factors we have considered, isolation from colleagues was associated with negative career outcomes in the new public professionals we studied.

THE INTERDEPENDENCE
OF WORK SETTING FACTORS

In concluding our discussion of variation in the work setting and its impact on new professionals, it should be noted that the factors we have discussed separately are usually interdependent. Work settings that were more supportive and less stressful on one dimension tended to be positive on many of the other dimensions as well. For instance, the jobs in smaller, less bureaucratic institutions tended to be characterized by smaller caseloads and more autonomy and variety. There also tended to be less conflict and ambiguity in goals and expectations, more active and considerate supervision, and a more positive and friendly social atmosphere. Although one factor (for instance, average caseload) may have been the "single cause" that determined all the other factors, it would be impossible to argue convincingly that this was true. For instance, in a large study of burnout in child abuse agencies (Berkeley Planning Associates, 1977), it was found that, although caseload size was correlated with degree of burnout, relatively large increases in caseload were necessary before any significant increase in the incidence of burnout occurred. This particular study found that leadership style was the factor most strongly associated with incidence of burnout (based on statistical analytic techniques applied to the data). But even leadership was only one of several factors that influenced staff burnout in agencies; other factors, as we have seen, could compensate for bad leadership or undermine good leadership. Also, as noted in the discussion of leadership and supervision, this aspect of a work setting is itself influenced by many other factors, such as the leader's attitudes and skill and role demands impinging on the leader from external factors.

Furthermore, there were often exceptions to the general rule. For instance, the social climate among staff members in large, bureaucratic institutions was sometimes warm and friendly, though the opposite was more often true. Similarly, there were small, homogenous agencies with relatively light workloads but with social climates characterized by considerable tension and competition. In any given work setting, the constellation of all these factors seemed to interact in complex ways, combining to form a unique *gestalt* that influenced the initial experience and career development of new public professionals.

Although the structure of the work setting seems to play a decisive role in the early career development of public professionals, individual outlooks and life situations of the professionals can also be important. In perusing the tables presented in this chapter, one can see that there are often certain "exceptions to the rule." For instance, Table 9.2 shows that the novices who remained committed generally enjoyed lighter workloads; however, there was one individual who remained committed while carrying a heavy load. Similarly, Table 9.1 shows that there was a new professional who seemed to "burn out" despite receiving a relatively good orientation to work. To explain these deviations from the norm, one must consider what the individual brings to the job. While there are probably many characteristics of our subjects that influenced their adaptations, especially important seemed to be their life situations outside of work and their personal goals, needs, and preferences concerning their careers.

10

THE RELATIONSHIP BETWEEN "WORK LIFE" AND "PERSONAL LIFE"

Although we often think of "work life" and "personal life" as representing separate worlds and often strive to keep them separate, in reality the two are always intertwined. For the professional especially, the psychological interdependency between one's personal and work lives is probably inescapable. In our study, we found that differences in the new professionals' life situations outside of work seemed to influence their career development in significant ways. As one novice put it, "When I have trouble with my job, I have trouble with my personal life, and when I have trouble with my personal life, I can't do any work." The opposite also was true: positive work experience seemed to have a positive effect on the quality of life outside of work, and stable, supportive, fulfilling commitments in one's personal life could help the novice professional better cope with the work situation. Thus, there was usually a strong interaction between the new public professionals' work lives and personal lives, and the nature of that interaction seemed to be associated with differences in career development and burnout.

THE IMPACT OF PERSONAL LIFE ON WORK LIFE

As a rule, those who had a significant, rewarding life commitment outside of work seemed less psychologically dependent on work and better able to cope with strain. The non-work commitment could be a satisfying, enduring relationship with another person, a family that provided pleasure and fulfillment independent of what happened at work, or even a meaningful hobby or community activity.

These commitments seemed to serve at least two potential psychological functions for the new professional. First, they could provide *additional psychological resources and support for coping with work-related strain.* For instance, a new teacher who was married could talk about the day's problems when he returned home, and his wife could offer support, encouragement, and even concrete advice. A new psychotherapist who was taking a class or participating in a sensitivity group in the evening could discover some valuable new techniques or approaches to use with difficult clients. A new lawyer could "work off" some of the anger and frustration generated by the job in her weekly karate class.

A specific example occurred in the life situation of Calvin Miller, the new chemistry teacher who, as we saw in Chapter 8, experienced considerable stress, frustation, and isolation from professional colleagues in his work. Fortunately, Calvin became involved in a local church and met an older, more experienced teacher there. Although this other teacher taught a different subject in a different school, he had worked with new teachers before and was sensitive to their anxieties and concerns. Calvin found that he could talk to him about his problems when they met at church, and, unlike his colleagues at school, this teacher responded with sympathy and helpful advice. Much to his surprise, Calvin's church work provided a source of emotional and technical support to help him better cope with his job. Although this outside support did not completely eliminate the stress and strain, it helped alleviate some of it.

Rewarding outside commitments and activities could also help the novice better adapt to the job by providing *alternative sources of affirmation and fulfillment.* When one's job was the only vehicle for achieving a sense of meaning, growth, and self-esteem in life, frustrations and dissatisfactions in work were especially threatening to one's psychic equilibrium. When, on the other hand, one had non-work commitments in which one felt successful, these could provide a sense of self-worth that might be missing at work. For instance, if a new lawyer was also a mother who felt she had been and could continue to be successful in this role, she would probably be less personally threatened and disturbed by the sense of professional inadequacy that often occurs early in one's career (see Chapter 2). Of course, she would not be indifferent to failures at work; unresolved questions about her professional competence would clearly be a source of distress. However, she could more easily separate her ultimate evaluation of self-worth from her performance at work if she could use other significant roles in her life as a basis for judgment.

However, if role commitments and activities outside of work could help ease the strain of work for new public professionals, they could also make the strain worse. Disruptions, difficulties, and traumas that occurred in one's "personal life" could adversely affect the novice's attempt to adapt to the work situation. For as stress increased outside of work, it seemed to consume valuable coping resources, making efforts to cope with work-related stress even more difficult.

Calvin Miller again offered a vivid example. When he began teaching, he had just moved from a distant community. He was new to town, completely disoriented. When he moved into his new apartment, less than a week before school started, he had no furniture and the carpet was still wet from being shampooed. He had to spend the first night sleeping in the bathroom on a borrowed cot with the windows open, a fan running, and the air conditioning on full blast so he wouldn't be overcome by the fumes from the shampoo. Needless to say, he was not as calm and "together" as he might have been when he met his classes for the first time. At the very beginning, when it was most crucial to be calm, confident, well-organized, and prepared, the turmoil in Calvin's life outside of work made it difficult for him to be so.

On the other hand, high school teacher Alice Harris was nicely settled in her personal life when school began. She had lived in the same place for at least a year, she and her husband were familiar with the community, their household was established and running smoothly, and they had friends and outside interests. For them, Alice's new job was the only major source of change, uncertainty, and possible turmoil in their lives. Because the overall level of change and stress for Alice was less, she had more emotional resources available for coping with the great demands that would soon be placed on her at work.

Thus, the individual's personal circumstances could have an important effect on work. Satisfying commitments and activities outside of the job could foster positive career development by providing alternative sources of affirmation and fulfillment. Direct support for coping with work-related stress could also come from outside of the job. However, strain in these external role commitments and activities could compete with work, adding to the burdens new professionals faced at this point in their careers.

THE IMPACT OF WORK LIFE ON PERSONAL LIFE

The interaction between personal life and work life is a reciprocal one: new professionals often reported that the strains of work could not be left at work, that they often seemed to adversely affect outside activities and relationships. More than one individual we interviewed felt that an important relationship with another person had ended in part because of the stresses generated by work. Many others reported that, although their marriages or love relationships were intact, the strains of work were clearly contributing to strain at home.

The Time-Bind Problem

For virtually every new public professional, work made heavy emotional and time demands at this stage of the career. Consequently, it was impossible to prevent one's work life from intruding on one's personal life. Managing the demands of work roles and other life roles in itself became a major source of stress and strain for many new public professionals, another facet of the career for which few had been prepared.

The competition between work life and personal life primarily became focused around the issue of *time*; the "time-bind problem" was a typical predicament of the new professional. Concerned about measuring up, so often feeling inadequate, the novice tended to devote more time to his or her work during this stage of the career. Not only did the novice tend to spend more time at work and bring work home, but, even when not actually "working," the novice was likely to be thinking and worrying about work. As Calvin Miller said, one can't "leave" the work at school because of the pressures and responsibilities. "You're involved with it, you take the job home with you, you live the job, really. It's not like other 9 to 5 jobs; like if you're working on the assembly line, no matter how monotonous that gets, when you punch out, you punch out. Here, it's just a constant involvement."

For some new professionals, life during this period became totally work-centered: they had virtually no outside interests. This was true for Calvin Miller. And, like most in this situation, he increasingly felt uncomfortable with how he allocated his time. It bothered him that he had virtually no life outside work. He was living in a new community, a university town rich with cultural, educational, and recreational opportunities of which he had not been able to take advantage. He had no friends, and his intense absorption in work made it difficult to make friends. Also, devoting so much time, effort, and thinking to the job was tiring; there was little variety in his life. He woke up, went to school, came home, prepared for classes, ate alone, prepared for classes, and went to bed. This pattern was repeated day after day. The sameness of his life was extremely wearing. And when work was full of frustration, there were no alternative sources of gratification to which Calvin and others in his situation could turn.

On the other hand, someone like Calvin was spared the problem of managing competition between different interests. Clinical social worker Sherman Reynolds was married and had many outside interests and hobbies. Also, his wife was a student and they shared the housework. For him, the time-bind was especially severe. The dilemma was, "How do I find the time for an absorbing job, my hobbies, my wife, and my share of the housework?" Sherman was at home so little, especially compared to the previous period of his life when he was a student, and when he was at home he was usually so tired and mentally preoccupied that it was hard to even keep up with the housework. His other interests became almost totally eclipsed. His wife came to resent his absence, an absence that could be mental even when not physical, and he, too, began to resent the conflicts and strains such a demanding job created.

When the heavy emotional demands of work made the new professionals less accessible to significant others in their lives, strains in those relationships could increase the conflict and stress experienced by the novice during this period. For instance, Sherman Reynolds admitted that he and his wife had a difficult time at first because he would come home from work in the evening and just want to be left alone for a while. He did not want to talk about anything, especially his work. Piotrkowski (1979), in a study of the impact of work on the family, found that this need to be alone, free of any outside demands, was a common pattern in workers whose jobs were difficult, frustrating, or especially demanding. The situation was especially difficult for Sherman because his wife was a student in the same field, and she was interested in his work. She wanted to talk to him about it when he came home, and also wanted to talk about her own, very much related, activities and experiences of the day. She became frustrated by his inaccessibility and often took it personally. She thought he was responding to something in her, not realizing that it was simply the demands of his job. In this case, Sherman reported that matters improved when his wife became more involved in her field-work and came to realize how demanding the work was. She then understood the need to be inaccessible for a time when first coming home at the end of the day.

The outcome was less positive in the case of poverty lawyer Shana Phillips. When she passed the bar and took her first job working in a poverty law agency in which the work demands were extremely heavy, she was living with a man who had also been a law student but who was not then engaged in a demanding job. In fact, shortly after she began her job, he quit his and was not working at all. She described with great candor how her work affected the relationship:

> We have pretty different outlooks on life: he's more into taking things slow and easy and enjoying himself and I'm more serious about my career. . . . He felt very threatened because of our different outlooks. Also, he was threatened by the job because it was a real time-consuming thing. He'd resent the fact that I wouldn't want to spend a couple of hours in bed in the morning, that I had to get up and go somewhere. He would just resent the time that I was putting into the job. . . . One thing that I think makes it more difficult for a male lover to accept is that I am so busy and oftentimes I can't spend the time that the other person wants to spend. If whatever they're doing in terms of their job isn't as time-demanding as mine is, it turns out that the time that we spend together is because I'm free; it revolves around my schedule and that's a valid criticism that Hank has had and that other men have had.

Not surprisingly, this relationship had broken up twice during the first four months since she began her job. And, on yet another occasion, she gave him money to take a vacation without her so that they both could have a "breathing spell."

These findings concerning the problems of time-binds between work, leisure, and personal relationships outside of work are consistent with those that emerge from a study by Mechanic (1962). In his study of graduate students facing difficult and important qualifying exams, he found that students who coped best tended to be married but childless, with the spouse also involved in school or having a satisfying job. In this situation, the outside demands and expectations for both members of the couple were congruent; thus, strains, conflict, misunderstandings, and the attendant guilt were not as great.

In addition to making one less accessible to significant others, time-binds can also lead to changes in one's interpersonal style. As an individual frequently tries to keep everything balanced, mood and behavior may change in ways that further strain personal relationships. As Shana Phillips indicated, the demands of work forced her to become regimented and controlled virtually all of the time. Even her leisure had to be carefully planned and organized so that it fit into the complex scheme of things. Spontaneity virtually disappeared:

> It really regimented me. I used to be pretty loose. In undergrad I partied a lot, but law school was like going through basic training for the Marine Corps or something. I really got regimented to leading a particular kind of life: up early, at school all day, then work and study, and not a lot of time to play. So when I wanted to relax, I'd just get loaded real fast just to unwind because I was really tense, and then I'd get loaded and pass out or something, so I couldn't really enjoy it. The first year of school was pretty bizarre.

Unfortunately, this pattern repeated when Shana finished law school and began working in her first professional job. The pressures and demands of work were once again intense, and once again her behavioral style changed as she became controlled, rigid, and brittle in her attempt to fit everything in. Ironically, leisure became just one more "need" or "demand" that had to be squeezed in and completed as quickly as possible so that it would not interfere with other commitments.

Thus, whether a new professional had relationships and interests outside of the job, the demands of work at this stage of the career created time-binds that adversely affected life outside of work. When work demands were excessive, the individual became depleted. Outside activities and commitments that could have been alternative sources of fulfillment became additional demands, competing for the overwhelmed novice's time and attention.

**Conflicting Goals and Commitments
in Personal Relationships**

Unfortunately, time-binds were not the only way in which the demanding work situations of new public professionals could strain personal relations outside of work. When the novices became full-fledged professionals, they had "careers" to which they felt both a personal and moral commitment. Spouses or friends might feel threatened by this new "competition," and the real or imagined conflict in loyalties could increase strain in a relationship. Becoming a new professional also marked a change in status for the novice, and this, too, could be a threat for an insecure spouse or friend. Again, the best example of this potential problem came from our interviews with poverty lawyer Shana Phillips. As noted, she was living with another law school graduate when she passed the bar and took her first professional job. He did not pass the bar, and that fact put a great strain on the relationship. As she put it:

> That didn't make his ego feel very good. I started feeling guilty for making it; he started resenting me for making it; and it's been a continuing problem since then. . . . I had money because I was working, and he didn't. And then there would be a certain amount of resentment on my part that he wasn't working because he could have gotten a job, and he would resent me having expectations for him. It was just kind of a circular thing. . . .
> [Interviewer: "It seems that without that support, that could be another draining factor on you as much as sometimes the job might be."]
> It was. I mean, it really was. I'm at a point now where I've asked him to leave . . . because it was just too difficult for us both being here. He took the bar in February and flunked it and didn't make it over on appeals. He's studying for the bar again and I finally just told him, "I don't want us to be together because it's too easy for you to use me as an excuse to get angry. Then you'll blow off your bar.". . . He's really got to pass it this time. If he flunks it twice, I don't know if he'll ever be able to deal with it and pass and practice law.

A similar situation occurred with another couple: both were lawyers, both were seriously committed to their careers. One person wanted to start a private practice in a distant community; the other (one of our research subjects) was working in a poverty law agency and wanted to remain there for at least two more years. As dual career, professional couples become more common in this society, such career conflicts are likely to increase. When one or both members of the couple are new professionals working in public institutions, the conflict becomes just one more that must be confronted during a difficult period in one's life.

To summarize, it seems clear that work lives and personal lives are inextricably connected for new public professionals. Like the blue collar workers studied by Piotrkowski (1979), these professionals simply could not maintain the impermeable boundaries between job and home that many increasingly sought. Like it or not, stresses, strains, and demands at work "spilled over," profoundly affecting relationships and activities outside of work. Similarly, stress at home made career adaptation and development even more problematic.

On the other hand, positive and stable relationships outside of work seemed to facilitate the coping process. Also, satisfying activities and commitments outside of work could provide an alternative source of fulfillment when fulfillment at work was rare. Whether the relationship between work life and personal life was ultimately positive or negative, however, such a relationship existed and strongly influenced the course of professional development at this stage of the career.

11

CAREER ORIENTATION AND PROFESSIONAL DEVELOPMENT IN THE NOVICE

In general, new professionals in public human service agencies share a common set of experiences and are similarly affected by variations in the work setting. For instance, most experience the strains associated with professional-client relations, which were described in Chapter 3. All must come to terms with the crisis of competence. Most respond negatively to a heavy caseload or poor supervision. In fact, we were impressed with how similar the strains, reactions, and personal changes were in different individuals engaged in different types of professional work. Nevertheless, there were clearly differences in individuals that influenced their responses to the first months of professional work. In addition to variations in personal circumstances at the time they began work (see Chapter 10), they also brought to their jobs differences in previous experience and in formal training, which resulted in different outlooks, values, and goals. Especially important was the divergence in their career-related goals and aspirations. Put simply, the various new professionals sought different kinds of rewards from their work. Work and career had different meanings for different people. These distinctions in *career orientation* seemed to be another factor influencing professional development and burnout at this point in the career.

THE CONCEPT OF CAREER ORIENTATION

Essentially, career orientation refers to the meaning of work for the individual. It includes an individual's short-term and long-term goals and values for his or her career. What does one want from one's present job? Why was that job chosen over others? What aspects of the job are most important for satisfaction and fulfillment? What are one's aspirations for the future? To what extent does one expect work to be the central life interest? These are some of the questions that define one's career orientation.

The concept of career orientation has been employed by other writers to further understand the work experience. Porter, Lawler, and Hackman (1975) suggested that all workers want certain things from their current jobs and have goals for the future, which they want their present work situation to help realize. However, while organizations provide opportunities to fulfill these goals, they also make demands on individuals and can impede or limit the attainment of career goals. Thus, an individual's attitudes toward work will be influenced by the congruence between the career opportunities offered by the organization and the individual's own career objectives. For instance, a mental health professional who is interested in doing child therapy will be dissatisfied in a program in which opportunities for such work are very limited and assigned on a rotating basis rather than by interest. On the other hand, Porter et al. also noted that career orientations are affected by the work situation as well as by other life experiences. So, the mental health professional might find work with families and adults more satisfying than he had expected and might change or broaden his goals, or he might decide that effecting more reasonable policies was so crucial to the quality of service that he would move into administration rather than remain in a direct service position. Thus, career orientation is not static; career goals can, and often do, change as a career progresses.

A much earlier work by Wilensky (1956) presented a formal typology of career orientations. Wilensky studied the careers of intellectuals employed by labor unions. During the course of his study, he developed a concept that he called "role orientation," and he identified four basic types. Missionaries were those primarily oriented to a political or religious philosophy. They were uncompromising idealists who saw their union as a means to a larger end. The Professional Service type included those who were oriented primarily to technical competence and professional standards. Their primary goal was to find a job in which they could utilize their technical skills and do quality work. The third group, Careerists, consisted of individuals oriented to material rewards and job security. Careerists were not concerned with either the technical quality of their work nor larger social ideals. The last group was the Politicos. They were attracted to the challenge and excitement of political contests and preferred jobs that provided opportunities for such contests. The Politicos liked the manipulative and jockeying characteristic of the political arena. Their primary goal in work was to win contests and increase their influence and clout.

By identifying these orientations and assigning his respondents to them, Wilensky was able to better understand how and why labor union intellectuals changed over time. He proposed that the appropriateness of one's orientation would vary with the type of job and with the stage of development of the labor movement. For example, Missionaries seemed to fit in better and receive more gratification in their work during the early days of the labor movement. As the movement developed, the Missionary became increasingly superfluous or even detrimental while the technical skills of the Professional Service intellectual became more valued. Thus, over time, Missionaries either left the movement or shifted their orientation. Wilensky found that Public Service and Careerist intellectuals were most stable in their orientations over time and that Missionaries were the least stable type.

Sometimes an individual's orientation changed in order to better fit the requirements of the job. For instance, some Careerists who moved into jobs requiring a high level of training and skill gradually shed their primary concern with rewards and security and assumed a Professional Service orientation, becoming more concerned with developing and utilizing skills and doing quality work. When Wilensky knew the type of job and the role orientation of the intellectual, he could usually accurately predict how the individual's career would develop.

In our own study of new professionals in public human service programs, four distinct career orientations also emerged. We called these the Social Activists, Careerists, Artisans, and Self-Investors. These four types were somewhat different from those identified by Wilensky. However, like Wilensky's, they helped us to understand and predict the individual's response to the work situation. For each career orientation, there was an optimal work setting, and the degree of stress, strain, and burnout was influenced by the "goodness of fit" between individual career orientation and work setting.

THE FOUR CAREER ORIENTATIONS
FOUND IN PUBLIC PROFESSIONALS

Social Activists

Those new professionals who were classified as Social Activists wished to do more in their work than just help individual clients. Personal security and status were of little importance to them. Their primary objective in their jobs was to bring about social and institutional change. They were the idealists and visionaries who defined work more as a crusade than as a career or job. They identified more strongly with a social and political ideology than with a theoretical perspective or their professional group. In fact, they were often highly critical of their profession and hoped to transform it through their work. They were impatient with the status quo.

The social significance of their work was the dominating criterion for the Social Activists' evaluation of a job. They could tolerate long hours and demanding work if they felt they were contributing to real social change. In evaluating co-workers, Social Activists were primarily concerned with their social values. They wanted to work with people who shared their ideology and commitment to social change.

A good example of a Social Activist in our research was Shana Phillips, the lawyer working in a special public defender program for indigent convicted felons who wished to appeal their sentences. By representing "underdogs" at the appeals level, Shana hoped that she would be making an impact on the legal system as a whole. In college, she had been active in S.D.S. and other radical social movements. At one point, she had even been arrested for the bombing of a building. When many of her comrades decided to go underground, she was faced with a choice: either go underground and become a fulltime revolutionary or go to law school and work for change within the system. She finally chose the latter course, but never wavered in her identification with the New Left and a commitment to radical social change.

When first interviewed, Shana had been working as a lawyer in this first job for about six months. She had become increasingly dissatisfied because of the heavy caseload and pressure of the job. She was also disillusioned by the competitiveness and careerism of other lawyers with whom she worked. She felt that, no matter what their views initially, lawyers seemed to become increasingly money-hungry and preoccupied with their own success. She also was disappointed by her clients, many of whom proved to be less grateful, sincere, and deserving than she had expected them to be.

Nevertheless, this young lawyer continued to work for social change. She eventually quit her job, but she took another in an agency engaged in class action reform law. She also became more active in political work outside of the job, helping to form a new feminist legal agency in which she volunteered time and service. For this Social Activist, her work continued to be a way of bringing about social justice and reform. Law was a tool of social change, not a profession.

Careerists

The Careerist sought success as conventionally defined. Prestige, respectability, and financial security were important to Careerists. In our society, the professions traditionally have been a route to these goals and thus have attracted many Careerists. The new professionals who were careerists were highly involved and motivated in their work. They wanted to make a good impression on colleagues, supervisors, anyone who controlled access to career advancement. Careerists were ambitious. The extrinsic rewards of a job tended to be more important for this group than for the other groups.

While financial security was important, the new public service professionals categorized as Careerists usually valued prestige as highly as salary. Careerists tended to be impressed by credentials from prestigious institutions, and most sought work in settings with especially good reputations. If Careerists felt they were not presently in the most prestigious setting, a primary goal was to do well enough to eventually move up to such a setting. Careerists also tended to be concerned about how they were performing in relationship to others. They assessed their performance by comparing it to that of others. They were the most competitive group.

Although this orientation may seem like an especially selfish and socially irresponsible one, Careerists were usually not purely self-seeking, unscrupulous characters. They generally were courteous and sympathetic toward clients. They might go out of their way to help a client with no expectation of a concrete reward for doing so. They might also support social change efforts and even work on behalf of them outside of work as private citizens. But their primary goal in their work was to secure recognition and advancement, the only sure routes to financial security and comfort.

Another lawyer we interviewed, Perry Curtis, typified the Careerist orientation. Like Shana Phillips, he worked in a public agency, defending the rights of indigent clients. However, for him this work was a stepping stone to a secure and lucrative private practice. He took the job because he believed that it would be a means of obtaining valuable experience. He especially liked his job because of the many contacts he was making with local judges and attorneys, contacts that would help him secure work when he set up his own practice.

This "poverty lawyer" did not have a history of student activism and involvement in social causes. Initially, he had not even sought this job as a legal aid lawyer. His first choice had been a job in the county prosecutor's office. That job fell through, however, and, with the tight job market, he was grateful when offered his present job. Taking this job was a purely Careerist decision. He was not attracted initially by the cause of serving the poor, nor was he attracted by the nature of the work and the opportunities to learn new skills. It was simply a job that offered good possibilities for future career advancement. Because the job helped him to further his Careerist goals, he was more satisfied with it than many others in the same job might have been.

Artisans

For the Artisans, issues of career advancement and financial success were less important than the intrinsic quality of their work. Performing well in terms of their own internal standards was the primary concern. Professional development and growth were also important. Artisans, more than others, sought jobs that provided opportunities for challenge, new experiences, and the development of professional skills. Prestige and recognition from others were not necessarily irrelevant, but the Artisans were more motivated to succeed in terms of their own inner standards of quality. If the job allowed it, Artisans would become absorbed in the process of work, taking delight in the skillful use of technique. For them, professional work was a craft that offered its own rewards merely in the performance of it. They wanted jobs that led to an inner sense of accomplishment and growth.

Artisans tended to be the most individualistic type. They valued independence and autonomy more highly than did others. They worked primarily for themselves, not others. Artisans might leave a job even when they were conventionally successful if they had become bored or were attracted to a different kind of work. Opportunities for advancement, supervisory or administrative responsibility, and increased power or influence had little appeal for Artisans. Co-workers were valued to the extent that they shared the Artisan's interest in the work itself and provided intellectual stimulation. Artisans tended to be less competitive than others. They enjoyed working with people who knew more than they and who had much to teach them.

When they did find interesting work in which there was a strong sense of accomplishment, Artisans focused on the present. They were not as future-oriented as Social Activists and Careerists.

A new high school math teacher, Victoria Goble, seemed to be a good example of the Artisan orientation. Most of the high school teachers interviewed had chosen teaching as a career late in college, often as a compromise because of difficulties involved in pursuing another, preferred career path. But Victoria decided she wanted to be a schoolteacher while still in high school, and she had remained committed to it. Teaching for her was truly a vocation and calling.

When she finally began teaching, Victoria threw herself into her work. Her standards were high, much higher than those deemed adequate by peers and administrators. However, even though she had to work much harder to meet her own, internal standards, she did not mind as long as she felt that she was succeeding and constantly improving. She seemed to work harder than others and to enjoy it more. Also, it was not enough for her to feel that she was reaching "most" of her students. She wanted to reach *every* student in every class and felt that eventually she could. She continued to experiment with new teaching techniques and approaches designed to motivate and involve those students who seemed to remain untouched by her efforts. She admitted that her goals were higher than other teachers', but she did not feel that she could lower them.

Competence was especially important to this teacher. She graded more strictly than other teachers, but also spent more time with the students, helping them improve their grades. She also went out of her way to "grade" herself; she was one of the few new teachers we interviewed who designed and used a student evaluation form to secure feedback on her teaching.

More than others, she sought out new ideas and knowledge that would help her be more effective. For instance, she was the only new teacher who spent time observing in the classrooms of more experienced, effective teachers. Other new teachers expressed a desire to see experienced teachers in action, but this Artisan was the only one who had found a way and the time to do so. Victoria was also unusual in maintaining contact with her critic-teacher from student-teaching days, seeking continued help to improve her teaching.

Her salary was not especially important to this Artisan teacher. She said that if she ever found she was teaching more for the money than for intrinsic satisfaction, she would quit and find another job. A sense of accomplishment was the greatest reward she could receive from this or any other job. She also had little respect for colleagues who seemed to be in teaching only for the money and who made minimal efforts in their jobs. She was especially critical of these teachers, saying that they lacked a "professional attitude," and she avoided interaction with them at work. She interacted with very few colleagues socially, feeling no need for it. But those with whom she did associate shared her high level of commitment and standards.

Not surprisingly, Victoria did not like the teachers' union of her school. She felt that many of the issues discussed at contract meetings were trivial. She deplored the attitude of more partisan unionists that, if the administration did not give them what they wanted, they would slack off and give less to their students. She was against striking just for money, but she said she would strike if working conditions made it more difficult to teach effectively. As an Artisan, her primary concern was meeting the high, internal standards she set for herself. A sense of growing competence and skill in her work was more important than a large, yearly increment in salary, prestige, or status.

Self-Investors

Self-Investors were more involved in their personal lives outside of work than in their careers. They tended to draw a clear line between personal development and professional obligation, and they invested themselves in the former. We created this category when we discovered that many of those we interviewed were simply not strongly engaged in their present work. They could not be identified with any of the other three orientations because those who were so identified had a strong commitment to their work, albeit for different reasons in each case. The Self-Investors, however, were not motivated by work-related concerns. Their primary loyalties and interests lay elsewhere. For some Self-Investors, families were at least as important, demanding, and/or gratifying as their jobs. For others, personal exploration and discovery through psychotherapy, yoga, encounter groups, or some other vehicle was a more central interest at the moment than the professional career.

Because work was not their primary interest, Self-Investors lacked the clear focus on their work possessed by the others. They were not working in order to "change the world," as was true for the Social Activisits, although Self-Investors might be engaged in such efforts *outside* of work as private citizens.

Self-Investors were also not strongly motivated toward career advancement and success. Unlike the Careerists, they were not particularly ambitious. They did not seek high status, prestige, or high salaries. They were content with modest increments in status, responsibility, and salary over time.

The Self-Investors were different from the Artisans in that they did not have unusually high internal standards of performance. Opportunities for learning new skills were not as important to them. In their jobs, they sought interesting work that was moderately challenging but not too demanding. They also wanted pleasant, friendly co-workers and supervisors. Once these minimal expectations for work were met, the Self-Investors were likely to be content for some time. If challenge, excitement, novelty, and a sense of accomplishment and growth were strong needs, the Self-Investor would look to activities outside of the career to gratify them.

Although Self-Investors were notable for their psychological detachment, none were totally indifferent about work. They did want to meet minimal standards of competence and might work very hard to improve their skill if they believed they were failing to do so. They were not indifferent about poor supervision, large caseloads, and other common sources of dissatisfaction. And they were not necessarily less sympathetic toward clients. However, their real concern lay elsewhere. Thus, when they encountered unpleasant working conditions, they seemed less troubled than others in the same situation. They could live with bad working situations (up to a point) because work was not as important a part of their lives.

The sources of the Self-Investors' disaffection from work were varied. In some cases, their present occupation might have been a second choice, something they "ended up in" because of convenience or the weight of external factors. In other cases, they might have become alienated in the face of discouragement, frustration, and disillusionment earlier in their training or careers. As we saw in Chapter 7, psychological retreat from work is one way of coping with the problem of unfulfilled expectations and goals. In still other cases, the Self-Investor's commitment to matters outside of work (for example, the family) might have preceded his or her entry into the present occupation.

A good example of the last case was a new high school teacher working in a small community some distance from her own. Eugenia Barnes had started and raised a family before securing her teaching credentials and beginning her career. Although her children were older and all in school themselves, they still lived at home and depended upon their mother for physical care and psychological support. Her husband had also become accustomed to her performance of a domestic role, and, although he verbally supported her work and career, he became irritable when her job demands required him to take on more domestic responsibility than he was used to. When she was ready to return to school, this Self-Investor initially wanted to go into social work or counseling. However, the training was longer and she felt it would not be fair to her family to be a "student" for so long. She thus chose teaching as a compromise, a field in which she could help others but which did not require graduate work.

When she started teaching, she found that she was woefully unprepared. She had to work long hours to catch up. However, by the second semester, she was considerably better organized and prepared for her work. She seemed satisfied with her progress and had reduced the amount of time spent on preparation. She wanted to perform competently, but she still felt a strong obligation to her family and friends. She did not become friendly with anyone with whom she worked, maintaining a very clear and limited involvement in the life of the school. As a Self-Investor, her loyalties lay elsewhere. She was at least as invested in her family as in her job.

Another Self-Investor we interviewed had different commitments, but he too was less psychologically involved in work than in other pursuits. Douglas Furth was the clinical social worker employed in a small mental health agency where he provided counseling to adults, children, and families. From the beginning, he limited the amount of time spent at work. He maintained a lighter caseload than many other staff members and eschewed commitments that would require extra time. He was concerned about his clients and conscientious in his work with them, but his standards were not particularly high and he seemed content with his progress.

The most important activity in his life was a personal growth group that took at least ten hours a week. He discussed this experience at great length during our interviews. He felt that the personal insights he gained through this experience sometimes helped him in his work, but he was not participating in this program primarily for the sake of his work or clients. He clearly saw himself as the main beneficiary. The rewards were personal satisfaction and fulfillment.

When work threatened to interfere with this personal growth program, he made efforts to change work. For instance, he liked his job because he could arrange his hours in a way that required him to work only four days a week. The fifth day was then free for day-long personal growth workshops and seminars. When some of the other staff members went to the agency director and objected to this arrangement, this Self-Investor became indignant. He said he would quit if he lost his extra day off.

Emotional nurturance was an important need of this Self-Investor. He hoped to receive a great deal of it from co-workers when he started his job. For a time, he worked hard to establish "support groups" for staff in the agency. When his efforts finally failed, he psychologically withdrew even more from work. In our interviews (which occurred on a regular basis for several months), he increasingly spoke about his personal life. His primary motivation was, from the beginning, to take care of himself and meet his own needs. He did this by becoming increasingly involved in life outside of work. As a Self-Investor, work was only one small part of a life in which his self-actualization and psychological growth were the primary concerns.

Mixed Types

In considering these four career orientations, it should be noted that one rarely finds an individual who is a "pure" case. In almost all of the individuals we studied, there was a blend of the orientations described above. Usually, it was easy to identify one of those orientations as dominant, however, there were often clear signs of another orientation in the same individual. Over time, the emphasis might change as the primary and secondary orientations became stronger, then weaker, and so on. In a few cases, it was not even possible to identify a single orientation as dominant. Two or three of the orientations seemed to exist in close balance within the individual.

Social Activist lawyer Shana Phillips provides an example of how career orientations can combine and change over time. Her primary desire for work was to bring about social reform. However, she was not indifferent about her status and career within reform law. She worked for one of the more prestigious poverty law agencies in the state, one that handled only appeals cases in the criminal courts. Her work enabled her to plead cases before the state supreme court on a number of occasions, and she seemed to find this an appealing "ego thrill." While complaining about the competitiveness and careerism of her colleagues in the legal profession, she admitted that she herself was not "innocent" of these "sins." She too was competitive and worked hard to do well and enhance her status among colleagues. So there was Careerism as well as Social Activism in her orientation to her work.

Over time, a third career orientation developed and became stronger. After working long hours and seeing few results for many months, she became increasingly discouraged and frustrated. Her personal life was adversely affected by her intense absorption in such demanding work. Finally, she decided it was time to make a major change. She consciously withdrew from work and became more invested in outside activities. She refused to bring work home or to work more than 40 hours per week. She lowered her expectations for what she could or would accomplish on the job. She became interested in yoga and spent more and more time on yoga classes and practice. She still felt a strong commitment to social change, but she increasingly pursued her social change goals outside of work. Thus, she also came to share some of the characteristics associated with a Self-Investor.

Most public service professionals share to some extent the goals and values characteristic of each orientation. The four types described are ideal types, and, in reality, an individual usually will best be described as a unique mixture of them. Also, there are certain values for one's job that are almost universal. Almost everyone prefers work that is stimulating, varied, and meaningful. Almost everyone appreciates support and guidance that does not excessively limit one's autonomy. It was both surprising and unfortunate that so few of the professionals we studied found acceptable levels of variety, autonomy, support, and meaning in their jobs, because these qualities are desired by almost all.

However, with these caveats in mind, there do seem to be at least four distinct career orientations in the new public professionals we studied. And, in most cases, raters were able to agree on a primary career orientation for an individual based on the interviews.

THE DISTRIBUTION OF CAREER ORIENTATIONS
IN NEW PUBLIC PROFESSIONALS

Once we had determined the career orientation of each subject,* we considered three questions concerning the distribution of career orientations: 1) What proportion of our sample of new public service professionals was accounted for by each type? 2) Did the distribution of individuals across types vary with professional group? 3) Finally, and perhaps most interesting, did career orientations change over time?

Date pertaining to the first question are presented in Table 11.1. The dominant type was Self-Investor; they accounted for 44 percent of the primary orientations. The next largest group was Artisans, accounting for 33 percent of the primary and 42 percent of the secondary career orientations. The Careerists constituted a much smaller group; 11 percent of the primary and 30 percent of the secondary career orientations. The smallest group was the Social Activists, accounting for 11 percent of the primary and 4 percent of the secondary career orientations.

The data in Table 11.1 also indicates how the distribution of career orientations varied with professional group, the second question in which we were interested. Looking at the primary career orientations, we found that career orientations did vary with group. The new mental health professionals tended to be Self-Investors; 71 percent of this professional group was placed in this category. Many new high school teachers (43 percent) were also Self-Investors, but just as many were Artisans. The new public health nurses tended to be Artisans (57 percent). Finally, all the Social Activists were found in the lawyer group; 50 percent of the new public service lawyers interviewed were identified with this orientation.

---

*Career orientations were determined in the following way. For each subject, at least two raters studied all of the interview transcripts, independently assigned a primary career orientation, and, if necessary, a secondary orientation. (One subject could not be rated because of insufficient data.) The raters also indicated whether there was any change in career orientation between initial and follow-up interviews. Reliability of ratings was high. All raters agreed on the primary career orientation in 57 percent of the cases. In another 29 percent, at least two out of three raters agreed. For the change ratings, there was full agreement for 59 percent of the cases and at least two of three raters agreed for 29 percent of the cases.

TABLE 11.1: Number of Subjects Identified with Each Career Orientation by Field

	Activist	Self-Investor	Careerist	Artisan	Total
Primary Orientation					
Lawyers	3	2	1	0	6
Mental Health Professionals	0	5	0	2	7
High School Teachers	0	3	1	3	7
Public Health Nurses	0	2	1	4	7
Total	3	12	3	9	27
Secondary Orientation					
Lawyers	0	1	2.5	1.5	5
Mental Health Professionals	1	1	2	3	7
High School Teachers	0	2	1	3	6
Public Health Nurses	0	2	2	3	7
Total	1	6	7.5	10.5	25*

Note: Fractions due to mixed cases. Data based on initial interviews.
*No secondary career orientation assigned for three subjects.
Source: Compiled by the author.

The final question concerned change in career orientation over time. The data for this question are presented in Table 11.2. For all raters and ratings combined (n = 93), there were 12 instances in which there was a perceived shift in a subject's primary career orientation during the course of the study. Thus, career orientations did occasionally shift, but not frequently during the limited time period we studied the subjects.

The least stable career orientation was the Social Activist. Of the ten initial Social Activist ratings given, five had changed to another category by follow-up interviews. Put another way, 42 percent of the changes were from Social Activist to another orientation. Also, there were no instances in which a subject changed *to* a Social Activist orientation.

The other career orientation that tended to be less stable was the Artisan.

Again, 42 percent of the changes involved Artisans changing to another orientation, and no individual shifted *to* an Artisan orientation. However, the Artisan orientation was more stable than the Social Activist. While half of the initial Social Activist ratings changed, only 19 percent of the initial Artisan ratings shifted.

By far, the most stable orientation and the one that became more dominant over time was the Self-Investor. Those who were Self-Investors when first interviewed remained Self-Investors. All but one of the perceived shifts (92 percent) were from another orientation to Self-Investor. Thus, to summarize, the Social Activist and Artisan orientations tended to weaken while the Self-Investor orien-

TABLE 11.2: Change in Primary Career Orientation

	Activist	Self-Investor	Careerist	Artisan
Change from				
Lawyers	3	0	1	2
Mental Health				
Professionals	2	0	1	1
High School				
Teachers	0	0	0	1
Public Health				
Nurses	0	0	0	1
Total	5	0	2	5
Change to				
Lawyers	0	5	1	0
Mental Health				
Professionals	0	4	0	0
High School				
Teachers	0	1	0	0
Public Health				
Nurses	0	1	0	0
Total	0	11	1	0

Note: Data based on total of all ratings collected from all raters. Numbers in this table do not necessarily correspond to those found in Table 11.1 because the latter was based on three pooled ratings. So, for instance, one rating of Social Activist was given to two different mental health professionals by a single rater. These ratings are shown here. However, the other two raters gave ratings of Self-Investor; thus, those mental health professionals were categorized as Self-Investors for the purpose of Table 11.1.

Source: Compiled by the author.

tation became stronger during the first year or so of these new public service professionals' careers.

Bearing in mind the restricted sample size, let us now consider these findings in more depth. The typology of career orientations presented here is similar to previous typologies, but in some ways it also is distinct. The Artisans in our study are much like the Professional Service type in Wilensky's (1956). Our Careerists and Wilensky's Careerists also are similar. And there are commonalities between our Social Activists and Wilensky's Missionairies. However, Wilensky did not describe a career orientation like Self-Investor, and we could not identify a new public professional who resembled Wilensky's Politico.

One reason for the disparity between our typology and Wilensky's undoubtedly has to do with the difference between public professionals and other occupational groups. We believe that public professionals are a distinct occupational group. Members of this group share many experiences, problems, motivations, and attitudes, differing in distinct ways from those in other groups. Different occupational groups "produce" different career orientations in their members through selection and socialization. Thus, one would expect to find differences in the career orientations of public professionals and those of labor union intellectuals.

Our data also suggest differences in career orientation between different kinds of public professionals. For instance, Self-Investors represented the largest group, but the proportion of Self-Investors varied widely with profession. More than 70 percent of the new mental health professionals were Self-Investors, while only 29 percent of the new public health nurses in our sample could be placed in this category. On the other hand, while the Social Activist group accounted for only 11 percent of our sample, half of the lawyers were identified as Social Activists. There were no Social Activists found in the other three groups. Thus, while public professionals share many characteristics, there also are important differences in career orientation between professional groups.

A potentially important finding concerns the size of the Self-Investor group. In the initial ratings, the Self-Investors were the largest group. More than two of every five subjects in the sample were Self-Investors, people whose primary psychological commitment was not in their work and career but in other domains of their lives (family, personal growth experience, community affairs, and so on). Further, there was evidence that, over time, this group grew still further. Between initial and follow-up interviews, more than 90 percent of all changes in career orientation were from another type to Self-Investor. (This pattern also is consistent with the data on psychological withdrawal from work presented in Chapter 7.)

The implications of this finding are important. The question of how psychologically involved in work one should be is ultimately a value-laden one. There is probably wide agreement that either extreme is undesirable. The "workaholics" who become so absorbed in work that they neglect their responsibilities to family, community, and their own self-development are certainly not ideal. However, the alienated worker for whom the job is simply a way of supporting oneself, a dreary period of the day when one marks time and waits for life to really begin, is also not something for which to strive.

Also, the optimal amount of psychological commitment to work should probably depend on the type of work. A worker on an automobile assembly line performing a routine task over and over again need not be highly involved in his or her work. In fact, workers in this position who are involved and who hope to gratify their needs for personal growth and competence through their work will probably suffer greatly. It simply is not rational to expect much from such work except relatively safe working conditions, decent treatment by co-workers and supervisors, and a good wage. On the other hand, one would hope that those who enter a public service profession such as teaching or social work would be highly involved psychologically. When the job becomes only a job for those in these fields, the quality of service and the welfare of clients probably deteriorate sharply. The burned out poverty lawyer and high school teacher may be able to compensate for frustration in the job by turning elsewhere for fulfillment and meaning, but, as they do so, what happens to their clients and students? Thus, the finding that the incidence of Self-Investors in new public professionals is large and grows still larger over time is certainly a disturbing one that should be investigated further.

CAREER ORIENTATION
AND THE PROBLEM OF BURNOUT

Although the concept of career orientation and the data concerning it presented in this chapter are interesting in their own right, their primary importance lies in what they can contribute to our understanding of professional burnout in the human services. The new professional's career orientation became a useful and important concept primarily because it helped account for individual differences in satisfaction and change early in the career. The data suggest that it is the interaction of career orientation and job structure that accounts for positive and negative experiences and attitude changes for new public professionals.

The career orientation defined the optimally satisfying and fulfilling job. When there was a bad "fit" between one's career orientation and the demands and rewards of one's job, a state of tension and disequilibrium existed. Eventually, some change occurred. Often, this involved accommodation to the job by the individual, that is, a change in career orientation. In other cases, the individual was able to change the job to make it more congruent with career orientation or left it for another that was more congruent. Of course, the most satisfied novices were those whose first jobs met their career values and goals. A good example of this proposition was poverty lawyer Jean Chalmers (see Chapter 8), who made an unusually good adaptation to her job during the initial stage of her career. More than any other Social Activist, she worked in a setting that allowed, even encouraged, her to pursue her primary career goals. If she had worked in a setting such as that of Margaret Williams, she might have experienced the same frustration, anger, and eventual apathy observed in Margaret.

This is not to imply, however, that there is one kind of optimal job situation for all public service professionals. To the contrary, the data on differences in career orientation within the sample of new professionals suggests the optimal job will differ. A job that is satisfying to one novice may contribute to considerable stress and burnout in another because the two bring different goals and preferences to their work. So, for example, a Careerist like Perry Curtis might have found Jean Chalmers' job intolerable unless it also provided a sure route to concrete rewards such as status, prestige, economic security, and opportunities for rapid advancement.

At the same time that there is no single optimal job situation for all public professionals and although jobs in the human services differ along important dimensions (see Chapter 9), it seems that the demands of public human service work make some career orientations generally more adaptive than others. The data on change in career orientation suggest that Self-Investors and Careerists probably will experience less job stress and burn out less often than Social Activists or Artisans. In fact, Social Activists would appear to be most "at risk" for burnout because their career orientation is most discrepant with the demands and rewards provided by public human service agencies. Artisans generally will find a better "fit" with their career goals, but they too are at some risk. What the data also suggest, however, is that, even though Social Activists may be the most likely to experience frustration, they need not burn out more than others if they can find jobs that allow them to fulfill their social change oriented goals.

It should be emphasized again that, despite the differences in career orientation brought by new professionals to their jobs, almost all of their work situations would contribute to high levels of stress in most individuals; the great similarities in work-related goals and preferences among novice professionals should not be minimized. However, marked differences in the experience of stress, attitude change, and burnout did occur in our sample, and it would seem that, by examining the demands and rewards of public service jobs and the career goals and values of the individuals in those jobs, we may be better able to understand, predict, and alleviate professional burnout.

CONCLUSION: THE "LABELLING" DILEMMA

Although the typology of career orientations presented here helped us to better understand the experiences of public service professionals, we are concerned about the dangers inherent in any system that affixes a label to an individual. The research on the social consequences of labelling suggests that the consequences are often negative for both the individual and society. For instance, labels in the form of psychiatric diagnoses or intellectual functioning are often used to justify coercive administrative actions limiting individual freedom. Labels can become self-fulfilling prophecies, reinforcing undesirable behavior. Labels may also be misleading: labels applied to individuals imply that people behave in the same way across different situations, a simplistic and erroneous conception of human behavior. In other words, labels can become stereotypes, oversimplifying the complexities of human behavior and experience. When individuals or groups are labelled, there is a strong tendency for everyone—including the labelled—to relate to them in terms of the label rather than the person.

In the past, it has been the helping professionals who have applied labels to their clients. And, over the years, the number of labels applied to clients in schools, mental health settings, and correctional institutions has proliferated. However, the professionals have rarely been labelled themselves. Nevertheless, we have not constructed a professional career orientation typology simply because it seems fair that the professional now become the object of labelling. The labels used in our typology can be abused in all the ways labels have been abused in the past. Hopefully, the typology will illuminate our understanding of the public service professional's plight, not distort it, sensitize our awareness of how the job and work setting influence the individual's experience, not blunt it.

12

RECAPITULATION: A MODEL OF PROFESSIONAL DEVELOPMENT IN PUBLIC INSTITUTIONS

In the previous chapters, we have seen that the lives of new professionals employed in public human service agencies are marked by many stresses and changes. They begin their careers with certain expectations and needs. They want to achieve a sense of professional competence, to work with motivated, cooperative, and grateful clients, to receive support and autonomy from their employing organization, to become part of a stimulating and collegial group of co-workers, and to engage in interesting and significant work. Their previous socialization has led them to believe that they will find these qualities in professional work, and that was a primary reason for choosing to extend their schooling by several years.

Unfortunately, many are sorely disappointed. They fail to find what they originally sought from professional work, and the initial "reality shock" contributes to frustration, anger, and depression. Over time, their outlooks begin to change in many different ways. They become less idealistic, less willing to critically evaluate and change their own functioning when confronted with failure, and less trusting and sympathetic in their attitudes toward clients. They lose much of their sense of mission and zeal, adopting more modest goals for themselves and their clients. And they increasingly withdraw psychologically from their clients and from their jobs, looking to other aspects of their lives for the fulfillment they had originally expected to find in their work.

However, these changes were by no means universal in our sample, and the major sources of stress and disappointment were not experienced equally by all of the subjects. There were many variations in both the work places and the personal lives of the people we interviewed, and these variations seemed to influence the extent to which they experienced stress and change during the initial phase of their careers.

The picture of early professional development and burnout in public institutions that has emerged from our research is a complex one not easily communicated in words and sentences alone. Thus, in order to summarize the ideas and themes discussed in earlier sections and indicate more clearly their relationships, we have constructed a schematic model. There is a potential danger in such an exercise, for social scientists have a tendency to confuse their abstractions with reality in ways that seriously impede understanding. This tendency to become preoccupied with the manipulation and analysis of abstractions often seems to be greatly encouraged when we create formal models. Also, we tend to feel a certain parental pride and overprotectiveness about a model we have created. If we become overly zealous in defense and advocacy for our model, progress toward new knowledge and greater understanding comes to a halt. Furthermore, some people simply comprehend everyday language more easily then boxes, lines, and circles. When we rely too heavily on such devices, we exclude an audience that has every right to learn what we have discovered.

Despite these potential dangers, a schematic model that helps organize our knowledge and thinking seems to have real value. Not only can one see more clearly and succinctly how certain structures, experiences, and forces are related to one another; one may also better perceive the implications for future research and social action. Hopefully, by becoming aware of the potential dangers of models, we can reap the benefits without paying too high a price.

The model of early career development based on the research findings contained in previous chapters is presented in Figure 12.1. In the middle of the diagram are the five major sources of stress that stood out in bold relief as the new professionals described their feelings about work. First, they complained that they frequently lacked both the resources and expertise necessary to perform their roles adequately. They became all too familiar with the experience of "falling short." Even when they were making a positive impact, lack of feedback made it difficult for them to experience a sense of competence. Consequently, they experienced great uncertainty and self-doubt about professional competence, and this became a major source of anxiety and tension. Second, clients often proved to be another source of strain. Many lacked motivation and ability, making the professional's task more difficult and impeding the quest for competence. Also, some clients were abusive and manipulative. In addition, many of the new professionals were uncertain about how informal and friendly they should allow themselves to become with clients; a closer, warmer relationship often seemed to facilitate the helping process, but there seemed to be risks involved in establishing such a relationship. Thus, the "personal involvement" dilemma was another source of strain associated with professional-client relations.

A third major disappointment and source of stress for the new public professionals involved bureaucratic infringement on their autonomy. Rather than

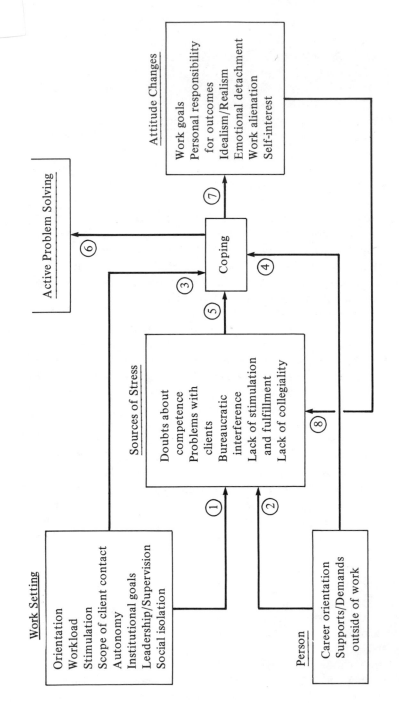

Source: Compiled by the author.

"free agents" upholding the value system they had learned during their training, many found themselves to be mere employees of large bureaucratic organizations that seemed to be guided by a very different set of values and norms. Organizational demands and client needs were not always congruent, and the new professionals often found themselves caught between. They quickly learned that the working life of a public professional is far more "political" than they had anticipated and that they were rarely captains of their own destinies.

Related to the lack of autonomy was a fourth source of strain: a lack of meaning and fulfillment in work, caused by oppressive routine and trivia. Initially, the work was novel and challenging, but it gradually lost this quality as one client followed another, one case followed another, one class followed another, and they increasingly resembled those that preceded them. The work was not actually boring, and in many respects the working conditions were pleasant enough so that the professionals were not really dissatisfied, but the work lacked the intrinsic meaning and intellectual excitement they had expected of professional work.

Finally, the new professionals had to cope with the disappointments associated with the lack of collegiality. Although a few of our subjects found colleagues who were a gratifying source of emotional support, technical guidance, and stimulation, most failed to do so. Major barriers to the development of collegiality among professional workers in public institutions included differences in values, age, and tenure in the profession; excessive workloads that created a sense of pressure and made social interaction seem an unaffordable luxury; intergroup conflict and rivalry within the organization; informal norms that seemed to make sharing and friendliness among colleagues somewhat suspect; and high turnover and instability in the staff. Whatever the causes, however, this lack of collegiality added to the stress, frustration, and disappointment that the new professionals were already experiencing.

In addition to the strain and pressure associated with these various factors, we found that many of the new professionals were going through important changes in attitude and outlook. These are suggested at the far right-hand side of Figure 12.1. First, many seemed to change their initial goals and aspirations. Sometimes they adopted new goals not directly related to the ones they initially emphasized, but more often they simply made their initial goals less ambitious and more modest. In other words, they increasingly settled for less. Related to these changes in goals was a tendency to change their perceived sense of personal responsibility for the outcomes of their work. They increasingly blamed the clients or the system when efforts to help fell short. A third set of changes involved increasing cynicism, pessimism, and conservatism about clients and people in general. The new professionals became less likely to see their clients as uniformly good and trustworthy. At the same time, they no longer saw the "bad guys," such as prosecuting attorneys or police officers, as being so uniformly bad. And some began to adopt more conservative attitudes and practices, such as

"Don't smile 'til Christmas" in the case of new teachers or stiff jail sentences for repeat offenders in the case of lawyers. In other words, idealism often gave way to realism, moderation, and cynicism.

A fourth change noted in many new professionals was increasing emotional detachment in the helping relationship. In other words, many chose to resolve the personal involvement dilemma by withdrawing and maintaining more formal and distant relations with their clients. A fifth change was increasing psychological withdrawal from work, a tendency to look toward non-work pursuits as the major source of fulfillment, meaning, and stimulation in life. And, finally, there was a growing concern with the self and a decline in the selfless concern for the welfare of others that many of the new professionals brought with them to their jobs. Of course, not all of the subjects changed in these ways, and some changes, such as the tendencies to feel less personally responsible and the lowering of goals and aspirations, were more pervasive than others. Also, there were individual differences in the extent to which the novices experienced the disappointments and sources of stress associated with the new public professional experience.

Factors both in the individual and in the work setting seemed to be associated with the differences in experience observed in the sample. These are represented at the far left-hand side of the model in Figure 12.1. Looking first at the work place, we noted eight different factors. First, the presence or absence of an orientation process, sensitive and responsive to the novices' needs, seemed to make a difference in their ability to cope with the initial stresses encountered in their work. Second, the size of the workload influenced both the degree of stress and efforts to cope with it. A smaller workload allowed the new professional to spend more time with clients or work assignments, thus increasing the chances that the efforts would be successful. And, if the professional did experience difficulty, a lighter workload allowed the time necessary to seek help and guidance from co-workers, supervisors, or professional workshops, journals, and books.

Third, jobs varied considerably in the amount of stimulation provided, and this directly affected the extent to which the novice became disappointed with this aspect of the work. Fourth, the scope of client contact also influenced the professional's emotional response to the job; those who were able to spend more time with individual clients and to relate to more aspects of the clients' life situations were more likely to feel a sense of accomplishment and less likely to react negatively to their clients.

The amount of autonomy available in the job also varied in our sample and was a fifth factor that seemed to influence the degree of frustration and stress experienced by the novices. A sixth factor had to do with the congruence of institutional goals with the professional service goals brought by the novices to their work; greater congruence between personal values and institutional goals and policies enhanced the professional's response to the job. Less conflict and ambiguity in goals also helped. Seventh, leadership and supervision practices made a great difference as well. New professionals responded well to supervisors who provided support without unduly infringing on autonomy. Finally, the degree of social isolation characteristic of the work setting influenced collegiality and the extent to which the new professionals could call on others for help. Thus, many aspects of the work setting influenced the degree to which the new public professionals experienced the major sources of stress characteristic of the initial stage of the career.

There were fewer personal factors associated with differences in experience, but at least two seemed to be critical. First, personal differences in initial outlook were especially significant; we identified four distinct career orientations that new professionals brought with them to the job, and differences in career orientation seemed to affect the individuals' career development. For instance, Social Activists and Artisans were more likely to experience disappointment and frustration than were Careerists and Self-Investors. Second, there seemed to be a strong relationship between one's work life and personal life. For instance, stress and difficulty at home seemed to impede adjustment at work. Also, lack of a close, stable, and available network of family and friends seemed to be associated with greater stress and more negative change during this initial phase of the professional career.

The eight arrows in the model suggest how the various aspects of the new public professional's experience are related; they define the *process* of change and development that occurs during this phase of the professional career. Arrows 1 and 2 refer to the potential effect that work setting and personal factors have on psychological stress. Arrows 3 and 4 suggest that these factors also influence the professional's attempts to cope with that stress. Arrows 5, 6, and 7 suggest that the sources of stress mobilize coping efforts in the new professionals; the professionals can deal with stress through direct action and problem solving (Arrow 6) or through internal changes in attitudes (Arrow 7). For instance, they can respond to inadequacies in performance by learning new techniques or assessing possible mistakes in their current actions, or they can lower their goals, adopt new ones that are more readily attainable, or reduce their sense of personal responsibility for outcomes. Both active problem solving and psychological defense are employed by new public professionals in response to the stress experienced during the initial phase of their careers.

Although the level of psychological stress drops over time for most new professionals, the attitude changes that helped bring about that drop probably remain for some time. In other words, even when the novice has developed a greater sense of professional competence, his or her work goals probably remain relatively low. The psychological defense remains even after the danger has passed. Of course, the validity of this interpretation must be decided by research that follows public professionals through their careers for a longer period of time than we did.

Arrow 8 suggests that changes in attitude, as coping efforts, do have some impact on the sources of stress. Emotional detachment, a decline in idealism, and other changes in attitude seem to reduce the degree of stress, frustration, and guilt experienced by the new public professionals. This is one reason they probably persist; the professional maintains the changes in outlook because they have been successful in reducing anxiety and tension.

The model presented in Figure 12.1 seems to capture in one way the dynamic process of disequilibrium, adjustment, and change that occurs in public professionals during the first stage of their careers. It provides a convenient way of summarizing the many patterns and processes that have been discussed in earlier parts of this book. However, it should be clear that the model falls far short of capturing the richness of the individual experience. Also, the factors and their interrelationships depicted in the model must be regarded as tentative, an attempt to sketch an initial, rough picture of a process that we still know very little about. We already know, for instance, that the model does not include other factors that contribute to attitude change during the initial phase of the professional career, such as social influence processes (identification, modeling, social pressure by supervisors, peers, and clients, and so on). The schematic model also does not include the individual's professional skill and knowledge, personal coping style, or other personality factors which are clearly important in shaping the experience. Nothing has been said about other methods of coping, such as support groups or behavioral strategies, that might reduce stress and strain; active problem solving and the attitude changes identified in this study are not the only means available for helping individuals cope.

However, the model—and the study on which it is based—was never seen as an exhaustive and complete analysis of the process of professional development and change in public institutions. We have at best a partial picture that is hopefully accurate as far as it goes and that enlarges to some degree our understanding of the phenomenon. But there is still one limitation of the model that must be addressed: the model only presents factors at the level of the individual and the work organization that seem to influence the novice's experience. The larger picture—cultural and historical forces that influence both individuals and their work organizations—has been neglected. We shall turn to a brief consideration of this larger picture in Chapter 15. First, let us consider how the results of this study can be used to reduce burnout and promote positive career development in new public professionals.

PART IV

IMPLICATIONS AND CONCLUSIONS

13

REDUCING PROFESSIONAL BURNOUT:
THE ROLE OF TRAINING

Many social scientists hope that their work will not only describe and explain phenomena, but also have some impact. However, to make a difference, the results of social research must be translated into social policy and social action. A good study always has the potential for making a difference; however, the findings must be translated into concrete recommendations for action if this is to occur.

Before presenting the practical implications of this study of new public professionals, some notes of caution are in order. First, the picture that has emerged from our research must be considered tentative. Our aim was to discover hypotheses for further verification, not to prove any particular conclusion. Those who use our findings as a basis for action must do so with great caution, for they are only untested hypotheses. In other words, any effort to reduce burnout in new public professionals should be carefully monitored and evaluated. Nevertheless, burnout in new professionals is clearly a problem in many human service programs; administrators, supervisors, and staff development specialists are already launching efforts to cope with it. The findings of our reaearch and the recommendations that follow from them may at least reduce some of the uncertainty and error that currently surround efforts to cope with the problem.

A second and related caution is that there will be risks involved in any attempt to alleviate professional burnout. As Maslach (1976) has noted, many techniques used to reduce stress and burnout in staff may do so at the expense of clients. We must always examine the unintended consequences for the client of any attempt to remedy burnout. For example, in some agencies, the staff are protected from being overwhelmed by clients through the use of special intake procedures. These procedures reduce strain on staff but add to the bureaucratic layers confronted by clients. Another example of unintended consequences was an experimental program intended to prevent medical students from becoming more judgmental, more pessimistic, and less empathic toward patients (Mendel, 1978). Students were assigned a chronically ill patient whom they followed for a longer period of time than usually occurs during training or even in many forms of practice. They were encouraged to focus on the human aspect of the illness and to develop an ongoing personal relationship with the patient. The program was carefully evaluated, and the results showed, that compared to other medical students, those participating in the program became more judgmental, less empathic, and more insensitive. Apparently, the ongoing personal relationship with an ill person was emotionally painful for the students. Rather than encouraging emotional involvement, it promoted emotional detachment as a form of psychological defense (Mendel, 1978). Other efforts to reduce professional burnout and enhance commitment could also backfire and should be evaluated carefully before being utilized on a large scale.

A third important point to keep in mind when evaluating the recommendations that follow is that there is probably no single best solution or remedy. In any given program, some experimentation will be needed to find the most reliable and feasible way of reducing burnout within the given constraints. In different professional fields, the solutions will need to be different. Each situation will be somewhat unique.

In many work situations, the options for doing something to alleviate burnout might be limited. What is possible in one setting may not be in another. However, even when the situation is dismal and the options limited, there are probably steps that could be taken to alleviate strain and burnout. Even in highly rigid, bureaucratic agencies with heavy workloads, difficult clientele, and limited resources, there is enough flexibility in the system and adequate resources to combat burnout and its negative effects on staff and clients.

For instance, protective service programs responsible for intervening in suspected child abuse situations are settings in which all of the ingredients for burnout can be found. These settings are usually part of large, underfunded, and bureaucratic state social service or child welfare system. The caseloads are heavy, and staff must frequently be on call 24 hours a day. They may be dealing with life and death situations. The families they must work with are often at the bottom of the socioeconomic ladder; their values are at odds with the staff person's, and they are resistant and hostile to the intervention. The economic, social, and psychological roots of the problems are usually complex, and the workers rarely feel they have the time or expertise to deal with them adequately. Nevertheless, a study of several child-abuse programs across the country (Berkeley Planning Associates, 1977) found that the level of staff burnout varied considerably from program to program. In at least some settings, things were being done that alleviated the strain and its impact on staff.

One final caution to keep in mind is that once the burnout cycle has begun, it usually is difficult to reverse. Burnout can be defined as a form of "learned helplessness." In the original studies on this phenomenon conducted by Seligman (1975), it was found that two or three mastery experiences were not sufficient to reverse the effects of experimentally-induced learned helplessness. In fact, animals in one study literally had to be dragged into responding constructively between 25 and 200 times before they began responding on their own. In other words, the motivational problems associated with burnout are highly resistant to change. A sustained effort is required to overcome them once they have become severe.

The difficulties involved in overcoming severe professional burnout point to the value of prevention and early intervention. Once a professional has burned out, a major rehabilitative effort is required. Interventions that attack the causes and contributing factors thus will be more economical and more effective. In the proposals that follow, the emphasis will be on prevention and early intervention.

Furthermore, it should be clear that any attempt to identify professional burnout as the individual professional's "problem" and to deal with it accordingly will be misguided and ultimately ineffective. Not all of the new professionals we interviewed experienced significant strain, and not all of them changed in the negative ways associated with professional burnout. However, at least 75 percent of them did. A phenomenon that affects so many is not a reflection of individual deficit or weakness; it is a reflection of *institutional* deficit or weakness. To use the terminology of sociologist C. Wright Mills, it is a *social problem*, not an individual problem. To be sure, individuals can be helped to better cope with the organizational, institutional, and cultural factors that contribute to detrimental stress and change in their careers. However, such efforts will have little impact on the problems we have identified here. Therefore, the recommendations that follow emphasize intervention at the organizational and institutional levels rather than at the individual level.

The results of this study, summarized in the previous chapter, suggest a number of guidelines for professional training, orientation, supervision, and the design of jobs and programs in human service organizations. Those related to training will be described here; the next chapter will focus on those involving the work place.

THE TRAINING PROGRAM

Despite lengthy and expensive training, all of the new pubic professionals had serious doubts about their competence and ability to handle their roles during the initial phase of their careers. The crisis of competence was one of the most pervasive and striking aspects of their experiences. Interpersonal difficulties in the professional-client relationship and organizational conflict were two other elements of the situation that seemed in part related to certain gaps in knowledge and skill. Although these sources of strain would probably occur no matter how well trained the novices were, many believed that their training could have been more helpful. There seemed to be some typical gaps in professional training programs that contributed to professional burnout early in the career.

Almost all of the new professionals interviewed criticized their academic training programs for not being practical, relevant, or useful. They complained that too much of the training experience occurred in a classroom setting rather than in the field, relied on abstract theories rather than practical knowledge, and was directed by college professors who had had little practical experience themselves rather than by skilled practitioners. And many believed that poor training was a major cause of their self-doubt and insecurity in their work. Mark Conner, a new school psychologist, seemed to be speaking for all new public professionals when he said:

> I just have found that the universities really don't prepare me or others in my field to go out in the field and feel competent initially. Maybe it's like that in other fields too. But it's really obvious you only learn when you're on the job, when you're doing it. That's when you really can get down and say, "Hey, I feel competent now." I really have known only a few people who have felt competent just getting out of school, and maybe they were really just putting up a front. I'd like to see more relevance in the system itself, at the university level: getting out, doing some of this stuff, then going back and relating it to the theory you learned.

The new lawyers were especially critical of their profession's lack of training in the "practicalities." Although many law schools have initiated "clinical law" programs in recent years, only three of the seven new lawyers we interviewed had participated in such experiences, and two of these three did not believe that the experience prepared them well for the demands of practice. For instance, law students in clinical law programs frequently did not have many opportunities to appear in court. As a result, they had little familiarity with courtroom procedure when they began practicing, and this gap in their training contributed to considerable insecurity. As Perry Curtis, the new lawyer working in legal aid, noted, "The scariest part in the beginning was the fact that I did not know court procedure. I did not know how to proceed in court, what side of the courtroom to stand on, how you get a motion upped for hearing, and then getting used to being in front of a judge and saying your spiel. All law school teaches you is how to research the law."

Another new lawyer, Margaret Williams, expressed the same idea when she observed that in law school the facts in a case are taken for granted and issues of law are in question. But in actual law practice, the issues of law are almost always clear-cut, and it is the facts that are being disputed. She lamented that she had had no training for this type of inquiry. Early in the interviews, she even claimed that law school had been totally useless. Later, she conceded that knowledge of the law acquired there did help her in initially evaluating the legal merit of her clients' cases; however, she continued to argue that law school was too exclusively theoretical, ignoring the practical knowledge and skills necessary for effective practice.

All of the other disciplines provided regular opportunities for field work of some sort during training. However, the new professionals in these fields also felt that there were gaps in their training. For instance, the psychiatric social workers had spent almost half of their two years of formal training in field work settings, practicing under the supervision of more experienced professionals. And yet they, too, complained that their training had not been "concrete" enough. In some cases, they felt that their training had been incomplete. For example, Diane Peterson, a new social worker employed in a treatment program for alcoholics, complained that she had learned to interview only by talking about her interviews with her supervisor after they were done. She had never *seen* others with more expertise do therapy or even conduct interviews, and no one with skill and experience had ever actually seen her conduct interviews.

In other instances, the training was simply inappropriate. As Diane Peterson said, her only preparation for group therapy was a theoretical course on group dynamics. She was never required to lead a group. But in her first job, she was required to lead several therapy groups. In fact, she found that she had to do more group therapy than individual therapy. Because of this gap in her training, her crisis of competence was particularly severe and disturbing.

"Getting started" was frequently one of the most difficult tasks for the new professionals, one for which they had never been prepared. In fact, as the first day of work approached, many realized that they had never received training for how to handle the "first" day of class or the "first" client. The specific and mundane tasks for getting started were usually not taught in professional schools. For instance, high school teacher Cynthia Noble observed that all her training in education courses and student-teaching prepared her only for teaching a class that had already been organized. She had received no preparation for *creating* a viable classroom setting. As the first day of school approached, she realized that presenting lessons to a group of attentive, eager students was very different from the task of social organization and planning necessary to begin the year, and she became increasingly anxious.

New professionals in other fields experienced similar tensions in anticipation of the first day of work. One might think that the first contact with a client in a neighborhood legal aid office would be far simpler and thus less intimidating than beginning a new term in a classroom. However, for one new lawyer in our study, Margaret Williams, the prospect was frightening. She said, "When I first got here, I thought 'What am I going to do when a client walks into my office?' And I was really scared." This new professional's anxiety was only somewhat relieved when she was assured that, for her first client, somebody who "really knew something" would be with her to help her out with the initial interview. Of course, the implication was that despite four years of college, three years of law school, and successful performance on the gruelling bar exam, in her own mind this new lawyer was not "somebody who knew something." And she was by no means unique in feeling this way.

GAPS IN INTERPERSONAL HELPING SKILLS

The most commonly noted gap in training involved the interpersonal basis of professional work. A characteristic of their work that these various types of professionals had in common was a helping relationship with clients, patients, or students. In doing their jobs, they frequently attempted to modify attitudes and behaviors or secure necessary information and cooperation from clients through the vehicle of personal contact. Interactions with other professionals, clerical assistants, and co-workers were also critical at times for effective work. Thus, to achieve a sense of competence, the new professionals working in public service settings needed some basic knowledge about interpersonal relationships and social influence, as well as skill in specific techniques and behaviors that seem to facilitate effective interaction.

Strong evidence of the importance of interpersonal skill in professional functioning came from the research of Schulman (1976). Schulman was interested in learning why so many people suffering from chronic hypertension fail to follow the prescribed treatment regimen. Previous explanations focused on personal or social characteristics of the patients. Those who dropped out were assumed to be less educated, more irresponsible, culturally deprived, and so on. However, research had failed to establish a strong connection between patient social class or personality characteristics and compliance with medical advice. Schulman believed that other factors, such as the quality of the patient-doctor relationship, were the major determinants of whether patients complied with the medical regimen. Her research and other recent studies have confirmed this view. When physicians or other primary caregivers explain procedures clearly to patients, involve patients in making decisions concerning their treatment program, and otherwise act in ways that make patients feel that they are significant and respected participants in the treatment, patient compliance greatly increases and blood pressure control is achieved much more often. Interpersonal skill enhances effectiveness in treatment of hypertension. Interpersonal skill of the helper is probably important in numerous other health, educational, and social service situations as well. The implications of Schulman's work are far-reaching. They suggest that skill in social relations is necessary for competent professional performance in a variety of fields.

Our own interviews with new public professionals provided further evidence of the importance of interpersonal skill and knowledge in professional work. Many of the new professionals spontaneously indicated an appreciation and desire for greater skill in interpersonal relations. They had quickly realized that to be effective in their work, they frequently needed to influence the attitudes and behavior of clients and also other professionals. Also, in many instances, they did not have the authority to make others think or act in desired ways. Instead, they had to influence them through their own interpersonal behavior. The professionals had to gain their trust and establish effective communication in order to gain their cooperation. There were also times when the professionals needed to reduce the anxiety, anger, defensiveness, or confusion in clients that interfered with effective communication and appropriate compliance with professional advice. For instance, a new public health nurse said that she felt particularly inadequate when she visited the home of a patient whose husband had recently been discharged from a psychiatric institution. He had become agitated and had grabbed a knife while the nurse was there. He brandished it about and threatened to kill his wife, his children, and the nurse. At that point, the personal safety of the entire household seemed to depend on the nurse's skill in establishing contact with the man and quieting him down. Although the incident ended without violence, the nurse felt uncomfortable with the way she handled it. She thought that she had been lucky. She believed that despite some courses and field work in psychiatric nursing, her skills for dealing with "mentally disturbed" patients or family members were weak.

Even when clients are not brandishing knives, considerable interpersonal skill is often necessary for effective performance. One new attorney, when asked what advice he would give to help other new attorneys just starting to work in legal aid, answered, "Patience and understanding. I think you should take the attitude that most of your clients are going to be a little nuts when they come in here because they're at the bottom of the heap, everything is piled up on them, and you're the last hope. Realize that you're not just an attorney, you're a counselor, a priest, a doctor." Although this lawyer correctly realized that one's attitude—how one defined one's role as a professional—was important for effective functioning, he also seemed to believe that skill was important as well. He said that he would have liked some training in attorney-client relations. How should one greet clients in order to gain their trust and confidence? What do you do with uncooperative clients? These were the sorts of questions he would have liked to have been addressed at some point in law school. These were the important gaps in his training.

Previous studies have tended to confirm that practicing professionals see interpersonal helping skills as critical in their work. For instance, most of the lawyers studied by Lortie (1966) believed that law school should provide more training in the social skills of practice. In a study of teachers' attitudes toward their work, 52 percent said that they had received too little preparation in "classroom management, routines, and discipline" (Lortie, 1975). They believed that

interpersonal and leadership skills "play a major part in the conduct of instruction." The teachers assessed peers largely on how they handled relationships
with students. The "ideal" teachers were noted for their leadership capacity:
"Loved or feared, they got their students to work" (Lortie, 1975, p. 118).

But what are these "interpersonal helping" or "leadership" skills that are
valued so highly by professionals in public human service institutions? As the
new professionals in our study acquired more experience and competence in the
area of interpersonal relations with clients, they realized that relatively simple
"communication techniques" could be extremely useful to them in their work.
For instance, public health nurse Sarah Prentiss said that initially it had been
difficult for her to adequately assess her patients' health status and current needs.
There seemed to be barriers to effective communication of important information. But she thought she had improved. When asked what she had done that
helped resolve the problem, she answered, "Just really listening and thinking
about what they're saying and maybe not talking so much, just letting them talk
to me and saying, 'I understand' or 'I see how you feel' and those kinds of communication techniques. It really helps, and people will just vent all kinds of things."

"Learning how to listen" also seemed to be useful in working with other
professionals. Another new lawyer, Reginald Smith, working in the juvenile
justice system, found that through his treatment of a judge, the judge could be
influenced to look at Reginald's client with favor. This was especially true in
juvenile court where proceedings were more informal and the referees acted as
judge, prosecutor, and juror. Reginald thought that recently he had been more
successful than others with one particularly stubborn and harsh referee because
Reginald was willing to listen respectfully to the referee and show that he understood the referee's point of view.

"Listening skills" also proved useful for lawyers when they wanted to
secure information from wary informants. Jean Chalmers, the new lawyer employed in a reform law agency, found that work on a case usually consisted of
two stages. Initially, the lawyer functioned as a fact finder. If the facts showed
that one's adversaries were violating the law, the lawyer became an advocate.
Jean found that during the first stage, listening skills are especially useful. She
said, "I generally find that it's easier for me to elicit more information if I'm
friendly and sort of easygoing, and just let them talk until they've revealed
everything. I mean, if you let people talk long enough, they'll just tell you what
you want."

However, interpersonal effectiveness in the helping relationship is influenced by more than just "an ability to listen." There is a large body of theory
and research on interpersonal and group behavior that could provide a technical
vocabulary by which novice professionals could "order the flux and color of
daily events" and notice crucial transactions that might not otherwise be perceived (Lortie, 1975). There are many conceptual frameworks for organizing
what occurs in interpersonal transactions that could provide a valuable way of

thinking about this aspect of professional work. Also, as Lortie (1975) has noted, studying theory and research in this area promotes a critical, analytical, inquiring orientation toward the interpersonal dynamics of the professional-client relationship, which helps reduce anxiety. Of course, to effectively use this knowledge, the student must have opportunities to apply it in realistic practice settings.

In other words, interpersonal awareness and skill can help professionals understand and control for their *own* emotional and motivational reactions as well as those of the clients. Maslach (1976) was correct in noting that professionals receive little preparation for coping with the emotional stresses associated with the interpersonal "dirty work" involved in their roles. For instance, they usually receive no training in the use of "detachment techniques" that could help maintain their emotional equilibrium without overly dehumanizing the professional-client interaction. Maslach (1973) concluded that psychiatric nurses were more resistant to burnout than other professional groups because they were more attuned to how the clients' behavior affected their own feelings and actions.

When a professional lacks the ability to understand and control his own feelings in the helping relationship, the results can be troubling for him as well as for others. As Lortie (1975) noted, teachers tend to be most upset by incidents in which they have "lost their tempers." They believe that losing their tempers weakens their influence on students. Unfortunately, they receive no training to assist them in managing themselves under provocation and stress. They are not trained to consider their own personalities and take them into account in work with other people. An analytic, open stance is not promoted. In Lortie's words, teachers are "moralistic rather than analytic and self-accusing rather than self-accepting" (1975, p. 159). He charged that the teaching profession has not yet come to grips with the "inevitabilities of interpersonal clash and considerations of how one copes with them" (Lortie, 1975, p. 159). The same could be said about many other professional groups.

To summarize, knowledge about interpersonal behavior and the ability to apply that knowledge in a number of professional situations seem to be important requirements of professional work in human service institutions. Most new professionals learned this early in their careers and gradually felt more competent in this area over time. However, few believed that they had received adequate preparation for this important aspect of their work during their formal training. As a result, they initially felt more insecure about their performance than was necessary. This gap in their training increased their sense of inadequacy and self-doubt during their first weeks and months of fulltime professional work.

Thus, the results of our study suggest that professional competence in interpersonal functioning should not be taken for granted. People are not born with it, nor do they necessarily acquire it automatically as they grow up. The knowledge and skill necessary for effective interpersonal performance in professional work can be, and sometimes is, taught. However, according to the new professionals in our study, this knowledge and skill generally was not well taught and frequently was not taught at all during their formal training. It was a gap in their training that made the transition from student to professional more difficult by preventing them from achieving the elusive sense of competence.

ORGANIZATIONAL CONFLICT RESOLUTION SKILLS

Another major gap in professional training concerned knowledge of the workings of complex organizations. These public professionals, by definition, worked in organizational settings, and, with one or two exceptions, the professionals we interviewed were employed in fairly large, complex, bureaucratic organizations. We all have some familiarity with such beasts, especially with the way in which they can acquire a life and purpose of their own, inconsistent with their stated goals and functions. Although some of the new professionals had taken courses on the "sociology of complex organizations" and all had come into contact with such settings frequently during their lives, their workable knowledge about how to negotiate and conduct themselves effectively as professional employees in these settings seemed slight.

As stated in Chapter 4, professionals working in large, bureaucratic public institutions are constantly required to manipulate the system in order to function effectively. For instance, public school teachers must learn how to acquire supplies they need from a system that is frequently stingy and complicated. Lawyers must learn the intricacies of plea bargaining and other courtroom skills. Clinical psychologists in mental health programs must often learn how to negotiate in a system characterized by feuding professional empires, each jealously guarding its prerogatives. Too often, however, the new professionals felt they lacked the competence necessary for this important aspect of their jobs.

Even when professionals are taught interpersonal helping skills for better coping with the professional-client relationship, they are not taught skills for handling interpersonal and organizational conflict with co-workers and administrators. They are unprepared for the large role that the "human side of the organization" plays in their work (Kramer, 1974). What Kramer (1974) observed in nursing is true in other fields as well; the typical trainee is prepared to work in a *professional* system, not a *bureaucratic* system. As noted in Chapter 4, the operating rules in these two systems are different. Ideally, the public professional should be able to practice in a way that is consistent with important professional standards and values *and* the basic demands of the organizational setting. In other words, public professionals must be skilled in the art of achieving satisfactory resolutions to conflicts that occur within organizations.

Teaching materials in organizational conflict resolution do exist (for example, Filley, 1975). Kramer (1974) described a program in which nursing students were exposed to the organizational conflict solutions developed by a "reference group" of particularly effective experienced nurses and collected in the field by the instructors. In this way, the students learned how one could handle on-the-job incidents involving conflict.

A rather different model, based on a training program developed for future teachers, has been suggested by Sarason, Davidson, and Blatt (1962). They proposed that, early in their training, students be exposed to field work experiences that would provide opportunities for systematic observation and study of professional work *settings*. Unlike most present internships, student-teaching, and field work practice, the emphasis would not be on the acquisition and practice of technical skills (though programs with this emphasis are necessary and should be expanded). Rather, the experience would focus on study of the institutional culture and its effects on clients and staff. The trainees would function much like anthropologists, observing, interviewing, and analyzing the social dynamics of the work setting, with the purpose of developing a more objective and accurate picture of the world of the professional. If the experience encouraged many trainees to drop out, this would not necessarily be bad. Turnover early in training is far less costly for all concerned than turnover during subsequent phases of a career.

There are probably other models that could be developed by those responsible for professional training. The rarity of training in organizational conflict resolution does not mean that such training cannot be offered. Materials, models, and programs do exist and can be used to better prepare public professionals and reduce burnout during the early stages of their careers.

CONCLUSION

To summarize, there seemed to be certain gaps in professional training that made new professionals feel that they were not adequately prepared for their work. Two especially common gaps in training were in the interpersonal aspects of the helping process and the organizational dynamics of public institutions. The new professionals became acutely aware of these gaps when they began their careers, and, until they acquired some practical knowledge and skill in these areas on the job, concern about competence and the stress associated with it were great.

Whatever form a training program for public professionals takes, there should be "a climate in which mutual criticism is an everyday part of the work of the faculty as well as for the students" (Freidson, 1977, p. 13). The world of professional practice is changing rapidly. The effects of training and socialization have become an area of active research, and new knowledge is emerging every year. Thus, no matter how effective a training program might be today, its effectiveness next year or the year after remains in doubt. Only by continually evaluating and changing themselves and their programs can faculty hope to remain effective.

Also, the "climate of mutual criticism" of which Freidson writes will help develop an attitude of inquiry and critical self-examination in students. Such an attitude should make them more responsive, flexible, and effective practitioners. But students will not incorporate this orientation unless it is practiced by their teachers and becomes a central characteristic of their training programs. Thus, self-awareness and mutual criticism must be central values in any professional training program.

Greater professional responsiveness and effectiveness can also be promoted by encouraging students to use the "scientific method" in *all* aspects of their practice. Lortie (1975) noted that schoolteachers rarely use the scientific approach in dealing with practical teaching matters. (Interestingly, this was as true for science teachers as for others.) By this, Lortie meant that "scientific modes of reasoning," such as observation, conscientious recording, comparison, rules of inference, testing alternative hypotheses through treatments, and so on, are not applied to pedagogical problems. The experimental attitude is weak in teaching, and it is weak in other fields as well, practically in dealing with the interpersonal and organizational aspects of work. Consequently, when the novice professionals confront new, unexpected problems in these spheres of their work, they are often at a loss for how to deal with them. If they find a solution that "works," they tend to continue using it uncritically. They rely heavily on "cookbook" solutions that may not be the most effective ways to handle these situations. Yet one cannot blame the practitioners, for their training usually has not encouraged them to use the scientific method in the practical aspects of their work.

Thus, gaps in training were a cause of burnout in new public professionals and should be a target for future intervention. However, the capacity to prevent professional burnout through training alone is ultimately limited. There are usually significant structural strains in the work place that must also be addressed if progress is to be made.

14

REDUCING PROFESSIONAL BURNOUT: INTERVENTIONS IN THE WORK PLACE

Although much can be done to better prepare new professionals through improvements in their training, the focus for intervention must ultimately turn to the work setting. One of the most consistent findings to emerge from the study was that the structure of the work setting greatly influenced the amount of stress and burnout experienced during the initial phase of a professional's career. Thus, the work place is an obvious and necessary point for intervention. Many useful improvements can be made in public human service organizations that do not require massive increases in funding. Of course, such increases would be desirable for many reasons. But, too often, administrators and staff come to believe that nothing can be done to alleviate stress and improve working conditions without increases in funding. This myth is a major obstacle to change.

The various types of intervention in the work place that can be used to reduce professional burnout may be divided into four general categories: staff development and counseling, the structure of the job, leadership and supervision, and organizational goals, methods, and norms. The literature on organizational change and development is filled with strategies and techniques for intervention in each of these areas.

.

STAFF DEVELOPMENT AND COUNSELING

Staff development programs represent a particularly useful way in which to influence professional goals and expectations, foster the development of useful coping skills, support effective problem solving, and provide opportunities for emotional catharsis and social support. Most human service programs sponsor in-service training and other kinds of staff development activities, but probably few have used staff development in a conscious effort to reduce professional burnout. Of the many methods that could be employed, four will be briefly discussed here.

Orientation Programs

A major factor in professional burnout in the career is "reality shock," the sharp discontinuity between the novice's expectations and the day-to-day reality of professional practice. Even when the novice has been involved in field work practice, the discontinuities usually exist, for students are rarely exposed to all aspects of the "back stage reality" (Kramer, 1974). Work places that hire the new professional can alleviate reality shock and burnout through carefully planned orientation programs based on what has been learned about the most typical strains experienced by new public professionals.

Most of the public human service agencies from which our new professionals came did not have such programs. The novices received some brief instruction on what forms must be completed, when, and how. Otherwise, they were left to fend for themselves. However, there were some noteworthy exceptions. Mental health professional Diane Peterson was hired before her training was completed and began working part-time in the agency, gradually working up to fulltime. During the first two months, she was involved in an intensive educational experience including reading, visits to other programs and agencies, seminars, and observations of experienced workers conducting interviews and other important functions. As she became more familiar with the field, the agency, and her new role, her responsibility and autonomy were gradually increased. After two months, she began to work with clients on her own.

The orientation of new public health nurse Sarah Prentiss was similarly extensive. During her first six weeks in the public health department, part of her time was spent attending seminars and workshops instructing her on various aspects of the agency's work. The other part of her time involved work in the field with a more experienced nurse who functioned as her "field advisor." As Sarah became more familiar with the role, her field advisor gave her more responsibility and autonomy. After four months, she functioned totally on her own.

Although Sarah and Diane, like all the professionals, had received considerable previous training, their orientation programs filled in many of the gaps that still existed. Also, because the novices were now real professionals employed in real jobs, the lessons learned in these orientation sessions seemed more important and meaningful. Therefore, they probably absorbed much more than they had in previous training experiences that may not have seemed as critical for successful role performance. Finally, and perhaps most important, these orientation programs communicated to the novices that they were not expected to know everything, to be finished products, to be fully competent from the very beginning. This message did much to alleviate the crisis of competence.

Of course, the work setting can expect too little of the novice professional as well as too much. Social worker Nick Fisher chafed when his supervisor gave him excessively elementary advice and suggestions. Nick, who had been a classroom teacher for five years before returning to graduate school in social work, felt that his experience and ability were being discounted. Orientation processes should be scaled to the individual needs of the participants and conducted in such a way that the participants do not feel infantilized. When this is done, it is unlikely that effects of an orientation program will be negative. In fact, our research suggests that the vast majority of new public professionals would gladly participate in relevant orientation programs.

Unfortunately, few public agencies with limited funding and crushing caseloads can afford such lengthy, formal orientation and socialization for new workers. However, most public agencies could probably do more than they do now—which is nothing at all. In fact, a modest but carefully designed orientation program, requiring only two or three extra work days for the new professional and even less time for more experienced workers who participate in it, would probably save time and money in the long run. The savings would occur because the new staff person could develop more realistic expectations, greater self-confidence, better coping strategies, and a more positive attitude toward the job and agency. Consequently, the new person could reach independent and adequate functioning sooner and remain in the agency longer, thus reducing the turnover rate.

In one published study of an orientation program, Gomersall and Myers (1966) reduced stress and greatly facilitated the initial learning process through an experimental program that required only one working day. In this program, the new workers were isolated with a few peers during their first day at work, and a relaxed and informal atmosphere was created. No work was done this first day. Instead, the new workers were shown actual data on the amount of time usually required to learn their jobs, were warned to disregard talk from older workers intended to "haze" them by scaring them, told how to take the initiative in communication with co-workers and supervisors, and were candidly told by other workers what kind of person their supervisor was.

An even more modest approach to orientation, one focusing particularly on expectations, has been described by Weitz (1956). He cited research suggesting that when new workers were given booklets describing typical, frustrating, "critical incidents" encountered on the job by experienced workers, they were less likely to quit during the first six months. Also, the "realistic" booklets, compared to the more positive booklets used to orient the workers in the past, did not lead the workers to drop out before they even began, as some supervisors had feared. There is an understandable concern that painting too grim a picture would chase away promising prospects. However, the use of a realistic orientation booklet did not seem to have that effect in this case.

The two orientation programs described here obviously would not be feasible or effective in every case. However, almost any human service agency has the means to study its existing informal orientation process and then to use this knowledge to develop its own program, best tailored for the specific job situation confronted by new professionals. The two main requirements for the development of effective orientation programs are first, an awareness on the part of the agency leadership that a new professional's initial experiences play a crucial role in her or his subsequent development and performance and, second, a willingness to devise and implement formal orientation programs that will make those initial experiences more constructive.

The "Burnout Checkup"

Periodic appraisal and evaluation of staff in human service agencies is common. Such assessments are generally used to determine merit pay increases, promotions, and so on. Sometimes they are used as a pretext for easing out unwanted staff. Occasionally, they can serve the positive function of providing staff members with the kind of feedback that fosters learning and growth. However, there is rarely an institutionalized, periodic assessment focusing on the staff person's current stress level in the job and future potential for burnout—a "burnout checkup." Mendel (1978) has suggested that such a procedure be instituted for every staff person as a way of decreasing burnout.

The typical evaluation of staff is conducted by supervisors. The focus is on the adequacy of performance. The process may be more or less formal, strained, and uncomfortable for those involved. However, the regular "burnout checkup" would be conducted by an individual who has no formal administrative authority over the staff person, and results would have no bearing on pay raises or promotions. The focus would be on the staff person's job satisfaction. The purpose would be to identify all the chronic strains and frustrations that might contribute to burnout and to plan appropriate action. For instance, it might be found that the staff person had taken on too many extra administrative responsibilities and that this was contributing to excessive levels of stress. Or, it might be discovered that the staff person's expectations were unrealistic and contributed to unnecessary stress and disappointment.

Thus, the burnout checkup would assess the current level of stress, strain, commitment, and satisfaction with work and identify factors that might lead to a decline in commitment and motivation in the future. If the person were found to be "at risk," some type of corrective action would follow. It could take the form of job restructuring, a change in supervision, personal counseling, or any of the other types of intervention to be described. Of course, there would also have to be a commitment on the part of the administration to act on the results of these checkups. For instance, staff are often *encouraged* to take on excessive work and responsibility and to maintain unnecessarily high standards. Supervisors and administrators must be prepared to change their own behavior in some cases.

Individual Counseling

Although professional burnout typically is a social organizational problem, not an individual one, there are sometimes situations in which the individual can be helped through individual counseling. It should be obvious that this does not mean a lengthy program of psychotherapy, involving all aspects of the person's life, aimed at a major restructuring of the personality. Such an intervention would probably be an expensive, inefficient, misguided approach and a gross invasion of privacy if it occurred within the work setting.

The counseling suggested here would be brief and focused on job-related attitudes and behavior. Like the burnout checkup, it normally would be conducted by someone having no formal administrative authority over the individual; however, it could be an integral part of supervision if the staff person's relationship with the supervisor were an open and trusting one.

A good example of this type of intervention was described by Schwartz and Will (1961). They claimed that burnout ("low morale syndrome") in a psychiatric nurse was reduced through a series of interviews conducted by an outside researcher. In these informal sessions, the researcher encouraged the nurse to ventilate her feelings, maintained an accepting and nonjudgmental attitude toward her, and encouraged the development of an "attitude of inquiry" toward the problem by asking detailed questions, paraphrasing, and offering occasional interpretations. Although only one nurse was involved in this counseling, the authors believed that her positive changes in attitude and behavior soon spread to other staff members. They believed that the development of insight into the problem that occurred during the counseling was the basis of the positive change.

Like orientation programs, personal counseling can encourage the individual to critically examine his goals and expectations and to give up those that are unrealistic. Counseling can also help the individual to adopt new work goals that provide alternative sources of gratification when progress toward other goals is temporarily stalled or difficult to detect. In our own research, poverty lawyers who saw their role as being educational and supportive as well as legal seemed to be more immune to burnout. Even when they could not solve a person's legal problems, they could feel that they were contributing to that person's well-being in other ways. Individual counseling could encourage such a change in goals and help monitor them so that the changes that did occur did not lead to a decline in commitment and effort that might be detrimental to clients.

Other functions of individual counseling with a focus on job stress and burnout include emotional catharsis, social support, and the provision of coping skills and strategies that could be used by the professional to alleviate work-related strain. For instance, the new professional could be taught how to most effectively use her supervisor and co-workers as sources of support and as means of coping with work demands. One new teacher we interviewed discovered on her own that she could spend time observing in the classrooms of more experienced teachers if she offered to help them in some way while she was there (for example, by working individually with a slower student who often disrupted class). In this way, she became a less obtrusive and threatening "observer," yet she was able to gain valuable ideas to use in her own classes. Individual counseling can help the new professional find viable means of obtaining opportunities for support, interaction, and the sharing of skills, thus alleviating burnout in several important ways.

Staff Support Groups

. Support groups for staff can often serve the same functions, and they may even do so more effectively. Many new public professionals in stressful jobs tend to feel their reactions are unique. They rarely discuss their feelings in any kind of sustained or systematic way with others. Thus, opportunities to regularly discuss and analyze burnout experiences with others working in similar situations can reduce burnout and its effects. Support groups provide ample opportunity for this to occur.

In a support group, professional staff from the same agency or different ones come together, usually on a regular basis, to talk about their work experiences.* There usually is not a formal leader and little structure or planned "agenda." Members share satisfactions, frustrations, and uncertainties. Those with specific problems can present them to the group and receive concrete suggestions. The climate is characterized by acceptance and mutual concern.

Research on stress supports the view that social interaction tend to help the individual cope, especially when one has a positive relationship with the persons with whom one interacts (McGrath, 1970). One function of interaction is to provide support for comforting beliefs and attitudes. Another is to allow individuals to compare their experiences with those of others in similar situations. Finding that one's difficulties are not unique and that one is coping as well

---

*Two of the public health nurses we interviewed had formed such a group with two other nurses working in different agencies. They had all graduated together from the same nursing program, and their regular meetings seemed to provide much emotional support to those interviewed.

as, or better than, others can be extremely comforting (Mechanic, 1962). Thus, it is not surprising that those who have written about professional burnout frequently point to the potential benefits of support groups (for instance, Maslach, 1976).

However, the research on the benefits of social interaction in dealing with stress is mixed, suggesting that sometimes support groups could be more harmful than helpful. The danger of "unintended consequences" is especially great here. For instance, McGrath's (1970) review of what is known about stress suggested that too much social interaction is aversive. Interaction, even in a "support" group, can itself become a source of stress. In the study by Mechanic (1962), talking to seemingly more competent or more anxious graduate students generated *more* anxiety, not less, in graduate students about to take prelims. More isolated graduate students actually tended to be less concerned and became concerned later because the stress of the other students was less visible to them. Social interaction can hurt rather than help.

Hopefully, a support group created with the explicit purpose of helping reduce stress and burnout would be more helpful than harmful, but this may not necessarily be the case. With little difficulty, such groups could become "bitch" sessions in which many mildly frustrated and annoyed staff members are encouraged to become angry and bitter without any sense of resolution or catharsis. As Schwartz and Will (1961) found in their study of psychiatric ward nurses, burnout can be highly contagious. When professionals who are already burned out come together to discuss their feelings and experiences, the outcome could well be even more burnout, whether or not the gathering is euphemistically called a "support" group.

Also, the support provided in support groups may encourage thinking and actions that are detrimental to the professional-client relationship even though they help alleviate stress and strain for the professional. For instance, Maslach (1973) noted that support from others could enhance the use of defense mechanisms that promoted dehumanizing emotional detachment from clients. An example was the mechanism of "joking on clients." Interaction with other professionals could encourage one to make fun of one's clients and to regard them in less positive and sympathetic terms. Support groups that encouraged such activity would clearly not be the best way to deal with the professional burnout problem.

Thus, support groups have great potential as a means of combatting burnout, but ultimate benefit or harm will depend on how they are structured. If the group becomes a "bitch" session or a way of avoiding action ("paralysis through analysis"), the members may leave feeling worse than when they came. However, if the feelings of members are accepted and they are helped to go *beyond* the expression of feeling, to formulate constructive attitudes and behaviors for dealing with problems, the support group can be a powerful method for alleviating burnout.

There are many other types of staff development activity that could be used to alleviate burnout. In-service training seminars or workshops on "stress management" and burnout are obvious examples. However, staff development is but one route of several. The structure of the professional staff person's job represents another promising area for change in human service agencies.

RESTRUCTURING THE JOB

Chapter 9 examined the factors in the work setting that seemed to be related to differences in degree of strain experienced by new public professionals. Several of these were related to the structure of the job, including the workload, amount of stimulation, the scope of client contact, autonomy—and, to some extent, social isolation. Is it possible to change the structure of a professional's job in a human service agency in order to modify it along the dimensions that seem to influence burnout? For instance, could the job be modified to increase stimulation, autonomy, and the range of client contact or decrease the workload or social isolation? The answer, of course, depends upon the setting. Programs that are part of large bureaucratic institutions in which job definitions are formally prescribed to a great degree by those at higher levels of the hierarchy (for example, social welfare offices) will be difficult to change. Also, settings in which the structure of the job has been established through strong tradition going back many years (for instance, the job of classroom teacher in the public schools) will be difficult to change. However, in most settings, there is some flexibility in the structure of staff jobs, and changes in job structure that alleviate burnout will be possible.

Modifying the Workload

Overload is probably one of the most typical sources of strain for public professionals. The professional is asked to do too much for too many clients, with little opportunity for even temporary escape. An obvious intervention, therefore, would be to decrease the workload by hiring more staff. Unfortunately, such a proposal requires a massive increase in financial support for human service programs (a laudable but politically unlikely event). It also requires a massive increase in the number of trained professionals, an increase that cannot occur very quickly given the existing capacity of professional training programs, no matter how much money is available for increasing the capacity. Thus, this obvious change in the job structure is also one of the more difficult changes to achieve, at least in the way we usually think of achieving it.

However, there are ways in which the workload of the public professional can be reduced without a major infusion of resources. For instance, paraprofessionals can be more fully utilized for service delivery. In schools, paraprofessionals in the classroom, working under the supervision of the teacher, could reduce the strain associated with teaching a large, heterogenous group of unwilling students. The teacher could spend part of his or her time working with the paraprofessionals, an activity that might be more rewarding or less stressful than working with the entire class of students. Also, the paraprofessionals could share responsibility for classroom management, allowing the teacher to take "time-outs" more frequently. (By time-outs, I mean short periods of time when the teacher could withdraw from the responsibility of maintaining classroom control and student interest to restore psychological equilibrium.) The scope of responsibility for paralegals in law agencies and mental health technicians in mental health facilities could similarly be expanded to reduce strain on professional staff.

In some settings, changing the way in which responsibility for clients is assigned could also reduce workload and strain for the professional. For instance, Maslach and Pines (1977) found that there were two models for assigning responsibility in day care programs: the children and staff could be divided into subsets, with certain staff regularly responsible for the same small subset or all staff could share responsibility for all children. The child/staff ratio could be the same in these two situations, but the strain on staff was less when they were responsible for only a small subset of the entire population. Not only did the workload seem less heavy in this arrangement, but the staff could also experience a greater sense of personal impact because the children to which they were assigned were "their" children. Thus, without any change in the client/staff ratio, a change in the structure of the staff job reduced the perceived sense of overload and increased the sense of personal impact and effectiveness.

Burnout in professionals can also be combatted by regulating the types of clients assigned to each staff person. In any human service agency, certain clients are going to be regarded as the "dirty work" of the agency. As Maslach (1976) has noted, these are usually the most resistant to change, the least cooperative, the least likely to improve, and so on. Involuntary, abusive, or demanding individuals would fall into this category. The unmotivated and "acting out" student, the multiproblem family, and the more severely disturbed and chronic client in a mental health agency would all be regarded as less rewarding and stimulating work situations by most professionals. Although it would be nice if professionals regarded these types of clients and work situations in a more positive way, that, in fact, is unlikely. Professionals want certain rewards from their work that these clients frequently do not provide. Yet these are the clients who are most likely to come to public human service agencies for help because they will not be accepted by private settings or practitioners.

However, not all clients in public human service agencies are unrewarding. And, if care is taken in the way clients are assigned to professionals in such settings, the more difficult and frustrating work of the setting can be shared. In fact, new professionals can be helped during this critical period of their careers if they are assigned a smaller number of the more difficult cases. Unfortunately, the assignment of cases is often done without any consideration for the impact on job stress and burnout, or there is an attempt to do it on the basis of blind equity or seniority, which increases the burden on the novice. For instance, in many public schools, the new teachers are given the most difficult and least desirable class assignments. As one's seniority increases, one "earns" the right to be assigned more rewarding or easier teaching assignments (Becker, 1952). Interestingly, the pattern is very different in large corporate law firms where the more difficult cases are typically assigned to more senior members (Lortie, 1973). The results of our research suggest that, to minimize burnout in public professionals, novices should be assigned the most motivated, rewarding, and least difficult clients. As they grow in skill and self-confidence, they can take on more difficult work. Because they are eased into it and take it on when they are more prepared to do so, the professionals in such a system might not be as negatively affected by their contact with the more frustrating and arduous work assignments. Also, these assignments assume a mark of distinction in such a system. Rather than being seen as bad luck, a particularly difficult class or client or case could be seen as recognition that one is a master professional who has demonstrated the capacity to work with such situations and to do so more effectively than most.

An institution for the mentally retarded described by Sarason, Zitnay, and Grossman (1971) was designed to reduce stress and to increase variety and stimulation for staff by changing the usual pattern of assigning staff to clients and programs. In their institution, all staff were required to work at least two programs. Thus, if a staff member worked part of the day or week or month in a difficult program, she would have the opportunity to work in a different, more rewarding setting at other times. Of course, some staff members preferred to work with the more difficult and frustrating programs, and they were allowed to do so. But it was assumed that even if one initially preferred working in such a setting, over time the impact would be negative unless there were some change in the staff member's assignment.

This approach to combatting burnout through the assignment of staff to different programs could probably be adopted in many other types of institutions, including the public schools in which new teachers might be placed initially in the "choicest" settings and then would spend part of their time in more difficult settings as they gained experience and confidence. In the case of poverty lawyers, the program could be designed in such a way that all the staff would have an opportunity to spend at least some time working in reform law or on more interesting and challenging cases. No lawyer should be forced to spend all of his or her time working in a setting in which many of the clients are abusive, the workload is crushing, and the cases are relatively small and insignificant. Legal work cannot always be exciting and rewarding, nor can teaching or public health or mental health work. But new professionals can be assigned to programs in a way that enables them to work in more rewarding situations.

Increasing Feedback in the Job

Building in better monitoring and feedback mechanisms represents another promising approach to alleviating burnout in new public professionals. The central concern of the new professional is competence. Unfortunately, even when the professional is effective, there is often no way for her to know this. This problem is especially acute in fields such as education and mental health. And, to a certain extent, the problem is inevitable. Uncertainty about outcome is an inherent dilemma in human service settings. Even when measures of client progress exist, such as pupil achievement tests in the schools, there is a cloud of controversy surrounding their validity and significance. Further, even if the outcome measures are accepted as valid by all involved, it is impossible to determine the professional's contribution to change (Hasenfeld & English, 1974).

Nevertheless, many human service programs could probably do more than they presently do to provide ongoing feedback to their staffs. For instance, the treatment of chronic schizophrenics is a field in which progress occurs slowly and is often difficult to measure. Real cures are few and far between. Most chronic schizophrenics do not get better and stay better. Staff members working in such programs badly need mechanisms that provide feedback on very subtle changes in the client functioning. In one experiment (Colarelli and Siegel, 1966), the staff of a psychiatric ward in a large state hospital were given such a mechanism in the form of a "levels system." This system categorized the clients as being at one of five levels of functioning. The first level represented a bare, vegetative existence. The next level was far from optimal self-actualization, but it represented real improvement that the staff person and co-workers could see. The system was developed based on careful study of the pattern of progress usually followed by chronic patients in the hospital, and it provided benchmarks that the staff could use to set realistic short-term goals for themselves and to experience a sense of efficacy and achievement when those goals were attained. According to the data collected on staff attitudes and changes, this "levels system" made a major contribution to staff morale and helped reduce what was becoming a serious burnout problem.

Reducing Social Isolation

Support groups represent one way of reducing social isolation and increasing collegiality among professionals working in public human service agencies. However, isolation also can be reduced by restructuring jobs to increase collaboration. For instance, Lortie (1975) has suggested several rather modest proposals for increasing collaboration among teachers, such as conferencing individual students, observation of special lessons taught by peers and visitors, and the occasional exchange of classes. These activities occur rarely in schools today, and the burden of social isolation is especially heavy for the new teacher. By building such collaborative activity into the teacher's job, by making it an institutional expectation, some of the pernicious isolation and lack of collegiality that hamper the adjustment of the novice could be eliminated.

In mental health settings, professionals can be encouraged to co-lead groups. Program development also provides an opportunity for collaboration, as when a team of mental health professionals or public health nurses work together to develop a mental health education program. In legal aid settings, lawyers could occasionally be allowed to collaborate on bigger cases that would normally be too involved for one lawyer to work on alone anyway. Thus, in any field, jobs can be structured to increase collaboration and decrease the social isolation that is particularly difficult for the novice.

Fulltime versus Part-Time Work

One final aspect of the job that deserves serious consideration is its "fulltimedness." The transition from student to professional is abrupt, in part because working 40 hours a week (it usually turns out to be 50 for the neophyte) in a fulltime job is so different from the schedule that has been followed during one's training. However, even if schooling became as rigidly structured and fulltime as the standard professional job, the strain on the novice would be great. All of the demands, frustrations, and uncertainties that have been discussed are exacerbated by the almost total involvement in work that is required by a fulltime job. It will be recalled that two of the new professionals who adjusted best to their jobs, who experienced less stress, more fulfillment, more sustained commitment and idealism (mental health professional Diane Peterson and high school teacher Alice Harris) began working on a part-time basis. Gradually, their involvement increased until one was fulltime and the other was four-fifths time. Their situations were unique in other ways as well, so we have no way of knowing to what extent beginning on a part-time basis contributed to more positive career development. However, it is likely that it did play a role.

Very few of the people who assume professional responsibilities in public human service institutions begin on a part-time basis. The jobs and programs are not structured to permit it. We live in a culture in which working fulltime is associated with virtue, especially when one has received extensive training to do what one does. The thought of well-trained professionals working only part-time is unthinkable to many. On the other hand, professional work in public institutions is filled with stress and frustration. The fulltime job promotes burnout by preventing one from escaping from the stress or participating in alternative forms of activity that might be more fulfilling. The "professional mystique" (Chapter 15) that encourages us to think that professional work is inherently stimulating, rewarding, and pleasant is undoubtedly a contributor to the belief that professionals, like most other workers, should work fulltime.

In many settings, there are institutional barriers to working part-time. For instance, in many organizations, professional personnel who work less than full-time lose all of their benefits such as health care and retirement. Working part-time becomes so difficult and unattractive that they feel compelled to work full-time despite the associated stress and strain.

Although the promotion of the idea of part-time jobs for professionals would be especially helpful to the novice, all would probably benefit. Working in a classroom or a mental health clinic or a poverty law office is difficult, frustrating, and frequently unrewarding. One often feels that one is giving much more than one is getting. To do this eight or more hours a day, week after week, produces an adverse reaction that not only affects the professional and his family but the institution and client as well. Philosopher Bertrand Russell recognized this fact many years ago when, in an essay discussing education and teaching, he wrote:

> Unfortunately, it is utterly impossible for overworked teachers to preserve an instinctive liking for children; they are bound to come to feel towards them as the proverbial confectioner's apprentice does towards macaroons. I do not think that education ought to be anyone's whole profession: it should be undertaken for at most two hours a day by people whose remaining hours are spent away from children. The society of the young is fatiguing, especially when strict discipline is avoided. Fatigue, in the end, produces irritation, which is likely to express itself somehow, whatever theories the harrassed teacher may have taught himself or herself to believe. The necessary friendliness cannot be preserved by self-control alone (Russell, 1976, pp. 209–210).

Although part-time jobs for professionals may seem like a hopelessly expensive and impractical proposal, we have already seen that at least two of the new public professionals participating in our study began their careers in this manner. Even if such arrangements do not become widespread, they clearly could be adopted more than they have been for the novice. However, such a change in the structure of the job, like the others that have been proposed, will help alleviate burnout best when accompanied by changes in the attitudes and behaviors of those who supervise new public professionals and their work settings. Management development is another area in which progress toward reducing professional burnout in human service settings could be made.

MANAGEMENT DEVELOPMENT

Supervision and leadership play a crucial role in the burnout syndrome in public human service agencies. Therefore, they also represent an important point of intervention. One of the earliest papers to mention the term "burnout" suggested that a major cause of burnout in nontraditional human service settings was "loss of charisma of the leader" (Freudenberger, 1974). Another, more rigorous study of the problem conducted in more conventional human service settings (child abuse programs) found that, of all the factors contributing to burnout in staff, leadership and supervision seemed to be most strongly associated with the problem (Berkeley Planning Associates, 1977). Furthermore, in a study of early career development in priests, Hall and Schneider (1973) found that the priest's first supervisor and the quality of the relationship between priest and supervisor strongly influenced the extent to which the new priest would experience "psychological success" and positive career development in the future.*

Supervisors serve several important functions for the new professional in a public human service institution. First, they provide information and technical instruction that are sorely needed to perform the role effectively and that cannot be fully acquired in earlier training and orientation. Second, the supervisor can provide the novice with the structure, organization, and direction that may be needed during the difficult period of transition from student to professional. It is through the supervisor that role expectations and agency goals are primarily communicated to the new worker. Thus, supervisors can influence the degree of role conflict, ambiguity, and strain experienced by the professional staff person.

Third, the supervisor is an important source of feedback for the new professional. Feedback is crucial at this stage of the career, as novices seek to learn how their performance fits the standards and expectations of their profession and work setting. Although there may be many potential sources of feedback, the new professionals usually look first to their supervisors. Unfortunately, they often are disappointed. For instance, studies of supervision in teaching and social work have found that supervisors frequently sidestep evaluation and feedback to subordinates and underestimate the extent to which subordinates want concrete feedback, negative as well as positive (Kadushin, 1974; Lortie, 1973).

The fourth important function of supervision for new professionals is social support. During a period of emotional turbulence, the novice looks to the

---

*While I use "supervision" and "administration" interchangeably, it should be clear that these are often separate functions and roles. In public schools, the principal is both the immediate supervisor for the classroom teacher and also the top administrator in the school. However, in a large mental health clinic or institution, a social worker's supervisor may have no other administrative responsibilities. The "administrator" is another, higher-level official. The recommendations concerning management development that follow are equally important and relevant for supervisors and administrators.

supervisor for help. Supervisors who are available to hear subordinates discuss their feelings about their jobs, especially frustrations, fears, and resentments, help alleviate the stress that contributes to burnout. Too often, however, the new professionals we studied did not develop the kind of open and trusting relationship with their supervisors that facilitated emotional support. Also, their supervisors concentrated on the surface task and discouraged the novice from discussing more personal, subjective, and emotional aspects of the work. Thus, supervisory behavior frequently did not provide the new professional with a means of dealing with stress and burnout.

One other important function of supervision is leadership. The supervisor provides a role model for the new professional, and the way in which the novice copes with work demands will be greatly influenced by the way in which the supervisor approaches demands. If the supervisor is calm, easygoing, and positive in his or her response to problems and obstacles, the new professional will tend to respond in a similar way. If, on the other hand, the supervisor is tense, irritable, and easily threatened, if the supervisor responds to frustrations by becoming perfectionistic and rigid, the new professional will tend to emulate this style and the potential for burnout will be greater.

Leadership also involves advocacy for one's staff and program. Supervisors who are able to effectively buffer their staff from excessive demands directed at the program by outside forces will help maintain a better work environment for staff. Similarly, the supervisor or administrator who is effective at "working the system," securing resources and policies that aid the staff in their work, will do much to reduce the strain that contributes to professional burnout. Supervisors and administrators within any organization vary in their real power and influence. Influential administrators who use their influence to modify those work factors that contribute to burnout in staff will make a great difference to the new professional.

In thinking about interventions to improve the quality of supervision provided to new professionals in human service settings, it is important to identify the factors that contribute to ineffective supervisory behavior. Unfortunately, there is little research in this area. In general, poor supervision may be caused by the supervisor's lack of knowledge or skill or by the demands associated with the supervisor's role. For instance, supervisors may not appreciate the value of allowing staff to work through their questions and problems on their own during supervisory sessions (Cherniss & Egnatios, 1978c). Consequently, they routinely give advice and interpretations, frustrating the staff member's needs for autonomy and growth.

However, if the supervisor is overwhelmed by demands to monitor paperwork, by constant cries that must be handled, or by too many workers to supervise, the quality of supervision will suffer. In fact, supervisors can experience burnout just as staff can; a burned out supervisor is one who has become indifferent and withdrawn in response to chronic role stress. Burnout in supervisors probably occurs frequently in public human service organizations because supervisors must juggle bureaucratic norms and organizational demands for control with professional norms and demands for collegiality and autonomy (Chapter 4). Thus, while attitudes and skills of supervisors are important and one should not assume that those in human service organizations possess the attributes required for effective supervision, role demands on the supervisor may make positive attitudes and skills irrelevant.

These possible causes of poor supervision suggest three types of intervention. First, there is clearly some need for training programs for supervisors and administrators in human service settings. These programs should have three objectives. First, they should convincingly demonstrate that professional burnout is an important problem deserving attention. Second, they should demonstrate that supervisors and administrators strongly influence the degree of stress and burnout experienced by professionals in their settings. Third, they should teach managerial personnel the skills and behaviors that seem to be most constructive in helping public professionals cope with stress and strain in their work.

However, training alone is probably not enough. Supervisors and administrators should also be helped to monitor their own performances as "agents of burnout control" through periodic feedback. Numerous studies (for example, Hegarty, 1974) have shown that when supervisors are provided with the results of anonymous ratings of their supervisory performance collected from staff through interviews or questionnaires, the supervisors frequently change their behavior in positive ways. Just as staff members often have little feedback, positive or negative, so also administrators rarely get good feedback. When feedback is provided, positive change often occurs.

The final type of intervention involves modification of the supervisor's or administrator's job. Many of the ideas presented previously about restructuring jobs apply here as well. One additional idea suggested by Abrahamson (1967) is the division or separation of technical and administrative aspects of supervision. When a supervisor in a human service setting must be responsible for administrative management and technical and emotional support for the staff, as is usually the case with the public school principal, the technical and emotional functions often are neglected or disrupted. On the other hand, when an administrator is charged with handling administrative aspects and there is also a supervising professional who is primarily responsible for staff support, these two functions tend to be better served. An example given by Abrahamson is the medical hospital in which senior physicians on the wards provide technical supervision while nonmedical administrative personnel assume responsibility for coordination and control functions necessary in any large organizational setting. In our own research, some of the mental health and public health agencies followed a similar pattern in which the new professionals met regularly and frequently with supervisors who continued to practice at least part of the time themselves and who were responsible primarily for staff support. Administrative and control functions were handled primarily by administrators who had no additional responsibility for the technical and social support of the staff.

The splitting of administrative and technical/emotional functions of supervision may well be the kind of restructuring of managerial roles that will alleviate burnout in staff. Only experimentation in individual work settings will clearly show whether the benefits of such an arrangement outweigh the costs, many of which are probably not known clearly at this time. However, even if this particular proposal proves to be impractical or harmful, there are probably other ways in which administrative and supervisory jobs can be modified in order to promote the kind of support needed to help all professionals, especially new ones, to work and grow in positive ways on the job.

PROGRAM GOALS, METHODS, AND TRADITIONS

A program's goals and guiding philosophy represent the final point of intervention for reducing professional burnout in the work place. As stated in Chapter 9, clear and consistent role expectations are particularly important for new professionals. As they develop greater self-confidence and a coherent, internal professional value system, clear external expectations may become less important. However, during the crucial initial phase of their careers, they look to the organization for guidance and structure. Conflict in program goals will inevitably lead to conflict in professional roles, and role conflict is a major source of stress and burnout. Similarly, ambiguity in program goals will lead to ambiguity in professional roles, another major source of stress and burnout.

The nature of human service organizations makes them inherently resistant to articulation of clear and consistent goals (Hasenfeld and English, 1974); however, some programs are clearly more successful than others in achieving clarity and consistency. For instance, the neighborhood legal aid agency in which new poverty lawyer Margaret Williams went to work seemed to lack a clear, singular sense of purpose. As a result, she entered with the expectation that she would be doing more reform work and "big cases" than she was actually able to do. The agency was not ready to accept the provision of routine legal services to the poor as its goal. Social change and other possible goals continued to be seen as vaguely relevant. On the other hand, the agency in which poverty lawyer Jean Chalmers went to work did have a single clear goal; to initiate and follow through on class action lawsuits that would modify the system in ways that would increase social justice for the poor. The agency was more specialized in its goals. The goals were clear and consistent. Beginning a professional career in such a setting was thus easier and led to more positive outcomes in professional attitudes and behavior. Articulating clear and consistent goals in a human service program can be a frustrating, difficult endeavor, but it is an important means of reducing burnout in new public professionals.

A second way in which program goals influence professional burnout is in their impact on role strain and overload. Programs that adopt overly ambitious goals are likely to be settings in which burnout is high. For instance, Mendel (1978) has argued that there is much staff burnout in programs for the care and rehabilitation of chronic schizophrenics because the goal of such programs, too often, is complete "cure" of the clients. But for many clients in such programs, even the ability to work fulltime in the regular job market for a sustained period of time may be too much for which to hope. Mendel argues that when staff attempt to attain such lofty goals and fail, as they almost always will, they become frustrated, demoralized, and ultimately give up altogether. They come to believe that the clients are hopeless and that no change is possible. Mendel advocates the adoption of what he calls the "rehabilitation model" in such programs. This model defines the goal of treatment as maximizing the individual's ability to function and minimizing dysfunction and emotional distress. Success is defined in terms of specific functions the client can perform rather than the abolition of all problems. In other words, permanently eliminating all delusions and hallucinations in a client is simply not seen as the program's goal. Helping that client learn how to take the bus to get around town whenever he wishes is the kind of goal the program strives to accomplish.

There is always the danger, of course, that, in their attempts to reduce strain and burnout, programs will adopt goals that expect too little of themselves and their clients. In the past, this has happened especially in work with certain populations assumed to be less able. For instance, less has been expected in the way of school achievement for poor children than for middle class children. To the extent that such expectations become self-fulfilling prophecies (Rosenthal and Jacobson, 1968), they can actually cause poor children to learn less and perform poorly in school. The same may happen in any human service program that adopts goals that are overly modest. (The custodial mental hospital or institution for the mentally retarded is a notorious example.)

Nevertheless, it is clear that programs that go too far in the other direction, that adopt goals that are totally unrealistic given the existing resources, expertise, and needs of the clients, will not do substantially better in the long run. Their staffs will burnout quickly and, as they do so, will adopt attitudes and behaviors toward clients that will ultimately be detrimental to the helping process.

Care must also be taken that program goals do not impose subtle, unintended demands on professional staff that contribute to burnout or harmful treatment of clients. For instance, discrimination in teachers' behavior toward students may be more related to role demands and program goals than to attitudes that the teachers bring with them when they begin teaching. As Lortie (1973) noted, when the demand for order in the classroom is high, those students who conform less to typical rules may become objects of discrimination. By making classroom order a less important goal, the school reduces the need for rule proliferation and enforcement. Pressure on both teachers and students is lessened, and teachers will be less likely to scapegoat and lash out against misbehaving students. Thus, reducing the importance of certain program goals, such as maintaining orderly clients or files, is another way in which human service administrators and policy makers can reduce staff burnout. The goals themselves, as well as their clarity and consistency, represent a possible point of intervention.

A related recommendation is that direct service goals be balanced with other goals in human service programs, especially knowledge and skill development. Providing service to clients is clearly the major goal of any human service program. But, as Goldenberg (1971) observed, when this is the only goal or when it totally dominates all other goals, staff and organizational problems are inevitable.

Balancing direct service goals with the goals of experimentation and the pursuit of knowledge combat staff burnout in at least two ways. First, the acquisition of new knowledge about service delivery represents an alternative source of gratification that helps keep professional staff going even when attempts to improve the lives of clients fail. If those service efforts are contributing to new knowledge at the same time that they are helping a particular client, resistance or slow progress in the client is less stressful for the professional. As long as the professional is *learning* and receiving recognition for that learning, the work can remain fulfilling and meaningful.

Second, there is an excitement about experimenting and learning that can keep professional staff involved in work for a long period of time. Direct service work becomes routine for many professionals. Each day seems to be much like the previous one, and it is all too easy to predict what will occur. When one is searching for new and better methods for alleviating suffering or promoting learning, one's work is no longer routine. Professionals who are experimenting and discovering new knowledge as they provide services to clients are more likely to feel that their work is open-ended, changing, creative, and absorbing. They are less likely to feel burned out and to direct their frustrations at clients and co-workers. However, this approach is unlikely unless experimentation and the pursuit of knowledge are formally defined as major goals of the program.

In our study of new professionals, there were a few individuals working in situations in which direct service and the search for new solutions were balanced. A conspicuous example was Jean Chalmers who, while helping individual clients to reverse their prison sentences and improve their lot in life, was conducting research and pleading cases in court that were changing the way in which the legal system worked. In essence, she and her colleagues spent much of their time looking for new solutions to the legal problems of their clients and others. They were breaking new ground. They were advancing arguments that had never before been advanced in courts of law. If they won, they found that those new arguments represented new "solutions" that other lawyers could use in the future. If they lost, they learned that the particular solutions they were testing did not work. In either case, they were performing "experiments" in which new knowledge was almost always an outcome. Thus, by making experimentation and the search for new solutions as important as the direct service goals of their programs, administrators in human service programs can alleviate professional burnout and promote positive career development.

Closely related to a human service program's goals are its "guiding philosophy." A number of writers on human service organizations have argued that a strong guiding philosophy enhances staff morale and motivation. For example, Reppucci (1973) wrote, "A guiding idea or philosophy which is understandable to, and provides hope for, all members of the institution, must be developed in conjunction with those members." The guiding philosophy links the general goals of a program to its day-to-day service delivery activities. For instance, an educational program might adopt the "open classroom" model, a framework for teaching that links general educational goals with the actual, specific behavior of teachers and students. Similarly, a mental health program might use psychoanalytic or behavioral theory as its guiding philosophy, and a halfway house for delinquent youth might adopt "reality therapy" or "positive peer culture."

Programs vary in the strength and centrality of their guiding philosophies. In many programs, there may not be a single, clearly defined framework for service activities. Each staff member is free to develop and use "any model that works." In other settings, there may be a formal model of treatment, "written down somewhere," that is brought out for public relations purposes but rarely discussed by staff or used as a framework for work.

In still other programs, there may be two or more guiding philosophies that become the basis of conflict and competition among staff members. For instance, in new professional Douglas Furth's mental health agency, one group identified with a psychoanalytic framework and another advocated a transactional analysis perspective. Although professional burnout is probably less severe in programs of this type than in those in which there is no guiding philosophy shared by a critical mass of staff, the unifying and motivating power of each viewpoint is weakened by the conflict and competition.

Finally, there are those programs that have developed a single, commonly shared, frequently reinforced guiding philosophy. It may be more or less elaborate, but some attempt has been made to translate the more general goals into operational guidelines and principles to which staff members frequently refer in their work with clients. In these programs, day-to-day pressures and the cause of expediency are not allowed to divert staff attention from its distinctive approach to service delivery. Staff members tend to be selected on the basis of demonstrated commitment to the established framework. There may be regular, ongoing orientation and educational programs for all staff members that help maintain commitment to that framework. In these programs, there is a sense of shared purpose and focus, which reduces much of the uncertainty that can contribute to professional burnout in the human services.

Unfortunately, a single, uniform model of service can also interfere with flexibility, innovation, and autonomy. Programs with strong guiding philosophies can be extremely resistant to change, even when confronted with strong evidence that they are failing or doing harm. An established framework may enhance morale and prevent burnout, but it may also be a shared delusion. If this orientation is imposed on staff and clients from above and they are allowed no voice in its development and given no opportunity to modify it, it can be a source of conflict that eventually leads to lower job satisfaction and motivation.

To maintain a strong, clear, guiding philosophy while minimizing potential abuses, two steps can be taken. First, staff members (and, when possible, clients) should be involved in the development, implementation, and periodic evaluation of the guiding framework. Second, what might be called the "experimental attitude" should be made an important part of a program's guiding philosophy and organizational culture. The experimental attitude, simply put, is that nothing is permanent; every decision, action, and policy must be regarded merely as an experiment, and change should occur continually on the basis of these experiments.

When a human service program's guiding philosophy is strong and well articulated, most of the staff and clients may believe that it is the only valid way of achieving the program's goals. However, it may well be the case that many other philosophies would be just as valid and effective as a basis for preventing burnout. What does seem to be important is the development of a single, unifying theme and model of practice that give the program a strong, unique, "institutional character," a clear reason for being the way it is (Selznick, 1957). Without a strong, distinct character, there is no spark, no fire, no zeal; without zeal, there is not sufficient confidence and motivation to resist the pressures that ultimately lead to burnout in many new public professionals. Thus, in addition to the development of clear and consistent goals that minimize role strain on staff and that balance direct service with the pursuit of new solutions and knowledge, creating and maintaining a strong, unifying guiding philosophy of service represents a promising way of alleviating professional burnout.

CONCLUSIONS: ADDRESSING THE LARGER PICTURE

The last two chapters have suggested a number of ways in which training programs and work settings of new public professionals could be changed in order to promote positive career development and alleviate burnout. However, it must be emphasized that these strategies will rarely work if they are imposed on staff in an arbitrary or dictatorial fashion. Job stress in the human services is a shared problem. Administrators, staff, and, when possible, clients should work together in developing strategies for alleviating stress.

For instance, a significant aspect of the monitoring and feedback mechanism developed in Colarelli and Siegel's (1966) mental hospital program was that it was not pushed onto a suspicious or unwilling staff. *It was a response to a clear call for help from the staff and it was developed in collaboration with the staff.* It was used to provide meaning and a sense of accomplishment to the staff, not as a weapon to increase "accountability" or productivity. In other words, it was developed in a spirit of trust and cooperation. The benefits of this feedback mechanism for staff would not have been realized if it had been developed and implemented without staff participation. Thus, strategies for combatting burnout should be the product of a joint effort by all affected.

One final caution for those who wish to alleviate burnout has to do with the importance of social forces beyond the immediate work setting or training program. These larger forces ultimately limit what can be accomplished through the reform of individual programs. Without changes at higher levels, accomplishments are limited. In the final analysis, burnout is neither a problem of the new public professionals, nor of the particular settings in which they work, nor of the particular settings in which they were trained. The problem of professional burnout inevitably relates to the idea of professionalism itself, the division of responsibility between the professions and the larger community for the general social welfare. The problem of burnout also relates to the way in which we tend to think about work and the relationship between work, leisure, and personal learning and growth. As long as the professions are structured as they are, as long as their role in society is defined as it is, as long as work is seen as a separate part of our lives that does not and should not have any relevance to how workers, including professional workers, spend the rest of their time, burnout in new public professionals will continue to be a problem.

At the very least, there must be a change in the way we think about the career development of new professionals in public institutions. New professionals simply do not have a secure sense of competence when they finish formal training and receive professional credentials. And, if they begin their careers in a public human service institution, they are confronted with a host of problems and dilemmas that exacerbate the crisis of competence, increase the sense of isolation and loneliness, and frustrate the quest for meaning and fulfillment in work. Until this picture of the public professional work experience replaces the professional mystique that now dominates our thinking, new public professionals will continue to burn out at an alarming rate. We shall consider these larger issues in Chapter 15.

15

PROFESSIONAL BURNOUT AND
THE SOCIAL HISTORICAL CONTEXT

The initial phase of a professional career in a public human service organization is characterized by stress, strain, and, for many, burnout. Our study of 28 new professionals from four different fields has identified factors in both the individual and the work setting that seem to contribute to this burnout. However, there are other factors, more subtle, but nevertheless important, that contribute to the phenomenon. These factors are part of the larger social historical context. They influence the individuals and the settings in which they work, and their influence is powerful, perhaps even more powerful ultimately than the factors with which we have been previously concerned.

THE PROFESSIONAL MYSTIQUE
AND THE PROBLEM OF GREAT EXPECTATIONS

People in our society have tended to view professionals and their work in highly positive ways. Although individual professionals might not live up to the cultural ideal, the archetypal professional in the past possessed more than his share of such positive human virtues as moral courage, honesty, compassion, skill, and independence. (I deliberately use the masculine third person pronoun because, among other things, the archetypal professional has been male.) For a culture in which so many of the basic values seemed confused and unattainable, there was solace to be gained from the professional as represented in the popular media (DeFleur, 1964). Here was one group of individuals in society for whom good still prevailed over evil, and the distinctions between good and evil had not become complex and ambiguous as they had everywhere else. As one social historian has put it, "The person who mastered professional discipline and control emerged as an emulated example of leadership in American society. He was self-reliant, independent, ambitious, and mentally organized. He structured a life and a career around noble aims and purposes, including the ideal of moral obligation" (Bledstein, 1976, pp. 91-92).

In the popular stereotype, professionals were rewarded for their virtue. Their work was more interesting, socially meaningful, and autonomous than anyone else's. Professionals were their own bosses. They were well paid and enjoyed greater job security than anyone else. Thus, in thinking about a career for their children, most parents felt that one could do no better than to enter one of the professions, and this value was transmitted to the children, affecting both their aspirations and expectations. To quote Bledstein (1976), "From the beginning, the ego-satisfying pretensions of professionalism have been closer to the heart of the middle class American than the raw profits of capitalism" (p. 289). For parents and their children, the professions seemed to fulfill needs for self-esteem, respect, honor, recognition, status, authority, power, and control, needs that are even stronger than the desire for material wealth. Fortunately, the professions also offered the secure prospect of fulfilling the desire for material success as well.

In some ways, the social and political unrest of the 1960s may have weakened this image, at least temporarily. Confidence in the honesty and ability of lawyers, physicians, teachers, and other professionals has eroded (Cherniss, Egnatios, & Wacker, 1976). Some young people from more affluent backgrounds seem to be hesitating about entering traditional professional vocations, choosing instead to seek "self-actualization," removing themselves from roles involving both material privileges and social responsibilities. Even among those who do enter professional occupations, some positive expectations concerning their future work seem to be given up early in their training (Sarason, Sarason, & Cowden, 1975).

Finally, there has been the growth of "anti-professional" approaches to professional practice, such as the "radical therapy" movement in the mental health field (Gross & Osterman, 1972). However, there is evidence that the attribution of positive qualities to professionals and their working conditions continues to occur. For instance, as one or two qualified youth decide not to apply to law school or medical school, a hundred others scramble for their places; applications have risen dramatically during the last five years. Also, despite a trend toward greater realism in the media, most lawyers, physicians, and other professionals depicted in television series continue to be portrayed as tough, honest, kind, good, and successful.

For many individuals involved in private practice in the most prestigious professions, the professional mystique may be valid. Thus, as for all mystiques, there is an element of truth in the professional mystique. In fact, for the mystique to maintain its strength, it must be valid for a certain number of individuals and work situations. Some professionals do feel competent; some professionals do experience high levels of autonomy in their work. But our data and the research of other investigators suggest that autonomy, stimulation, collegiality, and other aspects usually associated with professional work are not as typical as many people in our society believe, especially for professionals working in large, public institutions. An examination of several tenets central to the mystique highlights the disparity between the great expectations it generates and the reality of professional work in public settings.

The Elements of the Professional Mystique

Five aspects of the professional mystique are particularly important to new professionals. The first of these involves *competence*: a popular misconception about professionals is the confusion of "credentials" with "competence." What may distinguish new public professionals from other new workers is not their anxiety about performance, but rather the widely shared myth that they do not feel this way and *should* not feel this way because professionals are, unlike other workers, "finished products." There seems to be a strong expectation that new professionals will be competent and *feel* competent when they begin their first jobs. They have received the training necessary to assume professional duties and responsibilities. Their credentials signify to the world that they are ready. With added experience, they may become still more competent and effective. However, when they receive their degrees, it is assumed that they are relatively complete. It is in this way that professionals are most unlike other types of workers in the public view.

However, our findings suggest that these beliefs about competence and professionalism are not valid for most new professionals working in the public sector (see Chapter 2). They may have expected to feel competent when they walked into a classroom or consulting room, when they made their first home visit, or saw their first client. But they soon found that the sense of competence was elusive. With a rare exception, there was strong self-doubt and insecurity that dissipated only after many difficult months on the job, during which gaps in skill and knowledge were gradually reduced. For many of those we interviewed, complete confidence and mastery did not appear even after two years of fulltime professional practice. In conducting this study, we came to realize that professional status does not necessarily guarantee competence in every situation and that, contrary to the myth, professionals are never complete, finished products. However, these beliefs about professionalism and competence do not die easily. Because professionals are reluctant to express anxiety and self-doubt openly, many continue to think that they should feel more competent than they do and that the failure is a personal one.

Although the crisis of competence seems to be inevitable, these myths about professionals and their abilities make it worse. To use Sarason's (1977) phrase, the myths lead to "great expectations" for new professionals, expectations shared by co-workers, supervisors, clients, and the professionals themselves. They are expected to be confident, sure of themselves, efficient, and competent. They are not expected to be clumsy or insecure. For new professionals, these are great expectations indeed. When they fail to live up to them, they experience guilt, anger, and self-doubt. Anxiety increases as they repeatedly confront situations that suggest they are not the masterful, competent professionals of the myth. Great expectations inevitably lead to great disappointment and a sense of personal failure, at least for a short period of time. And they thereby increase the risk of burnout.

Thwarted expectations also exist around the issue of *autonomy*. Traditionally, professional status has been associated with freedom and control over the decisions affecting one's work (Abrahamson, 1967). Bledstein (1976) wrote:

> The professional person absolutely protected his precious autonomy against all assailants, not in the name of an irrational egotism but in the name of a special grasp of the universe and a special place in it. In the service of mankind—the higher ideal—the professional resisted all corporate encroachments and regulations upon his independence, whether from government bureaucrats, university trustees, business administrators, public laymen, or even his own professional associations. The culture of professionalism released the creative energies of the free person who usually was accountable only to himself and his personal interpretation of the ethical standards of his profession (p. 62).

A recent study of professional training and socialization suggested that the need for and expectation of autonomy continue to be major outcomes of the socialization experience. Bucher and Stelling (1977) found that new physicians in various specialities, as well as biochemistry graduate students, emerged from formal training with a heightened sense of autonomy and self-reliance. They saw themselves as capable of self-regulation and resisted the intrusion of others as critics or evaluators. They seemed to believe that the sense of mastery they acquired through training made them exempt from external supervision or criticism. Presumably, trainees graduating from these experiences would chafe under any restrictions on their autonomy.

Unfortunately, professionals in public institutions frequently find their autonomy severely restricted in numerous ways (see Chapter 4). For instance, they have little power to determine who their clients will be, and their power to effect change in their work settings proves to be limited. And, because the professional mystique led them to believe that things would be different, this lack of autonomy and sense of powerlessness are among the most stressful and disillusioning aspects of their work situations.

A third element of the mystique is the belief that professional work provides *stimulation* and *fulfillment*. It is supposed to be interesting, challenging, and varied. As Sarason (1977) observed, all educated American workers have come to expect more in the way of intrinsic fulfillment from their jobs. We have entered the "Age of Mental Health." Self-actualization is increasingly coming to be seen as a right, not just a privilege, and all aspects of one's life, especially one's work, are supposed to contribute to this goal. Of course, fulfillment and intellectual stimulation have always been associated with certain occupations in our society, particularly professional, scientific, and artistic ones. Now that everyone is coming to expect this kind of reward in work, the expectations that it will occur in professional work have become even stronger. What Lortie (1966) found in his study of lawyers is probably true to a greater or lesser degree for all new professionals: before they enter the "real world" of professional practice, they expect that the work will be heroic and charismatic, not routine and relatively insignificant. Thus, when new public professionals begin their careers, the professional mystique has led them to expect more stimulation, meaning, and fulfillment in their work activities than they actually find in most instances (see Chapter 4).

Collegiality is another mythical attribute of professional life. Members of the same profession do share much in common; when economically threatened, they can coalesce into a politically strong special interest (for example, the American Medical Association's influence in blocking enactment of national health insurance legislation for many years). However, the special collegial quality many novices expect to find when professionals work together is often missing, at least in the experience of many we have studied. As discussed in Chapter 5, the theme of social and professional isolation from co-workers was a dominant one in our interviews with helping professionals from a variety of fields. Sarason (1971) has eloquently described public school teaching as a "lonely" profession; after interviewing lawyers, nurses, psychologists, and social workers, we must conclude that teachers are not unique. Frequent contact with colleagues is rare in most fields, and the contacts that do occur are often characterized by a sort of undercutting rivalry, competition, and distrust, far from the ideal of professional collegiality.

A fifth element of the professional mystique concerns the *attitude of clients* toward the professional. The typical client is supposed to be grateful and cooperative. The typical client is supposed to know that the helping professional is concerned and invested in the client's best interests. The typical client is supposed to be honest and cooperative with the professional, recognizing that the professional cannot be helpful unless the client provides the necessary information and faithfully carries out the professional's prescriptions. To quote historian Bledstein (1976, pp. 102-103), professionals expect to receive "the client's unqualified gratitude. . . . In the professional order of values, no client merited a crueler fate, no client was quite so undeserving and detestable, as the one who betrayed his patron by appearing to be ungrateful." Unfortunately, as seen in Chapter 3, new professionals working in public human service bureaucracies found that a disturbingly large percentage of their clients failed to live up to the professional mystique's ideal for clients. Not only were clients frequently "ungrateful," but they made their lack of gratitude all too apparent by lying, manipulating, cheating, and resisting the professional's efforts to help. The initial expectation of compliance and gratitude simply did not withstand confrontation with reality, and one more part of the professional mystique was destroyed.

Thus, there are at least five highly positive characteristics commonly ascribed to professional work in our society that, for many professionals employed in the public sector, simply prove to be myths. However, these myths do not die easily. Together, they represent a mystique that continues to guide thinking and action. Also, while the mystique is least realistic for public sector professionals working in bureaucratic settings, they are probably the ones who are initially most tied to it; those who choose public sector employment often give up more lucrative career possibilities in private practice or industry because they expect that the nonmonetary rewards will compensate for lower incomes. But these expected compensations prove to be elusive in public sector jobs. Collegiality, autonomy, the gratitude of especially needy clients, and other rewards associated with public service careers are ephemeral. And most professional training programs unfortunately do little to provide a more realistic picture of professional work in public bureaucracies.

Professional schools rarely do much to modify the recruit's expectations concerning the nature of professional work. Professional school faculty, themselves separated from the professional workplace geographically, organizationally, and philosophically, indoctrinate the student with a professional value system emphasizing professional autonomy and the dignity of the individual client. They teach an idealized conception of professional practice, perhaps hoping that the students will adhere to the ideal when they leave school as a result of this strong indoctrination. But our interviews with new public professionals suggested that when the student does finally emerge into the "real world" of work, the differences between the expectations nurtured in professional training and the reality of the work place lead to considerable shock, disappointment, and disillusionment.

The Professional Mystique
and the Structure of Work

The professional mystique also affects the new professional indirectly through its impact on the job and those who structure it. For instance, because it is commonly believed that professionals experience positive, if not ideal, working conditions (high autonomy, variety, supportive and stimulating colleagues, and so on), there has been little concern about those working conditions. Most research and social policy on the quality of work has focused exclusively on blue and white collar workers in business and industrial settings (Sarason, 1977). The professional mystique has led most behavioral scientists, policy makers, and administrators to assume that quality of work life was not an important problem. Because the nature of work and its effect on the worker has not been recognized as a major problem in most service agencies and professions, little has been done to improve the situation through the redesign of jobs or other strategies.

A good example of this lack of awareness and concern with work in helping fields is the rarity of carefully planned orientation programs for new helping professionals in public institutions. The typical new professional we interviewed reported that, from the very first day on the job, it was assumed that the professional possessed all the knowledge necessary to function effectively. There was no orientation to the agency; the new professional in many cases simply found a stack of client files in his or her mailbox with a note to make contacts as soon as possible. Supervision focused on administrative control rather than professional development.

The assumption that professional credentials signify competence was also reflected in the selection process. Many of the agencies and institutions we studied engaged in the most casual selection procedure imaginable: a resume and an unstructured interview were the only screening devices employed. In numerous instances, the interview seemed vague and irrelevant. Although these procedures and criteria may have some predictive value, no agency seemed to be studying, evaluating, and improving its selection procedures. If a degree from a respected training institution means that the applicant is fully qualified, as the professional mystique suggests, why bother developing and evaluating elaborate selection procedures?

The design of jobs in service agencies seems to represent yet another area of neglect. If one assumes that new high school teachers, fresh out of college, are as skilled as more experienced colleagues, it makes sense to start them with a full teaching load and some of the most difficult students. However, if the myth of professional competence via certification were recognized by school boards and administrators, the new teacher's job would be redesigned. The first term of teaching might consist of only half the normal teaching load, smaller class sizes, and structured opportunities to observe more experienced teachers. Gradually, as competence and self-confidence increased, the job would become more demanding. Such a proposal might seem utopian in a period of fiscal crisis and shrinking support for public education; however, it really represents just one approach to the redesign of jobs based on a more realistic assessment of the needs and capacities of new teachers. In a sense, this proposal is probably no more "utopian" than the present arrangement in which so much is expected of the new teacher. In any case, innovative attempts to redesign jobs in teaching and other professions will not occur until the myth of satisfied, competent, and fulfilled professionals is abandoned.

Thus, the professional mystique permeates all aspects of the new professional's experience: it shapes the expectations and goals brought to the first job, as well as shaping the job itself. A legacy of our social history, these beliefs about professional work are unrealistic, at least for professionals working in public institutions. However, few novices are aware of the gap between the mystique and reality, and society and the work setting collude in obscuring this gap. Consequently, the new professional is unprepared for and unsupported in the first confrontation with the world of work, and career development is strongly influenced by the stress and burnout that so frequently result.

THE PROFESSIONAL CASELOAD
IN SOCIAL HISTORICAL CONTEXT

While the professional mystique provides a subtle set of expectations about which the novice is gradually, if painfully, disabused, the caseload represents a very tangible and continual source of stress and burnout. Most novices employed in public institutions find themselves responsible for an overwhelming number of clients. Furthermore, many of these clients are difficult: they are resistant to change; they suffer from so many different problems that the professional simply cannot make much progress on any; their problems are routine and uninteresting; they are often abusive and ungrateful.

The nature of the clientele and caseloads in public agencies make it more difficult for the professional staff to achieve a sense of efficacy and competence. The caseload also contributes to the staff's lack of time to explore various facets of work in a way that would make it more interesting and intellectually stimulating. In addition, strains caused by the clientele and heavy workloads represent one obstacle to the development of collegiality among staff; often feeling as though they are in a "combat zone," staff members simply do not believe they have the time to exchange ideas with, and provide emotional support to, colleagues. Thus, many of the strains experienced by new public professionals are related to the caseloads found in public human service agencies.

When the strain becomes excessive and professionals start to burn out, clients often become the target of their frustration. They blame the clients for the lack of meaning, fulfillment, and accomplishment in their lives. This tendency to blame the clients is not surprising, for they do contribute to strain. However, to blame the clients for the nature of the caseloads in public human service agencies is misguided. The clients are utlimately as much victims of the social historical context as are the professionals. There are reasons for the caseloads in public agencies that go far beyond the clients and their particular problems.

The Decline of Community

One historical factor that has contributed to the crushing caseloads and difficult clients found in many public agencies is the decline of community and the erosion of informal social support systems. As community support systems wither and are replaced by formal, bureaucratic human service institutions, the service demands on those institutions increase dramatically.

At one time, many of the services now provided by professionals and public institutions were available through informal support systems in the community. Those with personal problems or marital difficulties might seek help from clergy. Those with legal difficulties might go to the local ward heeler who could use his influence to grease the wheels of justice. Folk medicine dispensed by "drummers" accounted for much of the medical care. Spiritual renewal was provided by itinerant revivalists rather than professional encounter group facilitators. Obstetrical care was provided by midwives, and most babies were delivered at home. In other words, many of the services now provided by highly trained professionals working in special formal institutions were once provided by neighbors or nonprofessionals. In a very real sense, closely knit and integrated communities cared for themselves.

Of course, it is easy to over-romanticize about the human services provided by communities of the past. The fact is that the availability and quality of service were highly variable. However, as long as the community cared more for itself, burdens on the formal human service system were limited. But, with increasing industrialization, urbanization, and technological innovation, the sense of community deteriorated, and many of the traditional support systems and caregivers disappeared. They still exist and function well for many people in our society, but the trend has been for formal, bureaucratic, professional institutions to arise and assume responsibility for these functions. This shift in service delivery patterns ultimately puts great strain on the professional staff.

For instance, many of the mentally retarded citizens of a community were cared for by families and local institutions until a new, formal, professionally staffed agency was created to provide services to this population. Once this new agency was established, it usually relieved the local community of the "burden," assuming complete responsibility for care of many retarded individuals who had previously lived at home, helped by relatives, friends, neighbors, and so on. It is assumed the new agency provides better care at the same time that the families and community are relieved of the strain of caring for mentally retarded people. Unfortunately, as Sarason, Zitnay, and Grossman (1971) pointed out, the agency that assumes total responsibility for the care of the retarded usually staggers under the strain. Limited resources and a traditional pattern of service delivery lead to heavy caseloads and substandard custodial care.

What has happened in the field of mental retardation has occurred in many other social service and health care areas. As Lynn (1965) noted, there simply are not enough professionals to meet existing demands. Thus, the practitioner is burdened with too much work, jeopardizing standards and providing less rewarding working conditions.

The typical response to this problem of scarce resources is to call for a greater infusion of resources by the government. If the patient-staff ratio on a ward in an institution for the mentally retarded were 20-to-1 and a local newspaper uncovered the fact that residents had been beaten by frustrated and overwhelmed staff members, the state would be asked to increase its level of support so that the patient-staff ratio can be reduced to 15-to-1. However, the problem with this strategy is that relatively large increases in level of support provide relatively little relief for institution, staff, or clients. Also, when the problem is a shortage of *professional* staff, the practitioners may not be available even if the funds are. For instance, positions for mental health professionals in mental hospitals and correctional facilities often go begging, eventually to be filled by foreign-trained professionals whose competence may be questionable. In other words, the decline of community and the stinginess of an individualistic and materialistic society are not the only factors contributing to strain in professional work situations; the traditional structure of professional roles is also important.

Resistance to Change
in Professional Roles

There are no panaceas for the burdens and disappointments of professional work in public institutions; however, changes in professional roles could do much to ease the strain. Unfortunately, this is made difficult by the inherently conservative nature of American professions. *Technologically*, the professions in America have been relatively open to innovation, but *professional roles* have been resistant to change. Thus, changes in professional roles that could help ease the heavy service demands created by other factors are strongly resisted by the professions themselves. Ironically, the professionals become one of the greatest obstacles to change that could ultimately ease their burden and make their work more stimulating, meaningful, and rewarding.

For instance, when the community mental health movement began, one of its goals was to provide services to the thousands of emotionally troubled individuals in this country who could not previously be served because of the shortage of professionally trained personnel. Albee (1959), in an influential work on personnel availability in the mental health field, showed that as long as services were provided in the traditional fashion (for instance, long-term psychotherapy conducted by professionals with several years of post-baccalaureate training), the demand for service would not be satisfied. Thus, many observers began to write about the need for new kinds of personnel and new modes of service delivery, such as the use of paraprofessionals or mental health consultation with community caregivers (Sarason et al., 1966). But these changes in service delivery would require a major change in professional roles. Rather than providing services directly themselves, the mental health professionals would become "mental health quarterbacks" (Cowen, 1973), training and supervising paraprofessional service providers, offering mental health consultation to others, developing and running new programs, and so on.

Despite some enthusiasm and head-nodding about these proposed changes in the provision of mental health services, recent evaluations of the community mental health program suggest that there has been little change in professional roles and modes of service delivery (for examples, Chu and Trotter, 1974; Snow and Newton, 1976). True, there have been many new programs created, and there are many paraprofessionals now providing service of some sort in the centers. However, the role of the professional has not substantially changed. Most mental health professionals working in mental health centers continue to do what they were trained to do: long-term psychotherapy and counseling with single individuals or in small groups. Consequently, there are still long waiting lists in mental health facilities and many who need help are not receiving it. Also, the pressures this imposes on the organization mean that conflict, stress, and burnout continue to characterize the work lives of many professionals in these programs (Cherniss & Egnatios, 1978a).

One would probably find a similar pattern in other professions. For instance, the introduction of paralegals into the legal profession has done little to change the role of the attorney. Too often, paralegals employed by law firms—both public and private—function as legal secretaries or clerks. Similarly, the introduction of teacher aides in the public schools has had little impact on the traditional role of the classroom teacher. In many classrooms, the aides perform nonteaching clerical functions or "babysit" with individual children who teachers fear would be disruptive if an adult were not in close proximity.

It is not at all clear why the professions have been so resistant to changes in roles. Perhaps there is some fear that they will lead to a loss of status for the profession. There is certainly a belief that the quality of service will suffer if the traditional roles are modified, but there is usually little empirical justification for this fear. More to the point may be an unarticulated fear that the crisis of competence will become even more painful for the professionals; after struggling so much to achieve a modicum of efficacy in a particular role, professionals may be reluctant to assume new roles that may demand new knowledge and skill. Whatever the cause, the professions have been reluctant to ease the burden of heavy caseloads through structural changes in professional roles.

The Unequal Distribution
of "Dirty Work"

All professionals and professional organizations must cope with the dilemmas associated with human service work, but a subtle "class hierarchy" within each profession leads to a situation in which certain organizations and professionals are relatively more disadvantaged than others. The most difficult and unrewarding client problems in an American profession are usually not distributed evenly among professional practitioners. Because the public sector settings assume much more than their share of the least desirable work, the caseloads of their professional staffs generate more frustration and less reward than do the caseloads found in the private sector.

The more difficult, less rewarding work of the profession—the "dirty work"—tends to dominate the workloads in the settings lowest on the professional ladder. These settings are the "lower classes" of the professional class structure, the ones that *must* serve the bulk of those clients whose problems are routine and uninteresting, whose behavior and social background are most likely to be repugnant to the provider of service, and whose situations ensure that the provision of service will be relatively unrewarding. Thus, the professionals working in these settings face the most difficult working conditions while receiving the lowest financial remuneration. They are also likely to be accorded the lowest prestige. Consequently, they are likely to burn out more quickly and completely than their colleagues who work in "higher status" settings with more rewarding workloads.

It clearly is no accident that those working in the public sector, whether it be medical care, mental health, education, or law, are forced to take the work that is least desirable to the higher status sectors of the profession. Physicians and lawyers in private practice, teachers in select private prep schools, and mental health professionals in prestigious, university-based clinics and hospitals are able to pick and choose their clientele, control their workloads, and otherwise maintain more desirable working conditions. Those working in publicly supported institutions are left with the rest of the clientele and with relatively scarce resources with which to serve them. The new professionals who begin their careers in these settings are thus more likely to experience the stresses and strains we have examined. They are also more likely to burn out as a result. Therefore, the internal class structure of the American professions ensures that the frustrations will be greater and the rewards less in public settings. There are exceptions, of course, but the general pattern is unmistakable.

Thus, while the caseloads of new public professionals clearly represent a major source of strain and dissatisfaction, the sources of those caseloads are complex. Ultimately, they are the result of historical forces over which clients, professionals, and human service agencies have little control. These include the decline of informal community support systems and society's increasing reliance on professionals and bureaucratic institutions, the unequal distribution of "dirty work" within the professions, and the reluctance to change traditional professional roles in ways that would ease the strain placed on service providers in public institutions.

SOCIAL CHANGE AND
THE WEAKENING OF PROFESSIONAL AUTHORITY

One of the cardinal characteristics of our age is a basic mistrust of social institutions. Voters increasingly mistrust politicians, elected officials, and political institutions. Consumers increasingly mistrust larger chain stores and large corporations. The professions in America have not escaped this growing mistrust and alienation. They are caught in the same currents of social change. The fundamental assumptions on which professional authority has rested are being questioned by vocal detractors both within and outside of the professions. There is growing disenchantment with the professions, and this disenchantment has led to increased pressure for change.

This questioning of professional authority and pressure for change creates additional strains for all professionals, but new professionals are in a particularly vulnerable position for two reasons. First, as professional authority declines, achieving a sense of competence becomes more difficult because professionals no longer have a clear, unequivocal standard of performance by which to measure themselves. Second, because so many of the new ideas and methods are taught to professional students by the universities, those students enter professional work settings as "change agents." Consequently, they are more isolated from older colleagues and must cope alone with the strains of being new. Thus, as new professionals contribute to change in the professions, they are likely to be among those who are most adversely affected by it.

The Challenge to Authority
and the Crisis of Competence

The basic dogmas underlying work in every profession have probably been questioned and challenged to a greater extent during the last few years than at any time since the professions first emerged as distinct social statuses during the late middle ages. While the ferment and questioning takes a different form in each profession, there is one issue that cuts across all of them: What is the proper role of the professional in relationship to the client, to other professionals, and to society in general? In all of the professions, there is now an outspoken and increasingly influential faction that advocates radical change in the professional role; in some instances, changes are occurring.

The issue of professional authority is one area in which changes are having particularly significant implications for new professionals. Traditionally, professional status has been associated with authority based on expertise in a valued, difficult, and proven technology. However, the idea of professional authority itself is now under attack in many fields. One nurse with whom we spoke told us that many younger nurses are challenging the absolute authority physicians previously exercised in the doctor-nurse relationship. In mental health, many have come to doubt the relative superiority of professionally trained therapists compared with nonprofessionals who have no formal training but who are closer in status and experience to patients. And the growing willingness of patients to doubt a physician's word, even to the point of bringing suits against physicians in court, is but one more sign of the erosion of professional authority. As sociologist Robert Nisbet (1971) has noted, the widespread questioning of the authority and dogmas on which any social institution is based leads to an increasing sense of alienation and anxiety. For the new professional, the current questioning and criticism of professional authority often become an intensely experienced personal problem. As one young school social worker said, "I just don't know what I should *be*. Should I be a facilitator? A rescuer? An expert? Parents and teachers expect me to be a disciplinarian. But that's not consistent with my own values and goals."

The growing doubt of the idea that the professions are helpful and benign creates strain for all practitioners, but there is reason to believe that the strain is particularly great for novices. As discussed in Chapter 2, the achievement of a sense of competence is probably the major "developmental task" confronting professionals during the initial phase of their careers. The issue has by no means been resolved during one's formal training. The new professional is thus at a particular disadvantage during a period of rapid social change, because it is more difficult to have confidence in the tools provided by his or her training. The relevance and even the benefits of those tools can no longer be taken for granted by the novice. Consequently, the new professionals must proceed cautiously, testing and evaluating the results of their efforts as they go along, exploring and experimenting with various, competing modes of practice being proposed by different groups within the profession, thus delaying the time when one finally settles on a *modus operandi* and develops a sense of competence in it. How to "relate to" one's clients is but one area in which misgivings about the old way and the rise of many new options creates uncertainty and strain for the novice. While the questioning of professional authority may be a positive development in the provision of service, as long as the established ways within the professions are challenged, as long as the idea that the professions are benign is challenged, and as long as new professionals are not *prepared* for this by their training or their orientation to the new role, the crisis of competence for new professionals will be especially severe.

The Costs of Being
a "Change Agent"

Within most American professions today, the advocates of change in professional roles tend to be concentrated in the universities. Thus, professionals in training are exposed to the new concepts and often become advocates or representatives of the new ideas in the field. However, when they leave the universities and begin their careers in public institutions, they may find that institutional constraints do not permit them to perform their roles in the new ways they were taught. Also, they may find that their "new fangled" ways are not exactly welcome by older colleagues.

The conflict between old and new professionals discussed in Chapter 5 occurs in part because the new professionals are the carriers of new methods and ideas. For instance, mental health professional Douglas Furth noted that a major source of strain for him and other new professionals in his agency was continuing conflict between two staff groups. One group, composed of the older staff, favored the more traditional psychoanalytic model of therapy and was critical of innovative activities such as community education and mental health consultation. The other group, composed of the newer, younger staff, championed transactional analysis, a relatively new approach that differs from the psychoanalytic in several respects. The new staff was also eager to become involved in other kinds of activity not usually associated with the mental health professional's role, such as public education activities or mental health consultation. According to Douglas, there was constant friction between these two groups, and the conflicts created a tense social atmosphere in which collegiality and support suffered substantially. As representatives of the "new way" in mental health, the new professionals met with considerable antipathy from the older staff. As "change agents," they may ultimately contribute to progress in the field. But they were paying a price for it during a period of their careers when they could probably afford it least.

Thus, because there is no longer a strong, unquestioned concept of what the new professional should become, the process of becoming a professional is even more stressful for the new entrant. Caught between the old and the new, often clear about what they *do not want* to be, but not clear about how they can become what they *want* to be, many new professionals experience severe role conflicts. They feel more intensely than do many others the ambivalence, confusion, and uncertainty that characterize professional practice in America today.

CONCLUSION: COMING TO TERMS
WITH THE SOCIAL HISTORICAL CONTEXT

We have examined several social historical factors that contribute to stress, strain, and burnout in new public professionals. These are factors that affect both the individuals who become new professionals and the organizations in which they work. We live in a highly individualistic and optimistic society, one in which the prevailing assumption is that with enough effort, or training, or both, an individual can overcome any obstacle and succeed. There is much to be said for this attitude, for it can motivate individuals to try and succeed when a more pessimistic view might prevent them from doing so. However, a major shortcoming of this individualistic concept is that it leads us to ignore the "larger picture," the forces that constitute the social historical context and that strongly influence the behavior of both individuals and organizations.

As explored in the previous two chapters, there *are* actions that individuals and organizations can take that *would* ease the transitional crisis of new public professionals and reduce the incidence of burnout. However, there must also be changes in larger social structures and in the basic cultural ideas and attitudes that define our social reality. Changes on the level of society are more difficult to effect, and one can rarely see progress even when it is being made. This fact discourages many from confronting the larger social forces that influence their lives. However, to ignore them is to become a victim of history rather than an active agent helping to shape it.

APPENDIX A
RESEARCH METHODS:
GENERAL PROCEDURES AND RATIONALES

A trusim in social science research is, "Problem should determine method." The method used in this study of early career development in new, public sector professionals had several distinct features. It was longitudinal, comparative, and involved multiple in-depth interviews with a relatively small sample of subjects. The interviews were relatively unstructured, designed to let the subjects tell their own stories as much as possible. The subjects were interviewed several times during their first two years of professional work in public institutions. Four different professional groups were studied: poverty lawyers, mental health professionals, high school teachers, and public health nurses. This appendix describes in some detail the procedures used in the study and the rationales for using them.

RATIONALES FOR A LONGITUDINAL STUDY

In planning the study, one of the first choices that had to be made was whether to use a longitudinal or cross-sectional design. In a longitudinal design, the same group of subjects is studied over time. In a cross-sectional design, there are two or more different groups studied simultaneously: one group consists of subjects at the earlier period, the others consist of subjects at later periods of interest. One then examines how the groups differ in order to make inferences about how individuals actually change from one time to another. For example, in a study of the effects of college on students, a longitudinal design would test a group of entering students and then test them again upon graduation. (There could also be repeated testing and observation of the study group throughout college.) A cross-sectional design would test a group of entering students and, at the same time, another group of graduating seniors.

Clearly, each design has advantages and disadvantages. The cross-sectional design can be accomplished in much less time; one does not have to wait for the students to complete four years of college. However, in the cross-sectional design, changes that occur due to the passage of time or the impact of the institutional experience are confounded with changes that might occur for other reasons. For instance, differences between seniors and freshmen could be due to attrition during the college years rather than actual changes in attitudes that occur during those years. Also, in the cross-sectional design, one must assume that the seniors were comparable to the freshmen when they began college four years earlier, but there is no way of knowing that.

The longitudinal design avoids these pitfalls. By studying the same group over the period in which one is interested, one can say with greater certainty that differences that occur over time are due to changes occurring in the subjects during this period and not to selective attrition or differences between the groups that existed even before the study began. On the other hand, one must wait for the subjects to pass through time in the longitudinal design.

For our study of early career development and changes in new professionals working in public human service agencies, we chose the longitudinal approach for two basic reasons. First, we were interested in the *process* of accommodation, adjustment, and change. We did not just want to know, for instance, if new professionals with two years' experience were less idealistic than those who were just starting. We wanted to know *how* they got to be less idealistic and *why* they became less idealistic (if that was, in fact, a way in which they changed over time). Only by studying the subjects longitudinally, over time, could we examine in detail the process of becoming a professional. Secondly, we decided that considerable change would occur within a relatively short period of time in this group. As noted in Chapter 1, there was reason to believe that the first year or so of fulltime professional activity would be a period characterized by much change and that many of the changes that occurred during this time would be relatively stable, more stable than changes that occur during professional training. Therefore, we believed that a longitudinal design in which subjects were studied during as brief a period as four or five months would detect real change in attitude and behavior. Of course, this was a risky assumption to make. If the subjects did not change significantly during the relatively short time period studied, we would have invested considerable time and effort without obtaining the kind of information we wanted. Fortunately, our risk paid off.

RATIONALES FOR A COMPARATIVE STUDY

Another important aspect of the study was its comparative focus: early career development was studied not just in one professional group but in four. There were several reasons for this approach. First, we assumed that there was something important in the process of professional career development that all professions had in common, especially when that development occurred in the context of a public human service program. Clearly professional groups would differ in many ways, but we believed that there were sets of professional norms and institutional dynamics in this society so strong that virtually all professional groups and individuals would be affected. By studying several groups of professionals working in different institutional contexts, we hoped to better identify those forces.

Second, we believed that a comparative approach would make us aware of important aspects of the new professional's experience that would otherwise go unnoticed or not fully appreciated. For instance, new teachers typically receive minimal instruction, direction, guidance, or support from their supervisors (principals, department heads, curriculum specialists). This pattern is nearly universal in the public schools. Only by contrasting teaching with mental health settings, in which new professionals more typically receive regular supervision with a primary focus on professional development, does one begin to appreciate the importance of quality and quantity of supervision to the process of career development in a public institution. (Details on this point can be found in Chapter 11.) In other words, a comparative approach helps to sharpen one's focus, putting certain aspects of a phenomenon into stark relief, which, without a comparative focus, might not be discernible at all.

Our choice of the professional fields to study was not as clear-cut. The comparative approach required at least two different fields, but too many would make the tasks of contrast and comparison unwieldy. We also wanted to maximize the variety in training patterns, supervision practices, institutional contexts, task demands, client-practitioner relationship patterns, and so on. On the other hand, the fields had to have enough in common to make comparison manageable and meaningful. The purpose of the study dictated that any group should be engaged in human service work within a public institution. These considerations ultimately led us to study four professional fields: poverty lawyers, mental health professionals working in public agencies, public health nurses, and high school teachers.

THE PERSONOLOGICAL INTERVIEW
AS A RESEARCH METHOD

The method used for gathering the data was what we have come to call the personological interview. This approach has its historical roots in the work of Henry Murray and his colleagues and students at the Harvard Psychological Clinic (Murray, 1938). It is part of a more basic methodological tradition in social science, usually referred to as the qualitative-naturalistic approach (Glaser & Strauss, 1967; McCall & Simmons, 1969; Willems & Raush, 1969). It is usually contrasted with the other basic research tradition, the quantitative-laboratory approach.

A particularly good, general description of the personological interview is found in Levinson (1977). The approach he used in his study of adult male development was called "biographical interviewing," but in most of its particulars it is identical to our approach:

> A biographical interview combines aspects of a research interview, a clinical interview and a conversation between friends. It is like a structured research interview in that certain topics must be covered, and the main purpose is research. As in a clinical interview, the interviewer is sensitive to the feelings expressed, and follows the threads of meaning as they lead through diverse topics. Finally, as in a conversation between friends, the relationship is equal and the interviewer is free to respond in terms of his own experiences. Yet each party has a defined role as a sustained work task, which imposes its own constraints.
>
> What is involved is not simply an interviewing technique or procedure, but a relationship of some intimacy, intensity and duration. Significant work is involved in forming, maintaining and terminating the relationship. The recruiting of participants, the negotiation of a research contract, and the course of the interviewing relationship are phases within a single, complex process. Understanding and managing this process is a crucial part of our research method (Levinson, 1977, p. 15).

Choice of Method:
Discovery versus Verification

As noted, there are two research traditions in the social sciences, and our choice of the qualitative-naturalistic approach was based on four considerations. This method appealed to us first because we were studying a phenomenon that had seldom been studied before. Because early professional career development and, in fact, professional career development in general were largely uncharted, we did not want to predetermine the form the data would take through a forced-choice questionnaire or some other method that would limit both the options and focus of responses. Put another way, our goal was *discovery* rather than verification or proof. If good naturalistic description of the experience of being a new public professional had already existed, we would have chosen a different approach. But it is premature to begin testing specific hypotheses concerning isolated variables before one has a good, fine-grained description of the whole phenomenon. The premature use of quantitative, laboratory-based, hypothesis-testing research can lead investigators into many tangents and blind alleys. One can spend much time and effort establishing the existence of relatively insignificant processes and dynamics. As Tripodi (1974) and Northrop (1947) have cogently argued, the pursuit of knowledge should ideally be a developmental process in which descriptive research with the goal of discovery precedes the testing of correlational and cause-effect hypotheses. The paucity of good research on the new public professional's development led us to conclude that this phenomenon is still at the earliest stage of inquiry, and, therefore, a more descriptive, open-ended method such as personological interviewing was most appropriate.

Patterns, Processes, and Inter-relationships

A second reason for using personological interviews in our study was that we were primarily interested in the *process* of becoming a new professional in a public human service institution. An in-depth description and analysis of this process as it actually unfolds was the study's goal. We did not want a "static snapshot" (Kanter, 1977) suggesting how many subjects said "x" or did "y." We wanted to see all of the salient pieces of the patterns, and we wanted to observe and study how they related to each other. We wanted to see which parts of the pattern stood out in bold relief and which were relatively unimportant and how the parts fit together and dynamically ebbed and flowed over time. In other words, we wanted a moving picture of the whole experience from the perspective of the participant rather than a single snapshot of one fine detail.

One advantage of the personological interview is that it provides a good picture of how various attitudes and feelings fit together for the individual. It allows the subject to respond spontaneously and at great length, which suggests, better than a forced-choice format ever could, how even seemingly inconsistent and illogical ideas and beliefs make sense from the vantage point of the subject's own world. Rather than dividing up, fragmenting, and discarding large parts of the subject's personal experience, the personological interview seeks to absorb the whole of that experience in order to chart the underlying pattern of thoughts, feelings, and actions that give it meaning and coherence. Many social scientists, such as Freidson (1977), have argued that this close, "clinical" study of process is necessary in social research to determine the underlying causal connections when laboratory-like manipulation and isolation of the variables is ethically and logistically impossible. Thus, we chose to use the qualitative method of personological interviewing because we were interested in studying the patterning of attitudes, actions, and perceptions during the first phase of professional career development in a public institution and because we were interested in studying and describing the process as a coherent whole rather than an artifically isolated part of it that might or might not have social and theoretical significance.

Minimizing Experimental Distortion

A third consideration that lead to the choice of personological interviews was our desire to minimize the extent to which our own preconceptions would determine the outcome. To design an experiment or structured questionnaire, one must strongly rely on one's preconceptions. Based on our own experiences, it would not have been difficult to construct such instruments. We had studied the social science literature and were familiar with the various theoretical perspectives and concepts of social psychology (for example, role theory, self-concept theory, and so on). It would have been easy for us to use these previously formulated concepts to study the experiences of new professionals. For instance, we could have studied how the new professional's "self-esteem" changed over time in different professional fields and different institutional contexts. But what would we have learned from such a study? If we proceeded in the normal manner (that is, administer a questionnaire in which self-esteem allegedly is measured), we would never know whether self-esteem was an important or meaningful issue for the subjects during this period. And we certainly would not know how important it was relative to other aspects of the experience. In fact, by focusing on self-esteem in our research instruments, we could have made it seem more significant than it really is. Thus, if we had used existing theoretical constructs in social psychology as a basis for a more structured, focused, quantitative study of the new public professional's world, we easily could have distorted it.

One virtue of the personological interview is that it allows—in fact, if done properly, it *requires*—the subject to challenge and correct faulty researcher biases and preconceptions. The process of spontaneous interaction that occurs in the interview allows the subject to do this in a way not possible in a more structured, experimenter-controlled situation. The subject is active rather than passive. When a researcher asks a question that indicates a misconception about the subject's experience, the subject has more opportunity to correct the misconception than if the question were presented in a forced-choice questionnaire.

For this reason, the personological interview seems to have greater "ecological validity" than do many other research methods. Ecological validity refers to the extent to which a phenomenon studied in the research situation is similar to that phenomenon as it occurs in its natural context. For decades, psychology has been a science of the white rat and college sophomore. These have been the most typical subjects in psychological experiments, and the experiments have usually been conducted in isolated, artificial laboratories located in basements of college psychology buildings. Even research in social psychology has tended to follow this pattern. Gradually, however, many researchers in the field have begun to question the extent to which the findings generated in these laboratory studies would be replicated in more natural settings. Many of the findings produced in laboratory research *may* prove to be valid when tested in more natural social contexts, but, until this is done, the ecological validity of that research is in question.

Those who have written about the personological interview have noted that it is more ecologically valid than the more structured, experimenter-controlled alternatives. Raush (1969) advocated the use of more naturalistic methods, such as the personological interview, because they are more "ecologically representative;" they "yield information about the phenomenon under investigation rather than about the effects of the investigator's intervention." In a study of subjective response to the work experience, therefore, the personological method as a naturalistic approach seems to have greater ecological validity than many other alternatives.

Of course, we were not totally free of bias or preconceptions when we initiated the study. As suggested in Chapter 1, we did have certain notions about issues that would be important. No research method can completely eliminate the influence of researcher expectation and preconception. However, the less structured methods, such as personological interviewing in which discovery is the primary goal, minimize the negative influence of prior theoretical and personal bias. They also have an ecological validity that other methods lack.

The Problem of Candor

A fourth reason for preferring the personological method concerned the problem of candor. A study of how people feel about their work immediately runs up against this problem, for work is probably the most significant aspect of most peoples' lives, a major source of self-esteem, meaning, and identity. To know a person's work, especially her personal experience of it, is to penetrate to the core of her identity, a realm of personal experience with which even the person has not allowed herself to become completely familiar. As Sarason (1977) wrote, "The experience of work, like that of sex, is so extraordinarily complicated and private, so determined by culture and tradition, so much the organizing center of our lives, and so much a developmental process that it is small wonder we as individuals have difficulty taking distance from 'our work,' i.e., from ourselves" (p. 2). Another observer, writing from a more sociological perspective, expressed a similar point of view:

> [I]t is no simple thing to find out what meanings people attach to their work. Occupational groups are likely to fill the air with rhetoric which purports to explain the intentions of their members. . . . [T]o gain and give an accurate picture, [the social scientist] must penetrate the rhetoric of prestige seeking, defense, and public justification to identify the genuine sentiments of people within the occupation (Lortie, 1975, p. 107).

Although candor represents a problem for research on the nature of any work experience, there is reason to believe that this is especially so in the case of the *professional* work experience. Professionals, even more than most workers, are particularly invested in seeing themselves and their occupations in the most positive possible light and in presenting this view to the public world. Why? To quote Sarason (1977, p. 103):

> Work or career satisfaction is no easy matter for professionals to talk candidly about, *especially if the profession is seen by others as an endlessly fascinating and rewarding line of endeavor [italics Saranson's]*. To proclaim one's dissatisfactions or doubts is tantamount to questioning the significance of one's life and future, to appear to others as "deviant," and to raise questions in their minds about one's personal stability. How can you say you are frequently bored in, or feel inadequate about, or unchallenged by your work when the rest of the world sees you as meeting and overcoming one challenge after another, as a fount of ever-increasing knowledge and wisdom, as a person obviously entranced with his career? And it is not made easier when to proclaim such feelings to one's colleagues is perceived as sensible as Macy's telling Gimbels its problems.

These quotes suggest that no study of the professional work experience can completely solve the problem of candor, but we believed that the personological interview was better than most methods at minimizing the effects of self-serving reluctance to discuss such issues. In these interviews, the primary aim of the interviewer was to develop trust and rapport with a subject, to spend many hours talking and listening to him or her in order to gradually gain this trust and penetrate some of the defenses and resistance frequently maintained between important aspects of inner experience and the public world.

To summarize, there were several reasons for choosing the personological interview as the research method for our study of the new public professional's work experience. The lack of previous research on the topic and the exploratory nature of the study led us to look for a method that was more suited for discovery than proof or verification. Our interest in learning more about the processes that occur when one assumes a professional position in a public human service agency was also important, as was our interest in the total pattern of experience. Also, we wanted to use a method that would minimize the influence of common preconceptions and maximize ecological validity. The problem of candor was an important consideration. Given the many reasons for choosing a qualitative-naturalistic method, it is not surprising that psychologists are increasingly using such methods in their research. Even those who have been strongly identified with the quantitative-laboratory tradition have become impressed with the need to use qualitative-naturalistic methods as well. For instance, Richard Lazarus, an experimentalist who became best known for his laboratory research into the nature of psychological stress and the coping process, recently wrote:

> [T]he best strategy for such research on the cognitive mediators of emotion and coping is idiographic and naturalistic rather than nomothetic or normative and experimental. I no longer believe we can learn much by experimentally isolating coping processes, say, or personality variables, or situational demands, from the total context of the individual person in his usual environment. We need to study given classes of normally functioning persons longitudinally (1977, p. 158).

GUIDELINES AND PROCEDURES FOR THE STUDY

The Sample

The sample for this study consisted of 28 new professionals from four different occupational groups: public service lawyers, mental health workers, public health nurses, and high school teachers.* Most of the participants were identified through lists of recent graduates kept by professional training programs, although the majority of public school teachers were identified through the cooperation of a local teachers' union leader and a local principal. In a few cases, a participant gave us the name of a friend or co-worker who was also a new professional. Only two individuals (a high school teacher and a lawyer) refused to participate when initially contacted. Because the research was exploratory and the sample size small, there was no attempt to obtain a random sample.

An attempt was made to contact and begin interviewing participants as early in their professional careers as possible. However, there was some variability in the point at which interviews began. In one case, a subject was interviewed two weeks after beginning work. In another case, the subject had been employed 19 months when first contacted. An exception was the public school

---

*Most of the material on guidelines and procedures has been produced from Wacker (1979).

teachers, all of whom were in their first or second month of employment when interviews began.

Demographically, there was some variation in the sample. Table A.1 presents data on race, sex, age, and marital status for the four occupational groups.

TABLE A.1: Demographic Data on New Professionals

Group	Race		Sex		Mean	Marital Status	
						Single/	
	White	Black	Male	Female	Age	Divorced	Married
Lawyers	5	2	3	4	26.0	6	1
Mental Health Professionals	7	0	4	3	31.4	5	2
Teachers	7	0	2	5	25.3	3	4
Public Health Nurses	7	0	0	7	27.0	3	4
Total (Mean)	26	2	9	19	(27.8)	17	11

Source: Compiled by the author.

The participants were employed in a variety of work settings. One common characteristic of the settings was that they were all publicly funded agencies or institutions accountable to legislatures or citizen boards. The lawyers worked in neighborhood legal aid offices, state appellate defender offices, and reform law agencies representing the interests of indigent groups. Together they handled civil, criminal juvenile, and class action cases, but no single lawyer handled all of these types of cases. The sizes of their agencies varied from less than 10 professional and clerical staff members to more than 100 staff members. The lawyers had also been trained in very different types of settings, including very selective, academically oriented institutions and somewhat less selective, more practically oriented schools.

The mental health professionals worked in community mental health agencies, small family counseling agencies supported through the United Fund, councils on alcoholism, large state institutions for the mentally retarded, and public school systems. Six were clinical social workers holding the M.S.W. degree, and one was a school psychologist with an M.A.

All of the public health nurses were employed in visiting nurse agencies or local county health departments. Four of them, however, had received master's degrees in public health and were working as supervisors, while three were bachelor's level public health nurses. All of the supervisors had themselves been former nurses and had received their graduate training at the same institution.

The high school teachers taught a variety of subjects; two taught math, one taught consumer education and typing, one taught consumer education and math, one taught chemistry, and one taught art history. The sizes of their high schools varied from one with less than 700 students to others with more than 3,000 students. The locations were both urban (population 100,000) and rural.

Interview Procedures

Four interviewers conducted the interviews, which began in October of 1974 and continued through May of 1976. They interviewed each participant at least twice initially, and, in one case, four times. At least two months elapsed between the initial and follow-up interviews. The average length of time between the last initial interview and the follow-up was five months. The interviewer conducting the initial interviews also conducted the follow-ups in every case.

There were several rationales for conducting multiple interviews with each subject. First, we assumed that rapport between subject and interviewer would develop over time, and, as a result, more areas of subjective experience would become accessible during second and third interviews. Another rationale was that, in later interviews, we would be able to obtain information missed during initial interviews and clear up any misunderstandings or ambiguities. Third, we believed that, after studying the first interviews, the interviewer could use more precise, on-target probes during subsequent interviews. In other words, the insight acquired during the initial interviews could lead to more penetrating inquiry in subsequent meetings.

The number of interviews conducted with each subject varied. The decision was based in part on an assessment of the quality and type of information additional interviews would provide. This, in turn, seemed to depend to a great extent on the type of "working alliance" established between interviewer and subject, as well as the degree to which subjects were willing or able to discuss their feelings and experiences. In some cases, the decision was also influenced by practical considerations; for instance, some subjects felt that they could not afford the time for all of the interviews we would have liked. However, at least one initial and one follow-up interview were conducted with each subject.

In conducting the interviews, the interviewers attempted to keep them as informal and unstructured as possible. Developing rapport with the subject was considered an essential condition for obtaining accurate and meaningful material in the interview. Typically, the interviewer would begin on an objective, general level, obtaining factual information about various aspects of the work setting, reserving more sensitive, subjective questions until rapport and trust had had an opportunity to develop. Although ultimately the respondents' feelings about their work settings were of primary concern, it was important to obtain objective information about the conditions of that work in order to place its subjective experience into a meaningful context. As the interviews progressed and rapport was built, a respondent's report of certain facts or events was often followed up with probes as to how he or she felt about the situation. The interviewers attempted to adopt the role of learner, which was a very natural one, and to indicate sympathy and support in order to encourage the respondent to discuss his or her personal reactions and feelings at great length. Although emotionally laden material often emerged, the interview was structured as a learning situation rather than a therapeutic one. Inviting the respondent to assume the role of co-researcher in a collaborative venture facilitated the handling of sensitive topics and protected both interviewer and subject.

The location of the interviews was selected with the same concern for rapport and candor. In some cases, the subjects seemed most comfortable being interviewed on their "home turf." In other cases, they preferred to meet away from their offices, perhaps to avoid scrutiny by co-workers or supervisors. In these instances, the interviews were conducted in the interviewer's office at the university or on "neutral ground." Making the setting as relaxed and secure as possible seemed to be more important than using a fixed, standard location.

The interviews were semistructured in that interviewers had a "guide" or "mental list" of areas to be covered at some point in the interviews. Although there was no set order for discussion (the interviewer attempted to respond to the subject's perceptions and concerns), an attempt was made to discuss each topic at least once during the initial interview and again during the follow-up interview. An effort was made during the follow-up interview to learn how the respondents' attitudes and perceptions in each area had changed over time. The topics included pre-employment expectations, lifestyle changes (for instance, from student to work life), nature of supervision, perceptions of and problems with clients or students, relations with co-workers, influence of new career on personal life, sources of stress or dissatisfaction, changes in attitudes or values in general, and ideas about how to improve their present role, the structure of the work setting, and their professional training.

Specifying general areas in advance was necessary to obtain some consistency across subjects, yet the freedom of the format allowed the interviewer to enter the respondent's world, discovering each professional's important concerns and experiences without limiting or predetermining the data. As noted, we attempted to assume as little as possible in order to maintain the integrity of the subject's real life experience.

Each interview was tape-recorded and lasted approximately one hour, although some were much more lengthy. Some methodologists have argued against the use of tape-recording (for example, McCall & Simmons, 1969), however, we chose to use it for several reasons. First, it ensured that the interviewer would not lose important material through poor memory. Second, capturing all of the respondent's verbal behavior on tape would mitigate against the effect of "experimeter"; interviewers are always susceptible to recalling what they want to recall when writing up notes some time after an interview has taken place. Third, tape-recording left the interviewer free to be more attentive and responsive to the subjects during the interview. True, there was the possibility that some subjects would initially be insecure about the tape-recording and find the equipment intrusive. But we believed that, because tape recorders have now become inexpensive and commonplace, most subjects would not find the small cassette recorder to be particularly threatening. We found no reason to doubt the wisdom of this decision.

Almost all of the recordings were subsequently transcribed. Most of those that were not were due to technical failures. At least two of the interviews from each respondent were transcribed, an initial and a follow-up interview, and the audible interviews that were not transcribed were studied along with the others during data analysis. When a technical failure occurred, the interviewer would write detailed notes immediately after the interview.

Data Analysis Procedures

In sifting through the interview transcripts, certain themes began to emerge. A procedure called "thematic analysis" was used to discover underlying patterns in the research data. As Piotrkowski (1979) noted, "The object of thematic analysis is to allow the data to 'speak for itself' without the prior imposition of a researcher's schema." Of course, one cannot really come to a social phenomenon without any *a priori* assumptions. In thematic analysis, one uses a method called "serial hypothesis testing" (Rapaport, Gill, & Schafer, 1968) in which original hunches and emerging ideas serve as working hypotheses to be modified, discarded, or elaborated as new material is collected and studied. Original hypotheses are replaced by new ones. The hypotheses that remain at the end of this process have received strong validation from multiple sources.

When applied to personological research, thematic analysis and serial hypothesis testing proceed as follows. First, the researchers immerse themselves in the interview material for a single case, working toward what Levinson (1977, p. 16) calls an "intuitive understanding" of the person and his or her life. Then, one begins to develop "interpretive formulations," which are more abstract generalizations concerning underlying patterns and processes. As the theoretical conceptualization develops, it is applied to new cases and used to further our understanding of them at the same time that the new cases are used to modify, elaborate, or add to the theory.

In our study, the data were analyzed according to this general method. For each subject, an interviewer would read the transcripts and listen to the untrancribed interviews, recording significant ideas or "themes" on cards. Two criteria determined whether a particular idea or statement was "significant": first, the basic questions guiding the study regarding changes in professional outlook and the forces producing those changes and, second, personal significance and meaning for the respondent. Thus, if a statement or idea seemed to be emotionally charged or have particular importance for the respondent, it was noted even though the importance of the issue was unexpected by the researcher.

In general, a single interviewer would take notes on all of the respondents whom he or she had interviewed, usually the majority of a particular occupation. (There were four investigators and four professional groups.) Most interviewers also interviewed at least one or two subjects from other groups.

The note cards containing the significant ideas were then used to construct individual case studies and to identify general repeating themes. The order, however, varied with the researcher. In some instances, the case studies were written first, then a number of general themes or patterns were identified. In other cases the themes were identified first, without the benefit of the case studies.

The next step in the data analysis was "verification." After the first researcher had completed the case studies or the identification of general themes (whichever occurred first), a second reader, who had studied the same interview materials, would read the case studies or themes prepared by the first reader in order to determine their accuracy. Usually, only a few minor errors of fact were discovered, and both readers together easily resolved their disagreement. However, if there was disagreement about an interpretation or inference, it was discussed by the entire research group where the issue ultimately was resolved by consensus. Failing verification, the first researcher's questionable inference or interpretation would be rejected as unreliable.

Following this verification procedure, themes were identified if this had not yet been done, and a second verification procedure occurred to ensure that the themes were consistent with the case study. At this point, there was a set of verified themes for each of the occupational groups. The group themes and case studies then formed the basis for generalizations regarding the conflicts and strains experienced by all four occupational groups during the first year of their employment as public service professionals.

In general, the themes that emerge from this kind of research and that are presented in a written report should meet five criteria for internal validity. First, they should help us to *understand* the lives of the subjects; we should better comprehend the complex pattern of human experience as a result of the themes. Second, the themes should maintain the integrity of the original "data." Third, the interpretations should be internally consistent. Fourth, data that support the findings should be presented. Usually, these data will take the form of excerpts from interviews. Finally, the reported conclusions should be consistent with the reader's own experience. In qualitative research, the readers must critically scrutinize the results of the thematic analysis, playing a more active role in the process of "validation" than they normally would.

Undoubtedly, different researchers would arrive at different interpretations, and many of these interpretations may prove to have some validity when judged by these five criteria and put to more rigorous tests in future research. The primary goal is a theoretical understanding that "makes sense" and can be supported by the data without any claim that it is the only or even best possible interpretation (although the best possible interpretation is the ideal toward which we strive). Thus, if the findings are at variance with the readers' own interpretations, based on their reading of the data and their own previous experiences, this discrepancy can be the focus of further inquiry leading to even better formulations.

Although great pains are taken to minimize bias in inference and interpretation, it should be obvious that it remains possible in personological research. However, the same potential for bias exists in quantitative research. As Bakan (1969) has written, "All research activity requires that the research makes inferences." Sometimes, elaborate statistical analysis can deceive the readers into believing that the findings are more valid and objective than they really are. In general, there is no reason to believe that inferences based on qualitative research are any more or less valid and free of hidden researcher bias than those based on quantitative research. The best safeguard in both methods is the same: public dissemination of the findings and independent replication by other researchers.

APPENDIX B
ASSESSING CHANGES IN ATTITUDE

Change in attitude and perception was initially assessed in thirteen different areas. These areas were chosen on the basis of previous research and theory on professional socialization and subjective impressions formed during the interviews with new public professionals. The thirteen areas are listed in Table B.1.

In deciding whether a subject had changed, two criteria were used. First, direct self-report by the subject was an indicator of change. For instance, if a subject said that financial remuneration was more important to her than it had been when she first took the job, this was accepted as an indication that her concern with financial compensation had increased over time.

Second, ratings of verbal behavior during both the initial and follow-up interviews were used to determine changes in outlook of which the subject may or may not have been aware. This phase of the study was directed by Dr. Sally Wacker, and the following description of the procedure used is adapted from her report (Wacker, 1979). A Professional Attitude Scale was constructed to assess the following changes: goals or standards are modified; blames clients or system for failure; views clients as less motivated or able; trusts clients less; compartmentalizes work and private lives; emotionally detaches from clients; and less intrinsically motivated in work. Three undergarduate psychology students were hired to rate the transcripts of the respondents on these seven dimensions. Instances of each kind of attitude were extracted from the transcript, coded according to time of interview and dimension, and placed in random order for the raters to read and score.

Each rater had a personal copy of the excerpts and completed the ratings independently. When all of the ratings were finished, each respondent's state-

TABLE B.1: Attitude Changes Observed in New Public Professionals

Attitude	Mental Health Professionals			Lawyers			Public Health Nurses			Teachers			Total		
	C*	NC*	?*	C	NC	?	C	NC	?	C	NC	?	C	NC	?
Changes goals or standards	4	2	1	4	1	2	1	1	5	6	1	0	15	5	8
Concentrates on a few clients	2	3	3	3	2	2	1	1	5	2	5	0	8	11	9
Trusts clients less	0	5	2	4	1	2	1	1	5	5	2	0	10	9	9
Views clients as less motivated or able	0	5	2	3	2	2	2	0	5	6	1	0	11	8	9
Blames clients or system for failure	3	2	2	4	1	2	2	0	5	6	1	0	15	4	9
Becomes more specialized	1	4	2	3	2	2	2	0	5	2	5	0	8	11	9
Compartmentalizes work and private lives	6	1	0	4	1	2	1	1	5	4	3	0	15	6	7
Emotionally detaches from clients	1	4	2	4	1	2	2	0	5	4	3	0	11	8	9
More concerned about financial compensation	3	2	2	3	2	2	0	2	5	1	6	0	7	12	9
Becomes more conservative about social issues	0	5	2	3	2	2	1	1	5	4	3	0	8	11	9
Values autonomy more	6	1	0	3	2	2	2	0	5	3	4	0	14	7	7
Identifies more strongly with profession	1	4	2	1	4	2	0	2	5	0	7	0	2	17	9
Less intrinsically motivated in work	3	2	2	4	1	2	6	0	1	0	7	0	13	10	5

*"C" denotes number of subjects who changed in that way; "NC" denotes number who did not change; "?" denotes number of subjects for whom there is not enough information.

Source: Compiled by the author.

ments had been rated three times. The three ratings of each statement were compared, and, if one of the raters disagreed with the other two on a particular statement, the majority ruled and the discrepant rating was eliminated. If each of the raters had scored the statement differently, however, which was possible for five of the seven dimensions, or if two of them had been unable to rate it at all, the statement was thrown out as being too ambiguous. Of 881 statements, 46 or 5 percent were eliminated from consideration.

The ratings from each dimension were then grouped according to time of interview. Ratings from the first three interviews on a particular dimension were collected and an average pre-score for that dimension was obtained. The same process was followed for statements pertaining to that dimension from the follow-up interview. If there were fewer than two statements from either initial or follow-up interviews, the entire dimension was eliminated for that subject. By comparing the score from the initial interviews with the score from the follow-up interview, it was possible to obtain a measure of change over time (Wacker, 1979).

Thus, there were two sources of information concerning attitude change: the subject's self-report and the independent ratings of statements made during initial and follow-up interviews. For each of the 13 attitudes listed in Table B.1, a determination was made concerning each subject's change. One of three assessments could be made: 1) the subject had changed in that way; 2) the subject had not changed in that way, based on the available evidence; and 3) it was unclear whether the subject had changed. Because the sample was small and non-random tests of statistical significance seemed to be inappropriate. Therefore, only the frequencies were computed. These are shown in Table B.1.

A careful examination of Table B.1 will reveal that information on attitude change was not available for a large number of the subjects: information was often lacking for as many as 9 of 28 subjects. This problem was primarily a function of the unstructured nature of the interviews. Although the interviewers were interested in assessing change, especially during the follow-up interviews, they did not follow a rigid, structured format. Therefore, adequate report by a subject on a particular change dimension was sometimes missing in the initial interviews, the follow-up, or both. When this occurred, no assessment of change could be made.

REFERENCES

Abrahamson, M. *The professional in the organization*. Chicago: Rand McNally, 1967.

Albee, G. W. *Mental health manpower trends*. New York: Basic Books, 1959.

Anderson, J. G. *Bureaucracy in education*. Baltimore: Johns Hopkins Press, 1968.

Bakan, D. *On Method: Toward a reconstruction of psychological investigation*. San Francisco: Jossey-Bass, 1969.

Becker, H. S. The career of the Chicago public school teacher. *American Journal of Sociology*, 1952, *57*, 470–477.

Becker, H. S., Geer, B., Hughes, E. C., & Strauss, A. *Boys in white*. Chicago: University of Chicago Press, 1961.

Berkeley Planning Associates. *Evaluation of child abuse and neglect demonstration projects 1974-1977* (Vol. 9: Project management and worker burnout). Unpublished report, National Technical Information Service, Springfield, Va., 1977.

Bledstein, B. J. *The culture of professionalism: The middle class and the development of higher education in America*. New York: Norton, 1976.

Bucher, R., & Stelling, J. G. (Eds.) *Becoming professional*. Beverly Hills: Sage, 1977.

Caplan, R. D., Cobb, S., French, J. R. P., Harrison, R. V., & Pinneau, S. R. *Job demands and worker health*. Washington, D.C.: U.S. Department of Health, Education and Welfare, Public Health Service, Center for Disease Control National Institute for Occupational Safety and Health, 1975.

Carlin, J. E. *Lawyers on their own*. New Brunswick, N.J.: Rutgers University Press, 1962.

Cherniss, C., & Egnatios, E. Clinical supervision in community mental health. *Social Work*, 1978, *23*, 219–223. (a)

Cherniss, C., & Egnatios, E. Is there job satisfaction in community mental health? *Community Mental Health Journal*, 1978, *14*, 309–318. (b)

Cherniss, C., & Egnatios, E. Participation in decision making by staff in community mental health programs. *American Journal of Community Psychology*, 1978, *6*, 171–190. (c)

Cherniss, C., Egnatios, E., & Wacker, S. Job stress and career development in new public professionals. *Professional Psychology*, 1976, *7*, 428–436.

Cherniss, C., Egnatios, E., Wacker, S., & O'Dowd, W. The professional mystique and burnout in public sector professionals. Unpublished manuscript, University of Michigan, 1979.

Chu, F., & Trotter, S. *The madness establishment: Ralph Nader's study group report on the National Institute of Mental Health.* New York: Grossman, 1974.

Clark, B. R. *The distinctive college.* Chicago: Aldine, 1970.

Coelho, G. V., Hamburg, D. A., & Adams, J. E. (Eds.) *Coping and adaptation.* New York: Basic Books, 1974.

Cohn, J. E. *Noncompliance with a judicial order: The effect of school administrator attitudes.* Ph.D. dissertation, University of Michigan, 1978.

Colarelli, N. O., & Siegel, S. M. *Ward H: An adventure in innovation.* New York: Van Nostrand, 1966.

Corwin, R. The professional employee: A study of conflict in nursing roles. *American Journal of Sociology*, 1961, *66*, 604–615.

Cowen, E. L. Social and community interventions. *Annual Review of Psychology*, 1973, *24*, 423–472.

DeFleur, M. L. Occupational roles as portrayed on television. *Public Opinion Quarterly*, 1964, *28*, 57–74.

Dohrenwend, B. S., & Dohrenwend, B. P. (Eds.) *Stressful life events.* New York: Wiley, 1974.

Eron, L. D. The effect of medical education on attitudes: A follow-up study. In *The ecology of the medical student.* Evanston, Ill.: Association of American Medical Colleges, 1958, 25–33.

Filley, A. C. *Interpersonal conflict resolution.* Glenview: Scott, Foresman, 1975.

Frank, J. D. *Persuasion and healing.* Baltimore: Johns Hopkins University Press, 1973.

Freidson, E. *Profession of medicine.* New York: Dodd, Mead, 1970.

Freidson, E. Preface. In *Becoming professional,* edited by R. Bucher & J. G. Stelling. Beverly Hills: Sage, 1977, 7-13.

Freudenberger, H. J. Staff burn-out. *Journal of Social Issues,* 1974, *30,* 159-165.

Freudenberger, H. J. The staff burn-out syndrome in alternative institutions. *Psychotherapy: Theory, Research, and Practice,* 1975, *12,* 73-82.

Glaser, E. M., & Strauss, A. *The discovery of grounded theory.* Chicago: Aldine, 1967.

Goldenberg, I. I. *Build me a mountain: youth, poverty, and the creation of new settings.* Cambridge: Massachusetts Institute of Technology Press, 1971.

Goldenberg, I. I. *Oppression and social intervention.* Chicago: Nelson-Hall, 1978.

Gomersall, E. R., & Myers, M. S. Breakthrough in on-the-job training. *Harvard Business Review,* 1966, *44,* 62-72.

Grinker, R. R., & Spiegel, J. P. *Men under stress.* Philadelphia: Blakiston, 1945.

Gross, R., & Osterman, P. (Eds.) *The new professionals.* New York: Simon and Schuster, 1972.

Hall, D. T., & Schneider, B. *Organizational climates and careers: the work lives of priests.* New York: Seminar Press, 1973.

Hasenfeld, Y., & English, R. A. (Eds.) *Human service organizations.* Ann Arbor: University of Michigan Press, 1974.

Hegarty, W. H. Using subordinate ratings to elicit behavioral changes in supervisors. *Journal of Applied Psychology,* 1974, *59,* 764-766.

Kadushin, A. Supervisor-supervisee: A survey. *Social Work,* 1974, *19,* 288-297.

Kahn, R. L., Wolfe, D. M., Quinn, R. P., Snoek, J. D., & Rosenthal, R. H. *Organizational stress: Studies in role conflict and ambiguity.* New York: Wiley, 1964.

Kanter, R. M. *Work and family in the United States: A critical review and agenda for research and policy.* New York: Russell Sage Foundation, 1977.

Katz, D. The functional bases of attitudes. In *Attitude change*, edited by M. A. Malec. Chicago: Markham, 1971, 48–65.

Kramer, M. *Reality shock*. St. Lorris: C. V. Mosby, 1974.

Lasch, C. *The culture of narcissism: American life in an age of diminishing returns*. New York: Norton, 1979.

Lazarus, R. S. *Psychological stress and the coping process*. New York: McGraw-Hill, 1966.

Lazarus, R. S. Cognitive and coping processes in emotion. In *Stress and coping: An anthology*, edited by A. Monat & R. S. Lazarus. New York: Columbia University Press, 1977.

Lazarus, R. S., & Launier, R. Stress-related transactions between person and environment. In *Perspectives in interactional psychology*, edited by L. A. Pervin & M. Lewis. New York: Plenum, 1979, 287–327.

Levinson, D. J. *The seasons of a man's life*. New York: Knopf, 1977.

Lortie, D. C. Laymen to lawman: Law school, careers, and professional socialization. In *Professionalization*, edited by H. M. Vollmer & D. L. Mills. Englewood Cliffs, N.J.: Prentice-Hall, 1966, 98–101.

Lortie, D. C. Observations on teaching as work. In *Second handbook of research on teaching*, edited by R. M. W. Travers. Chicago: Rand McNally, 1973, 474–497.

Lortie, D. C. *Schoolteacher: A sociological study*. Chicago: University of Chicago Press, 1975.

Lynn, K. S. *The professions in America*. New York: Houghton-Mifflin, 1965.

Maslach, C. *"Detached concern" in health and social service professions*. Paper presented at American Psychological Association Convention, Montreal, Canada, 1973.

Maslach, C. Burned-Out. *Human Behavior*, 1976, 5, 16–22.

Maslach, C., & Pines, A. The "burn-out" syndrome in the day care setting. *Child Care Quarterly*, 1977, 6, 100–113.

McCall, G. J., & Simmons, J. L. *Issues in participant observation: A text and a reader*. Menlo Park: Addison-Wesley, 1969.

McGrath, J. E. (Ed.) *Social and psychological factors in stress*. New York: Holt, Rinehart and Winston, 1970.

McPherson, G. H. *Small town teacher.* Cambridge: Harvard University Press, 1972.

Mechanic, D. *Students under stress.* New York: Free Press, 1962.

Mendel, W. M. *Staff burn-out in mental health care delivery systems: Diagnosis, treatment and prevention.* Paper presented at the annual conference of the National Council of Community Mental Health Centers, Region 7, Overland Park, Kansas, November 8, 1978.

Moore, W. E. *The professions: Roles and rules.* New York: Russell Sage Foundation, 1970.

Murray, H. A. *Explorations in personality.* New York: Oxford, 1938.

Newcomb, T. M., & Feldman, K. A. *The impacts of colleges upon their students.* New York: Carnegie Foundation for the Advancement of Teaching, 1968.

Nisbet, R. A. *The degradation of the academic dogma.* New York: Basic Books, 1971.

Northrop, F. S. C. *The logic of the sciences and the humanities.* New York: Macmillan, 1947.

Oppenheimer, M. The unionization of the professional. *Social Policy*, 1975, *5*, 34–40.

O'Toole, J. *Work in America.* Cambridge: Massachusetts Institute of Technology Press, 1973.

Pearlin, L. I. Alienation from work: A study of nursing personnel. In *The professional in the organization*, edited by M. Abrahamson. Chicago: Rand McNally, 1967, 110–125.

Pearlin, L. I., & Schooler, C. The structure of coping. *Journal of Health and Social Behavior*, 1978, *19*, 2–21.

Piotrkowski, C. *Work and the family system.* New York: Free Press, 1979.

Porter, L. W., Lawler, E. E., & Hackman, J. R. *Behavior in organizations.* New York: McGraw-Hill, 1975.

Prottas, J. M. *People-processing: The street-level bureaucrat in public service bureaucracies.* Lexington, Mass.: D. C. Heath, 1979.

Rapaport, D., Gill, M. M., & Schafer, R. *Diagnostic psychological testing.* New York: International Universities Press, 1968.

Raush, H. L. Naturalistic method and the clinical approach. In *Naturalistic viewpoints in psychological research*, edited by E. P. Willems & H. L. Raush. New York: Holt, Rinehart and Winston, 1969, 122–46.

Reich, C. A. *The greening of America*. New York: Random House, 1970.

Reppucci, N. D. Social psychology of institutional change: General principles for intervention. *American Journal of Community Psychology*, 1973, *1*, 330–341.

Rosenthal, R., & Jacobson, L. *Pygmalion in the classroom*. New York: Holt, Rinehart and Winston, 1968.

Roszak. T. *The making of a counterculture*. New York: Doubleday, 1969.

Russell, B. *In praise of idleness*. New York: Touchstone, 1976.

Ryan, K. (Ed.) *Don't smile until Christmas*. Chicago: University of Chicago Press, 1970.

Ryan, W. *Blaming the victim*. New York: Vintage, 1971.

Sarason, S. B. *The culture of the school and the problem of change*. Boston: Allyn and Bacon, 1971.

Sarason, S. B. *The psychological sense of community: Prospects for a community psychology*. San Francisco: Jossey-Bass, 1974.

Sarason, S. B. *Work, aging, and social change: Professionals and the one-life, one-career imperative*. New York: Free Press, 1977.

Sarason, S. B., Davidson, K. S., & Blatt, B. *The preparation of teachers: An unstudied problem in education*. New York: Wiley, 1962.

Sarason, S. B., Levine, M., Goldenberg, I. I., Cherlin, D. L., & Bennett, E. M. *Psychology in community settings: Clinical, vocational, educational, social aspects*. New York: Wiley, 1966.

Sarason, S. B., Sarason, E., & Cowden, P. Aging and the nature of work. *American Psychologist*, 1975, *30*, 584–593.

Sarason, S. B., Zitnay, G., & Grossman, F. K. *The creation of a community setting*. Syracuse: Syracuse University Press, 1971.

Sarata, B. P. V. *Job satisfactions of individuals working with the mentally retarded*. Ph.D. dissertation, Yale University, 1972.

Schein, E. H. *Professional education: Some new directions.* New York: Mc-Graw-Hill, 1972.

Schulman, B. Socio-organizational determinants of patient participation in the treatment process with special attention to the control of hypertension. Unpublished manuscript, University of Michigan, Ann Arbor, 1976.

Schwartz, M. S., & Will, G. T. Intervention and change on a mental hospital ward. In *The planning of change,* edited by W. G. Bennis, K. Benne, & R. Chin. New York: Holt, Rinehart and Winston, 1961, 564-583.

Seligman, M. E. P. *Helplessness.* San Francisco: W. H. Freeman, 1975.

Selznick, P. *Leadership in administration.* New York: Row, Peterson, 1957.

Snow, D. L., & Newton, P. M. Task, social structure, and social process in the community mental health center movement. *American Psychologist,* 1976, *31,* 582-594.

Stotland, E., & Kobler, A. L. *Life and death of a mental hospital.* Seattle: University of Washington Press, 1965.

Tripodi, T. *Uses and abuses of social research in social work.* New York: Columbia University Press, 1974.

Veysey, L. Who's a professional? Who cares? (Review of *Advocacy and Objectivity: A Crisis in the Professionalization of American Social Science, 1865-1905* by M. O. Furner.) *Reviews in American History,* 1975, *3,* 419-423.

Vollmer, H. M., & Mills, D. L. (Eds.) *Professionalization.* Englewood Cliffs, N.J.: Prentice-Hall, 1966.

Wacker, S. W. *Job stress and attitude change in teachers, lawyers, social workers, and nurses.* Ph.D. dissertation, University of Michigan, 1979.

Warnath, C. F. Calling a spade a spade. (Review of *Perspective and challenge in college personnel work* by J. F. Penney.) *Contemporary Psychology,* 1973, *18,* 478-479.

Weitz, J. Job expectancy and survival. *Journal of Applied Psychology,* 1956, *40,* 245-247.

White, R. W. Competence as an aspect of personal growth. In *Primary prevention of psychopathology, Volume III: Social competence in children,* edited by M. W. Kent & J. E. Rolf. Hanover, N.H.: University Press of New England, 1979.

Willems, E., & Raush, H. *Naturalistic viewpoints in psychological research*. New York: Holt, Rinehart and Winston, 1969.

Wilensky, H. L. *Intellectuals in labor unions: Organizational pressures on professional roles*. Glencoe, Ill.: Free Press, 1956.

INDEX

structure, 254–56
Professional Service career orientation, 190, 191, 202
program goals/methods/traditions, 243–47
Prottas, J.M., 67
psychoanalytic approach, 246, 263
psychologists: autonomy of, 168–69; boredom of, 68; caseloads of, 159; colleagues of, 83–84, 90, 92; and commitment, 128; training of, 218, 219
psychotherapists: autonomy of, 61–62, 65–66; conviction in, 8; and personal life, 182; and self-doubt, 32
public relations functions, 147

radical therapy movement, 250
Rapaport, D., 277
Raush, H., 268, 271
reality shock, 206, 228
reality therapy, 246
reference groups, 225
rehabilitation model, 244
Reich, C.A., 125
Reppucci, N.D., 170, 246
reputation and competence, 25–27
roles: conflict in, 4; effectiveness of, 114; expectations in, 172; models for, 152–53; orientation to, 190; stress in, 241; structure of and collegiality, 86–88
Rosenthal, R., 244
Roszak, T., 125
Russell, B., 239
Ryan, K., 42, 43, 83
Ryan, W., 105

salaries: concern over, 126–27; perceptions of, 14
Sarason, E., 250
Sarason, S.B., 4, 9, 10, 58, 66, 82, 225, 236, 250, 252, 253, 255, 257, 259, 271, 272
Sarata, B.P.V., 23
scapegoating, 81, 108, 115
Schafer, R., 277
Schein, E.H., 2
schizophrenics: chronic, 244; treatment of, 237
Schneider, B., 9, 104, 173, 240

Schulman, B., 220
Schwartz, M.S., 93, 231, 233
scientific method in professional practice, 226
self-actualization, 14, 69, 237, 250, 253
self-doubt, effects of, 31–36
self-esteem: and responsibility, 23; and self-doubt, 32–33; and self-orientation, 132; and work, 22
Self-Investor career orientation, 191, 195–97, 198, 199, 201, 202, 204, 211
Seligman, M.E.P., 217
Selznick, P., 247
semiprofessions, 2
sexuality, attitudes on, 177–78
Siegal, S.M., 237, 247
Simmons, J.L., 268, 276
Snow, D.L., 259
Social Activist career orientation, 191–92, 198, 199, 200, 201, 202, 204, 211
social change and professional authority, 261–63
social ecological perspective, 11–12
socialization: and burnout, 7; and career orientations, 202; conservative aspects of, 9; and goals, 104; of medical students, 8; and professions, 2; in public agencies, 229
social workers: autonomy of, 59, 64, 169; career orientations of, 197; and clients, 39; colleagues of, 77, 86; commitment of, 120–21; idealism of, 99; personal life of, 184–85; and specialization, 101; supervision of, 174; training of, 216, 219
specialization and goals, 100
Spiegel, J.P., 92, 173, 175
staff development and counseling, 227–34; burnout checkup, 230–31; individual counseling, 231–32; orientation programs, 228–30; staff support groups, 232–34
Stelling, J.G., 170, 252
stereotypes of professions, 250
Strauss, A., 8, 268
stress: and coping, 211–12; measurement of, 130; and self-orientation, 132; sources of, 12–14

ABOUT THE AUTHOR

CARY CHERNISS received his Ph.D. in psychology from Yale University in 1972. Since then he has been an assistant professor of psychology at the University of Michigan, Ann Arbor. He has conducted research and published papers on the topics of mental health consultation, job satisfaction in community mental health centers, clinical supervision, and professional burnout. He has also served as a consultant to public schools, mental health agencies and correctional programs for youth.